R. Pethig U. Schlieper (Eds.)

Efficiency, Institutions, and Economic Policy

Proceedings of a Workshop held by the Sonderforschungsbereich 5 at the University of Mannheim, June 1986

With 21 Figures

Springer-Verlag Berlin Heidelberg New York
London Paris Tokyo

Professor Dr. Rüdiger Pethig
Fachbereich 4
Universität Oldenburg
Postfach 25 03
D-2900 Oldenburg

Professor Dr. Ulrich Schlieper
Lehrstuhl für VWL und Ökonometrie III
Universität Mannheim
Seminargebäude, A5
D-6800 Mannheim 1

ISBN-13:978-3-642-73066-5 e-ISBN-13:978-3-642-73064-1
DOI: 10.1007/978-3-642-73064-1

Library of Congress Cataloging in Publication Data.
Efficiency, institutions, and economic policy : proceedings of a workshop held by the Sonderforschungsbereich 5 at the University of Mannheim, June 1986 / R. Pethig, U. Schlieper, eds. p. cm.
ISBN-13:978-3-642-73066-5 (U.S.)
1. Welfare economics–Congresses. 2. Public goods–Congresses. 3. Institutional economics–Congresses. 4. Institutional economics–Congresses. I. Pethig, R. (Rüdiger), 1943.-
II. Schlieper, U. (Ulrich), 1936-.
HB846.E34 1987 338.9–dc 19 87-27294 CIP

2142/3145-543210

Preface

The traditional benchmark model for allocative efficiency has been neoclassical theory. Its *implicit* assumptions on institutions, transaction costs and information distribution lead most economists to spot several sources of inefficiency, e.g. public goods or nonconvex technologies. (It is only the adherent of rigorous Panglossian economics who would deny *any* type of allocative inefficiency). Once it is acknowledged, that the resource allocation in modern societies depends very much on basic forms of cooperative behavior, on transaction costs and on property rights, broadly conceived, the efficiency issue turns out to be crucially interrelated with institutions and with their capacity to adjust to changing social environments. Olson's key word "institutional sclerosis" expresses nicely the view being shared by a growing number of institutional economists that allocative efficiency and prevailing social institutions are *not* identical twins.

The present volume addresses the issue of 'efficiency and institutions' from a number of different angles. The first three papers by *Streit, Schlieper* and *Wickström* constitute straight analyses of the *"fundamentals" of modern welfare states:* As self-interested politicians are likely to give in to pressure groups, the market process is complemented and/or impeded by competitive rent-seeking activities of special-interest groups and redistributive coalitions. In this view, government activity is assumed to be predominantly redistributive. This is not only so, because "social justice" is considered an important social goal by many groups, but also because public actions and institutions being not primarily implemented with redistributive intentions nonetheless do have a strong redistributive impact.

In the first contribution of the present volume *Streit* focusses attention on the institutional sclerosis (Olson) of modern welfare states. He argues that the indeterminateness of the principle of social justice generates all kinds of legislature that is predominantly redistributive, and therefore elicits rent-seeking activities which in turn tend to cripple the power of parliament. One way to curb this tendency could be constitutional constraints restricting activities of parliament. Another could be neocorporatism. *Streit* doesn't see great chances for the enforcement of constitutional constraints, and he rejects neocorporatism because of its misperception of market order. He points to a few self-correcting forces, such as international competition, technological innovations and the shadow economy, but he concludes that the institutional sclerosis represents "a threat to welfare states which should not be ignored".

According to *Schlieper*, the competitive market mechanism is characterized as some unstable mix of competitive behavior and cooperation. These behavioral patterns are interrelated and none of them is unambiguously efficiency-enhancing. For example, "beneficial" cooperation is impeded by self-interest behavior; on the other hand, cooperation is also sought by redistributional coalitions to resist the harsh winds of competitive change. Since macroeconomic policy has important distributional consequences it can be among the prominent targets of rent-seeking special interest groups. To be more specific, *Schlieper* elaborates on the relationship between rent-seeking and macroeconomics in the context of a scenario in which the labour unions seek to increase real wages by way of an aggressive wage policy whereas the government pursues an accommodating fiscal policy. In *Schlieper*'s model the medium term effects of these strategies are superficially favorable both for the unions and the society but since the market sector declines in the long run, the rent seekers may destroy the source of their rents.

Wickström approaches the issue of rent-seeking activities by competitive pressure groups within a formal model in which government intends to redistribute a given "cake" (tax money) to a set of pressure groups such that each group's share depends on its relative pressure. Neglecting coalition formation among pressure groups the Cournot-Nash equilibrium appears as an appropriate solution concept being interpreted as a state of equilibrating forces in the pressure groups' tug of war. The advantage of keeping the model simple is that a unique Nash-equilibrium exists. This, in turn, allows for economically meaningful comparative-static analysis. Government growth is "generated" in *Wickström*'s model by successive exogenous increases of the size of the cake. *Wickström* not only shows that each group's share of the cake is positively related to its power but also, and more importantly, perhaps, that the number of active pressure groups increases as the cake grows.

So far the efficiency of modern welfare states was studied on a quite general level, focussing in particular on rent-seeking inefficiencies. Very important institutions of welfare states are their social security schemes that usually imply intergenerational transfers. *Breyer* and *von der Schulenburg* turn their attention to these institutions. But rather than being preoccupied with institutional design they investigate the efficiency-related issue of acceptability under majority rule of such a scheme. Their model takes its institutional setting from the German statutory health insurance system. Whether a voter fares better under a social health insurance scheme or under a private one depends on the size of his or her family. Hence the family structure, i.e. the distribution of children across families becomes decisive for the outcome of the vote (along with the population growth rate and the rate of time preference). Their numerical comparative-static calculations contradict a number of widespread beliefs concerning the acceptability of intergenerational transfers via social insurance.

Another major topic of the present volume is the *effciency of law* (*Witt; Rowley and Brough; Monissen and Wenger*). *Witt* wants to explain the emergence of property right regimes and starts form the wellknown Demsetz hypothesis that private property rights emerge out of a regime of free access whenever the latter is less efficient than the former. *Witt* points out that Demsetz privided only a necessary condition for the transition between the two property-rights regimes because Demsetz's institutional comparison is incomplete. Regulated communal rights should be considered as a further option. Starting from free access private-property-rights regimes may well be - and historically sometimes were - efficiency-dominated by regulated-communal-rights regimes. Of course the latter regime generates costs of negotiating and policing the internal rationing/maintenance scheme. But on the other hand, a balanced view requires also to take the social costs of private right enforcement into consideration.

Rowley and *Brough* embark on a careful comparative institutions evaluation of the efficiency of the common law. They start with a detailed outline of the medieval origins of the common law and then trace its evolution to the presence. After that, their main effort is to scrutinize the modern institutions of common law with respect to its efficiency-enhancing incentives. The paper puts forward a number of strong indications and (a priori) arguments in favor of the efficiency of the laws of property and contract. However, in sharp contrast to these findings, in the case of the US tort law the authors' conclusion is that the "combination of juries and contingent fee lawyers..., together with the invasion of certain benches by 'public interest' judges, ensures that rent seeking losses will be imposed upon society."

Monissen and *Wenger* investigate the comparative efficiency of various institutional arrangements in the labor market with respect to the function of firmspecific human capital. They argue that collective workers' codetermination might be efficiency-enhancing provided that it helps to lower the costs of information exchange between workers and managment. But they also conclude that the codetermination arrangements in Germany fail to meet this condition. In the last part of their paper *Monissen* and *Wenger* approach the issue of efficient firm-specific human capital formation by suggesting a somewhat "radical" reform of the labor market: Suppose the German law were changed in such a way that contractual arrangements are made legal by which the workers' rights to unionize (to strike) and their codetermination rights could be excluded and by which competition-restraining clauses were feasible. Then labor contracts stipulating efficient and "exploitation-free" wage paths could be expected to emerge.

So far, the problem of the free rider and the allocation of nonexclusive public goods have only been mentioned occasionally. We now tyrn to this issue.The first contribution is the paper by *Güth* and *Hellwig*. The authors study the "competitive supply of a nonexclusive public good as a sequential game with incomplete information. Each potential supplier is assumed to design and announce a direct revelation mechanism which may be vetoed by the consumers. Once one of the suppliers obtained the "franchise" to supply the public good, the consumers play a noncooperative strategic game in which their strategy is their reported (not necessarily true) willingness-to-pay. In an earlier paper Güth and Hellwig showed that in the absence of potential competition efficient revelation mechanisms imply negative profits while profit maximizing revelation mechanisms lead to positive profits and to an undersupply of the public good. Taking these results as a starting point the principle issue of their present paper is whether Bertrand competition eliminates the inefficient monopoly solution.

They find, in fact, equilibria of "potential competition" in which the mechanism selected provides the supplier with zero expected profits, but there are also equilibria in which each supplier proposes the monopoly mechanism. The intuition is that given the other buyers' votes for the monopoly mechanism, a single voter expects his vote for the preferred (i.e. the zero-profit) mechanism to destroy unanimity and hence to lead to the non-supply of the public good.

This social choice element in each individual's decision problem which is absent in competitive provision of private goods prevents (potential) competition from wiping out expected profits and the pertaining inefficiency. The authors are right in pointing out that their analysis has a direct important impact on the theory of natural monopoly questioning the efficiency claim of awarding the franchise to the "best" bid.

Pethig develops an allocation procedure for those group-specific nonexcludable public goods which are provided by organizations or associations raising their funds through membership dues. By comparing this procedure with both the standard Cournot-Nash approach of voluntary contributions and with exclusive market provision it turns out that uniform membership dues reduce free-rider incentives implying that the relevance of Olson's postulate concerning the exploitation of the great by the small is considerably weakened. It is also shown that decreasing the dues leads to increasing membership and increasing total amount of public good supplied. Assuming that dues are determined by majority vote of the organization's members the procedure yields a stable membership size and tends to discourage high-demand members' incentives to offer gifts in addition to their dues.

All contributions to this volume have been presented at a *workshop* held in June 1986 at the University of Mannheim. Each paper has been thoroughly discussed, and the result of this discussion is reflected both in subsequent paper revisions and in the *comments of formal discussants* being included in this volume. The editors wish to thank all participants of the workshop for their stimulating and constructive discussion. They are also grateful for the *financial support by the Deutsche Forschungsgemeinschaft* provided through the *Sonderforschungsbereich 5* at the Universität Mannheim. Last but not least the authors wish to express their deep gratitude to Mrs. Börresen, Mrs. Peschla and Mrs. Rössler whose help was indispensable not only in organizing the workshop but also in preparing the final versions of all typescripts.

Oldenburg and Mannheim,
August 1987

Rüdiger Pethig
Ulrich Schlieper

Contents

Economic Order and Public Policy
- Market, Constitution and the Welfare State

by

Manfred E. Streit*

> "if democracy be a real form of government, the sort of system in which all things are regulated by decrees is clearly not even a democracy in the true sense of the word, for decrees relate only to particulars."
>
> Aristotle

I. Introduction

It is the purpose of this essay to argue

- that the lasting economic development problems of Western welfare states can be explained by a basically common pattern of causation;
- that the pattern begins to reveal itself when taking into account the lack of attraction which any policy to secure a market order normally has for so-called political entrepreneurs;
- that the diagnosis suggests corresponding structural reforms of the political decision-making process which are not very likely to be carried out;
- that an improvement and legal formation of the political bargaining practice of welfare states cannot provide a workable economic constitution;
- that there are at least some spontaneous forces at work which may prevent the economic problems of welfare states from becoming insuperable.

Elements of the explanatory pattern can be drawn from corresponding studies particularly in economics, political science, philosophy and sociology of law. The same holds true for the possibilities to reform the democratic decision-making process. Analytically and from an economic point of view it appears necessary to merge mainly

- an evolutionary and institutionally oriented view of the market process;
- an interpretation of political decision making as it is attempted in public choice;
- an understanding of the legal and institutional framework of present democracies which can be found in the philosophy and sociology of law.

* The present paper is partly based on a more recent analysis of mine (M.E. Streit, 1986a). I am grateful to P. Golz, G. Wegner and H. Wenzel for valuable criticisms and suggestions.

Pethig Schlieper (Eds.)
Efficiency, Institutions, and Economic Policy

Although it will be sometimes argued with reference to historical and institutional developments and structures in Germany, this should not reduce the relevance of the explanatory pattern to a special case.

II. Framework requirements of a market order

The order of economic activities emerging from a market process is the evolutionary product of two factors, self-coordination and self-control through a tâtonnement in the proper sense of the word.[1] Self-coordination takes place within a network of exchange transactions between autonomous (legally competent) individuals or institutions (mainly companies). The network itself is very complex, diversifiable and ever changing. Furthermore it is highly informative in the sense that, as a concomitant of very transaction, information on scarcity is procured, processed and disseminated. Self-control becomes effective as soon as potential partners of a transaction are in a position to assess the conditions of an envisaged exchange in the light of possibilities to substitute partners (and objects) of transaction, i.e. as soon as there is effective competition. Self-coordination and self-control produce transitory patterns of allocation and of distribution reflecting an economic order which Adam Ferguson succinctly described as "the result of human action, but not the execution of any human design."[2]

Taking into account the two core-elements of a market process - self-coordination and self-control - any policy to establish and safeguard the order generating this process requires two types of framework activities: With respect to self-coordination it is necessary,

- to define and secure private property rights as potential objects of exchange and as elements of demarcation of individual spheres of influence which can be used by the holders of such rights in a self-responsible way;
- to establish the autonomy of all economic agents (in the sense of equality before the law) in order to induce them to coordinate their economic plans only by means of negociated contracts in all those cases in which they require the cooperation of others in pursuing their individual (economic) objectives;
- to guarantee the economic freedom of the private agents by granting them corresponding economic basic rights which are protected against state interference.

Ultimately self-coordination of decentralized economic decision makers requires to establish and guarantee what David Hume summarized as "the stability of possession, of its transference by consent, and of the performance of promises."[3]

1) Such a view of the market process was characteristic for the Great Scottish moral philosophers. It was particularly F.A. Hayek (e.g. 1963, 1964, 1968, 1973) who took up this tradition of thinking. The evolutionary determination of the economic order has probably first been emphasized in modern times by A.A. Alchian (1950). That this view may require to revise the relevance of the neo-classical paradigm for understanding and justifying the market order has, for example, been discussed more recently by E. Streissler (1980) and J. Röpke (1980).
2) The quotation was found in F.A. Hayek (1967a), p. 96.
3) D. Hume (1886), p. 293.

With respect to self-control it is necessary to secure and promote competition by law. A corresponding legislation becomes imperative because it cannot be excluded,

- that the interdependence of private economic agents, reflecting the division of labour, degenerates in some cases to a lasting dependence as a source of economic power which then remains unchecked by possibilities of substitution;
- that the freedom of contract will also be misused to reduce this very freedom by restricting competition;
- that economic agents obstruct their competitors by resorting to unfair practices instead of trying to supplant them by offering superior substitutes.

The execution of this legislation creates regulation problems. They tend to increase the more discretionary power the regulation authority receives, i.e. the more restraints of competition are subjected to the rule of reason or the less the per se-rule is applied.

III. Economic properties of framework activities

The two complementary framework activities have much in common with those structural elements of the political constitution of democracies which are designed to secure the rule of the law ("Rechtsstaat"). On the one hand, autonomy is granted to those who are entitled to make laws and to govern. But since, on the other hand, autonomy tends to provide opportunities to exercise power, a sophisticated system of checks and balances has been devised to prevent an arbitrary use of such political power. Similarly, the legal and institutional structure of a market order consists of secured opportunities to act in an autonomous, self-responsible way. But equally, legal and institutional arrangements are required to prevent an arbitrary use of the concomitant economic power.

Because of this structural similarity it can be argued that a constitutional state requires a political and an economic constitution.[4] The modern welfare state emerged from the constitutional state with the attempts to pursue in addition the objective of social justice ("Sozialstaatlichkeit"). However, as will be set out later (section 5), the pursuance of this objective has led to political and legislative activities which tend to produce conflicts with the objectives of the constitutional state, i.e. rule of the law and economic freedom. And most of these activities are rather discretionary interventions than framework activities.

Considering, first, the framework activities which aim at establishing and securing a market order, these activities manifest themselves mainly in rules (law) with the following characteristic properties:

- They refer to an unknown number of persons and cases; this implies that their application is independent of the economic results which they may help to bring about in any particular case.

4) For a more recent elaboration on the concept of the economic constitution c.f. E.J. Mestmäcker (1978), pp. 27 ff.

- They do not provide a direct benefit to the individual who decides to stick to them if one leaves aside a possible moral satisfaction; from an individualistic point of view law-abiding produces pure external economies.
- They tend to gain quality in the course of time they are accepted and their enforcement corresponds to a reinvestment in order to preserve their preventive capacity; the gain in quality is related to their durability because time is required to adjust to them by developing stable patterns of behaviour and thus stabilize expectations with respect to social (economic) relations.

From an economic point of view rules with such properties have to be considered as pure and durable public goods or as public capital.[5] In Weberian terms it is formal law establishing abstract rules.[6]

IV. Framework activities and political competition

Given these properties, the provision and enforcement of such rules by the state is a most convincing case when judged with respect to allocative efficiency. However, this does not mean at all, that such a function of a state is rated equally high politically in a competitive democratic process. On the contrary, applying political economy, it is exactly the abstractness or the "formal rationality" (Weber) of these rules which turns them into "products" rarely considered by political entrepreneurs to be competitive. The supply of such products does hardly help to attract and preserve any particular group of clients (supporters) under every-day political conditions. This is much more reliably achieved by providing group-specific privileges. With regard to the economic constitution such privileges may consist, for example, of exemptions from the anti-trust legislation. Taking into account that law-abiding exerts a pure external economy, exemptions from the rules represent cases of legitimatized free-riding. And as will be argued later (section 10), the prevailing structures of democracies are such that there exist no barriers to prevent a permanent erosion of the economic order through this type of free-riding.

Whereas the political value of legislation depends upon the extent to which it promises to provide economic results to particular individuals and groups, the formal law of the order does not allow to assign specific economic results to anybody. A policy to establish and secure a market order allows at best "to improve for any member of society selected at random the chances to gain a high income..."[7] To offer such chances by a corresponding rule-setting is probably most attractive to political entrepreneurs in periods of reconstruction after a major crisis. During those times - to borrow from Rawls and Buchanan - the "veil of ignorance" covering achievable economic and social positions is particularly dense for many if not most

5) C.f. J.M. Buchanan (1974), pp. 108 ff.
6) M. Weber (1921), pp. 396 f.
7) F.A. Hayek (1967b), p.28. ("Eine optimale Politik in der Katallaxie kann und sollte darauf abzielen, für jedes zufällig herausgegriffene Mitglied der Gesellschaft die Chancen zu verbessern, die es hat, ein hohes Einkommen zu erzielen,...").

members of society.[8] Consequently, a programme for establishing a market order as it was offered in Germany after the second World War, can become temporarily a vote-winning political supply. However, in an established market order under every-day political conditions it is much more likely that "the order is of interest to the individual particularly to the extent to which it does not apply to him."[9].

V. Political competition and social justice

The legislation preferred by political entrepreneurs is characteristic of democratic welfare states. As a consequence of their aim to assign particular results to specific groups, formal law becomes "materialized" (Weber). "Ethical imperatives or utilitarian or other rules of expediency or political maxims"[10] are substituting abstract norms. The ethical imperative which is predominantly employed to justify material legislation and to acquiesce in activities of interest groups which are likely to have a pernicious effect on the market system is the principle of social justice.

To the political entrepreneur this principle has two crucial advantages. Firstly, it has neither a definite meaning nor generally agreed limits; this allows to justify an almost indefinite number of group-specific privileges. Secondly, the attribute "social" comes close to lending properties of a taboo to any project to which it is attached; this allows to ignore respectively to play down even in more obvious cases conflicts between equity and efficiency as they are usually involved when social justice is stressed.

To the average citizen (voter), however, such conflicts between equity and efficiency are not only difficult to trace in most cases. It would also not be rational to do so since his personal return would be normally negligible compared with the costs he would have to bear to become informed and to exploit his minute chances to influence a pending decision in a significant way. And this gap between benefits and costs tends to widen the more an issue is removed from the individual sphere and the more dominant are either its public-good features or - in the case of negative effects on allocative efficiency - its public-bad features. Basically it is the same reason which explains why he is mainly interested in exceptions from the order as far as they are favourable to him and not so much in the order itself.[11]

8) G. Kirsch (1981), p. 272.

9) G. Kirsch, ibid., p. 262. ("; die Ordnung interessiert den einzelnen besonders in dem Maße, wie sie für ihn nicht gilt.")

10) M. Weber (1921), p. 397. ("Denn diese letztere (die materiale Rationalität, M.E.S.) bedeutet ja gerade: daß Normen anderer qualitativer Dignität als logische Gerneralisierungen von abstrakten Sinndeutungen auf die Entscheidung von Rechtsproblemen Einfluß haben sollen: ethische Imperative oder utilitaristische oder andere Zweckmäßigkeitsregeln oder politische Maximen, welche sowohl den Formalismus des äußeren Merkmals wie denjenigen der logischen Abstraktion durchbrechen.").

11) This explanation based on the concept of "purpose-rationality", to employ again Weberian terminology, does not exclude individual efforts founded on a "value-rationality". And it may be quite symptomatic to observe that mainly some political movements operating at the fringes of the political spectrum focus on issues with dominant public-good features like environmental protection and international security.

VI. Atrophy of the market system

Economically, the legislation predominantly passed in welfare states is redistributive at least by intention. Thereby it does not necessarily take the form of outright redistribution by taxation and transfers. Although the motive of envy is exploitable for some political entrepreneurs, a redistributive effort which does not require to mention a loosing group - even if it were merely in terms of statutory incidence - has the competitive advantages flowing from reduced transparence. Hence redistribution only too frequently comes in the disguise of regulations like one-sided restrictions of the rights to give notice, non-tariff barriers, tax reliefs, directed expenditure programs and exemptions from the anti-trust legislation. The latter is also the constitutional basis to which politicans like to refer to when they acquiesce in agreements between organizations of the labour markets which are most likely to deprive others of employment opportunities.

With regard to the market process, the various redistributive interventions are designed either to compensate particular groups for or - more frequently - to protect them against the substitution effects of competition.[12)] As an important side-effect, the almost incessant stream of additional regulations tends to confuse and to reduce the predictability of those property rights which are necessarily affected by them. Insecurity and uncertainty of property rights, however, constitute disincentives to invest.[13)] The effects of this kind of interventionism regarding the evolutionary market process are that both, its capacity to select and to restabilize through adjustment are reduced. And this reduction of the capacity to change can hardly be balanced by equally restraining the evolutionary forces of variation; factors like changes in tastes, in natural resources, in demographic trends and in comparative advantage can - if at all - be manipulated only to a limited and costly extent. As a consequence, lasting problems of employment and growth begin to emerge in developed democratic countries. They have been convincingly explained by Mancur Olson[14)] as an "institutional sclerosis" which can be traced to the influence and political encouragement which special-interest groups or "distributional coalitions" tend to enjoy. And there is growing empirical evidence, in favour of the basic hypothesis.[15)]

Important to the economic as well as to the political process is a diversion effect which is part of the institutional sclerosis. Given the propensity of political entrepreneurs to intervene into the market order on distributional grounds it may pay to individuals to devote resources to the formation and to the activities of distributional coalitions in order to capture the monopoly rents which are created by redistributive regulation. What has by now become

12) This is succinctly demonstrated, for example, by T. Scitovsky (1980).

13) S. Brittan (1978), p. 265 f., who takes up a similar argument brought forward by Henry C. Simons.

14) M. Olson (1982a,b).

15) Such empirical evidence - as far as it can go in view of the qualitative aspects of the hypothesis and its suggested consequences - can be found, for example, in S. Brittan (1978) who explicitly refers to an earlier version of Olson (1982a), in D.C. Mueller (1982) - particularly in the contributions by Choi, Lady Hicks and Mueller himself - and in E. Weede (1984).

more clearly analysed as "rent seeking"[16] and turned out to be a wasteful substitute for profit seeking within a process of dynamic economic competition, has already been envisaged by John Stuart Mill who was not opposed at all to distributional considerations: "Every function superadded to those already exercised by the government causes its influence over hopes and fears to be more widely diffused, and converts, more and more, the active and ambitious part of the public into hangers-on of the government, or of some party which aims at becoming the government."[17]

VII. An overburdened democratic procedure

The accumulation of protective and redistributive regulation in favour of specific-interest groups means that chances to obtain incomes as well as incomes themselves are increasingly influenced or even determined by a process of political bargaining. Thereby redistributive manipulations of the market process are traded against political support. However, there are reasons to expect that democracy as a procedure to come to decisions over the provision of public goods will become overburdened if more and more distributional conflicts have to be settled by applying the majority principle. In terms of bargaining theory the common cause of the difficulties can be seen in the property of the distributional bargaining process of being at best a zero-sum game for which no stable solution (core) exists.

In other words, there is no way of establishing which outcome of the bargaining process could be considered to be "collectively rational". The principle of social justice certainly does not lend itself to establish such a result. It suffers from the fundamental weakness of being indeterminate. Hence it is not even possible for political decision-makers to argue irrefutably with the beneficiaries of a distributional decision that they ought to be content. And even if they were it would not pay to them and to their functionaries to signal such content because this would place them in a strategically weak position at the beginning of future bargaining rounds. In addition the functionaries have a personal interest in playing down the results of their lobbying just enough to be asked by those they represent to carry on. As far as privileges provided to one group are considered detrimental to the interests of other groups this will induce them to exert defensive political pressures. Furthermore, any special treatment of a group is likely to be used by others to claim at least an equivalent treatment for themselves. Already because the normative basis for this kind of decisions does not provide a stopping rule, there is a danger that political decisions are becoming more difficult with each round of bargaining.[18].

The forementioned difficulties manifest themselves in a legislation which tends to become the more complex and ephemeral the more log-rolling and political side-payments are re

16) J.M.Buchanan (1980), p. 11.
17) J. St. Mill (1859), p. 165.
18) For a similar line of reasoning compare D. Usher (1981), p. 31.

required to recruit majorities. The immediate economic consequence of this kind of legislation is an increase in transaction costs which have to be incurred in order to comply with such a legal infrastructure. To these costs have to be added the already mentioned economic consequences of property rights made more insecure and uncertain. However, the bargaining process itself is already riddled with characteristic deficiencies: a strategically determined distortion of those informations which are fed into it, the costs of a delay of decisions which is not technically necessary but is part of the rituals of the game, the initiation and conduct of bargaining with the help of notoriously inflated bureaucracies and the equally notorious impredictability of the outcome in many cases.[19]

No wonder that many find such a process disgusting and silly at least as long as their own interests are not involved. However, it is important to recall that political bargaining about distributional issues is the consequence of a discontent with the distribution patterns produced by the market process. But to burden the political decision-process with more and more equity problems rationally presupposes that it is really capable to handle such a rising tide. This must be seriously doubted in view of the sturcture of the equity problem and of the properties of a political bargaining. Consequently, it is likely that more distributional conflicts between groups are piled up than are solved. As an instrument to reduce or even solve equity problems in an open and personalized way, the democratic procedure is far from being in general preferable to an effective market process where such conflicts tend to be handled in an impersonal and decentralized way.[20] It is the relative anonymity of competitive calculatedness allowing to apply the principle of exit (Hirschman) and the reduction of moral requirements to a minimum which explain both, the high level of productivity of a market system as an allocation mechanism and its low level of conflict despite of the pressures of scarcity.

Symptoms of an overburdened political process can be most prominently found in high courts. For example in Germany, it is observable that the constitutional court frequently takes over the task to produce at least some kind of principles allowing to systematize an ephemeral legislation, supposedly conductive to social justice, and to discipline lower courts, particularly those deciding on matters of labour relations, in producing legislation outside parliament. This has led to the accusation, that the constitutional courts are establishing themselves as a superior legislator. From an analytical and structural point of view there is something to be said in favour of this verdict (section 10). However, this is less convincing when it is propagated by those who are basically the cause of such a shift in the distribution of public powers. There are sufficient indications that not only parliamentary output is deteriorating in quality when measured by judicial standards, but also that conflicts which emerge during the process of legislation are left unsettled because a settlement may alienate potential

19) For a brief interpretation of the problems of a society which relies increasingly on bargaining compare L. Johansen (1979).

20) This is an essential part of the message of D. Usher (1981).

supporters. This is probably done in the hope that the courts and ultimately the constitutional court will take over the responsibility to solve politically unpleasant problems.[21]

VIII. A cornered welfare state

Considering the joint effect of the economic and political consequences of a built-in preoccupation with equity problems, democratic welfare states may find themselves in a tight corner: The pressure of expectations[22] on political entrepreneurs to solve the lasting problems of employment and growth has to be answered. Inflation as a social mollifier[23] has largely lost its charm. Given the poor performance of the tax base, the budgetary room to manoeuvre is permanently squeezed by the financial legacy of public engagements strongly influenced by equity considerations like health care, old-age pensions, unemployment benefits, housing and the protection of ailing industries and regions. And political entrepreneurs who consider to attack the problems at their roots by questioning group-specific privileges will mainly have to face a public outcry because of an unpleasant ratchet effect (section 9) which will most likely prevent them from pushing too hard.

However, what Lester C. Thurow diagnoses as a paralysis of the zero-sum society[24] cannot go on for ever. It is much more likely that the political order will fall into disrepute if it should not be possible to strengthen again its economic basis.[25] Such possibilities to stem self-destructive tendencies of democracies[26] will be explored in the following sections.

IX. Feasibility problems of market-oriented reforms

If the diagnosis is accepted, a causal therapy would require to revitalize the market forces by reducing the institutional sclerosis. In the meantime economists have made numerous propositons to this respect.[27] And it may be worth mentioning that many of the propositions made with respect to the German economy do not simply ask to abandon redistributional interventions. In a number of cases substitutive arrangements are offered which promise to be conductive to the declared social objectives but do not interfere so much with the market process.

21) Compare to this point, for example, the former judge of the German constitutional court H.H. Rupp (1979), p. 101.
22) K. Borchardt (1981), p. 48.
23) M. Bronfenbrenner and F.D. Holzman (1965), p. 75.
24) L.C. Thurow (1980), p. 24 f.
25) One of the first who stressed the complementarity between democracy and a market order was probably F.A. Hayek (1944, p. 52): " If 'capitalism' means here a competitive system based on free disposal over private property, it is far more important to realise that only within this system democracy is possible. When it becomes dominated by a collectivist creed, democracy will inevitably destroy itself." A more recent elaboration of this position has been tried by D. Usher (1981).
26) Examples for early warnings about such tendencies are provided by S. Brittan (1975), pp. 146 ff.
27) As an example may suffice the collection of proposals edited by H. Giersch (1983).

However, even in these cases scepticism regarding their political feasibility seems to be justified.

Considering feasibility, it could be plausibly argued that the sclerosis may create a gap between actual and potential output which could grow enough to make reforms Pareto-superior, i.e. that the gains from reforms will suffice to compensate the losers and to have something left over.[28] However, even if the losers and the size of the losses were well defined, there are at least two interrelated reasons to expect reluctance from political entrepreneurs and resistance from special-interest groups:

- A ratchet effect: It consists for a political entrepreneur of an unattractive reversal of the public-choice option which initially favoured a distribution-oriented manipulation of the market process. To take away group-specific privileges creates identifiable (private) losses on the one hand and widely dispersed and not clearly identifiable allocative (public) gains on the other hand. Because of this perception problem it will be difficult to win the support of the beneficiaries and hence of a majority.
- A prisoner's dilemma. Since a market-oriented reform would hurt the interests of many different distributional coalitions, particularly the functionaries of special-interest groups have to face a dilemma: They have to take into account the possiblity that some groups may prefer to keep the old privileges and oppose a corresponding reform successfully. This may give those who consented to reforms the image of losers even if some compensation was received.

Besides these more specific arguments against the feasibility of market-oriented reforms there are two general problems:

- To return to more coordination and gratification of individual efforts through the market process necessarily means to reduce the power-base of both, political entrepreneurs and functionaries of special-interest groups acting as their direct or indirect counterpart in many if not most cases of political bargaining. Hence both groups have a vested interest in the status quo.
- To secure a larger influence of the market process on economic affairs also implies a value judgement in favour of more (economic) freedom which is not necessarily shared by a majority. Societies seem to reveal - in the jargon of economists - a high income elasticity of demand for (economic) security; that the arrangements which are chosen to provide more individual security and which frequently involve a manipulation of the market process tend to imply less collective security and less freedom rarely helps to convince majorities. Even more important seems to be the value of distributive justice which not only favours a "creeping socialism"[29] supported inadvertedly by non-socialists but

28) E.g. S. Brittan (1978), p. 267 and M. Olson (1982a), p. 46 who also points at the requirement that the loosing group and the size of the losses must be well defined.

29) To quote a reminder by E. Weede (1983, p. 353): "In dedicating his 'Road to Serfdom' to socialists in all parties, Hayek (1944) underlined the capability of non-socialists to commit socialist errors. As a matter of courtesy, one might mention that socialists believe in a benefical impact of their strength on both, growth and employment."

also provides the ethical foundation of ideological socialism and its opposition against a market order.

How extremely high and clearly visible to the average citizen the shadow price of an inefficient, distribution-oriented arrangement can become without producing a sufficient incentive to reform, is demonstrated by agricultural policy. It cannot be excluded that this also reflects a majority willing to pay such a price for values like distributional justice and economic security. However, even if this is granted, it is remarkable how little support widely discussed proposals of a reform receive which would allow to pursue these objectives at significantly lower budgetary and non-budgetary costs.

X. Missing constitutional constraints

Any market-oriented reform of welfare states would be short-lived without taking into account the normative and institutional causes of the institutional sclerosis. They can be traced to

- a high propensity to intervene derivable mainly from the indeterminate principle of social justice which to pursue appears to form part of the legitimacy of modern democracies;
- an authority of parliament which is practically unlimited because it is merely constrained by constitutional principles in many cases open to interpretation and modifiable by parliament itself.

The first causal element opens up rent-seeking opportunities and provides the economic foundations to most special-interest groups. The fact that parliament is an almost absolute sovereign has been criticized by von Hayek as "the fatal defect of the prevailing form of democracy."[30] Besides representing a problem on its own, practically unlimited authority does not necessarily involve corresponding power. In the prevailing form of democracy the power is only too easily lost to special-interest groups and to the public administration in charge of preparing and executing most of the legislation. Political entrepreneurs in general and those in parliament in particular tend to lose much of the autonomy required to exercise power

- because the majority in parliament has to compete with the minority to preserve and to gain the support of special-interest groups by providing or at least by promising distributional privileges,
- because no political decision maker can point at a democratically legitimatized institution or procedure which could prevent himself to give way to the usual pressures of interest groups.[31]

30) F.A. Hayek (1979), p. 3.
31) Fcr an elaboration on most parts of these two points compare F.A.Hayek (1979), pp. 15 ff.

What appears to be missing is a constitutional constraint regarding the activities of parliament. To leave it to the constitutional court to define explicitly or implicitly such constraints does not only require at least a constitutional decision in favour of a market order. It also raises a question of legitimacy and it invites more political interference with the nomination of the judges. To try to clamp down on special-interest groups would simply mean to confuse cause and effect. This also explains why already all efforts to make the activities of interest groups more transparent, to set against their pressure public hearings as well as the advice of experts and to reveal their financial support for politicians and parties are hardly more than cosmetic operations on the body politic. Furthermore, restrictions of interest-group activities would unnecessarily violate the civil liberties of expression, association and assembly besides suppressing useful functions which interest groups might serve. The involved conflict between political equality on the one hand, which becomes distorted because not all interest of the electorate have equal access to the legislature, and the forementioned civil liberties on the other has to be solved in a different way.

XI. Little hope for a bounded legislature

Two types of constitutional constraints on parliament have been suggested so far:
- to reduce the authority of parliament or at least to render its use more difficult,
- to break up the authority and assign it partly to a second chamber.

The first possibility is in the tradition of Wicksell[32] who proposed to require for parliamentary decisions on taxation the approval of at least a qualified majority because he had to give up the requirement of unanimity on practical grounds. More recently various possibilities to introduce constitutional constraints on taxation[33] and on deficit spending[34] have been discussed. A further possibility would be to introduce or to enlarge the list of political questions which have by constitution - to be referred to a direct vote of all citizens. However, the efficiency so such proposals can be doubted because of the possibilities to circumvent these constraints. Corresponding manipulations would have to occupy the constitutional court which, in turn would be anticipated and would politicize (even more) the nomination of the judges.[35] What seems to be equally important is the implication of constraints of this kind, that they hardly operate in a context sufficient to prevent systematically the market order from being eroded.

The second possibility is in the tradition of Mill[36] and was considered by von Hayek[37] with

32) K. Wicksell (1896), pp. 115 ff.
33) E.g. G. Brennan and J.M. Buchanan (1977) and J.M. Buchanan (1979).
34) J.M. Buchanan and R.E.Wagner (1977); particularly the proposal on pp. 180 f.
35) For an elaboration of reasons doubting the efficiency of constitutional amendments of this kind compare D. Usher (1981), pp. 120 f.
36) J.S. Mill (1859), pp. 324 ff. ("Of a second chamber"). Although Mill begins with the verdict to "set little value on any check wich a Second Chamber can apply to a democracy otherwise unchecked" (p. 324) he reflects on how the assembly could possibly constructed in order "to moderate and regulate dcemocratic ascendancy" (p. 328). But he still remains quite sceptic about the restraining power of a second chamber.
37) F.A. Hayek (1979). Major elements of his"model constitution" can be found in part 17 (pp. 105 ff.).

more hopes than Mill was prepared to set into such a solution. Von Hayek's proposal requires to establish two representative bodies with distinct functions and - correspondingly - distinct democratic procedures to recruit their members. As a third institution, the constitutional court would have the task to control whether each chamber acts within the boundaries of its authority. The division of functions would be a vertical one in the sense that the Legislative Assembly would have to produce the abstract rules forming and preserving the order of society. The Governmental Assembly would practically serve governmental tasks of the kind present parliaments and governments are preoccupied with. However, it would be bound by the rules laid down by the Legislative Assembly. This would imply with respect to economic and social policies that their conduct would have to be in line with the rules of the economic constitution developed by the Legislative Assembly.[38)]

Even without going further into details of the Hayekian proposal[39)] it can already be safely argued that its implementation would require the solution of a quite difficult problem which it has in common with propositions in the Wicksellian tradition. Both types of propositions have to include a delimination:

- A concept in the tradition of Mill would require the legislative assembly to develop explicitly criteria as to which rules and regulations with distributional objectives are acceptable; whether these criteria are very narrow - as von Hayek prefers to see them - or not is of secondary importance.
- Propositions in the tradition of Wicksell are implicit and less determinate with respect to which distribution-oriented rules and regulations are acceptable; this applies to fiscal constraints as well as to decisions specified in advance of requiring approval by referendum.

However, both types of propositions to reform the institutional structure of prevailing democracies have hardly a chance to be realized under normal political conditions. If at all, there are chances for a few isolated steps to be made in the Wicksellian direction as suggested by the American experience. The major reasons for being sceptical have already been mentioned (section 9): Such reforms would require a constitutionally binding decision of self-restraint by those who neither have a vested interest nor are very likey to face a massive electoral pressure to do so.

38) To see the implications more clearly it may be helpful to assume for a moment that the constitutional court of Germany in the case of the Law to Aid Investment ("Investitionshilfegesetz") of 1954 had come down with the verdict that the constitution of the Federal Republic definitely envisages a market order instead of declaring it "neutral" towards the economic order; the position was reinforced in a further verdict concerning pharmacies in 1958 where the court declared the "mixed economic constitution" as imperative according to the basic rights granted in the constitution (Grundgesetz). Although the court is not equivalent to a legislative Assembly, the consequences of a verdict in favour of a market order probably would have been considerable. Quite a number of legislated infringements on property rights and on economic liberties in the name of social justice hardly would have stood up to the test of conformity to a market order. And as a consequence, the court would have had to delimitate in one way or the other which "social" legislation is reconcilable with this order

39) A thorough analysis trying to take into account also those elements of the proposals to be found in other publications of Hayek has been provided by F. Nienhaus (1982). A brief evaluation from the point of constitutional law has been provided by H.H. Rupp (1979).

XII. From neo-feudalism to neo-corporatism?

So far there seems to be no escape from seeing the state becoming to a large extent instrumental to representatives of special-interest groups as the feudal barons of our time. However, at least some observers hope for or see already positive examples of such a "neo-Feudalism on a functional basis"[40] being replaced or altogether avoided because organized interest groups "become incorporated within the policy process as recognized, indispensable negotiators and are made co-responsible (and occasionally completely responsible) for the implementation of policy decisions, which then take on a characteristically semi-public or para-state quality."[41] In the case of Germany, signs of the emergence of such a neo-corporatism (of the "medium" category) are supposed to be observable; as examples are quoted the so-called concerted action with the objective to establish something like a macroeconomic incomes policy which came to an end in the seventies when it could have been most useful and a similar exercise to stem the cost inflation in the public health service which still has to prove itself.

However, not only the forementioned examples but also the experience of more elaborate forms of interest intermediation in economic affairs do not come close to something which could be called a lasting success. They rather confirm the theoretical reservations concerning distributional bargaining (section 7). Even seemingly positive examples like the case of Austria begin to look different in the long run when the costs of concealed unemployment begin to show. Already a sober analysis of the experience of the seventies cannot avoid to make an important reservation, namely that corporatism "does not dispose of capacities to cope systematically with crisis-displacement effects and unintended second-order consequences of political interventions in the market economy."[42] And if the diagnosis of institutional sclerosis is correct, it is highly unlikely that the "second-order consequences" which are produced by this type of political decision-making will be reversed (section 9).

Could it be that neo-corporatism cannot work because a corresponding legal structure is still missing? This seems to be suggested by "neo-evolutionary theories about law".[43] To quite a few economists who still set much hope in the possibilites of rational intervention along conventional lines, the basic diagnosis of this theoretical development may come as a surprise: Interventionism has to face a "rationality crisis" (Habermas). The substantial or material rationality of interventionist law as opposed to the formal rationality of the rules of the market order (sections 2-4) turned out to be inadequate. "Social processes and economic arrangements are simply too dense, complex and potentially contradictory to be adequately accounted for in the kinds of interventionist control mechanisms that have been created."[44]

40) P. Bernholz (1982), p. 584.
41) P.C. Schmitter (1982), p. 263.
42) M. Schmidt (1982), p. 256.
43) To quote a title chosen by G. Teubner (1983), p. 239 - My interpretation of these developments in the sociology of law is mainly based on the forementioned attempt to bring into perspective corresponding theories developed in Europe but also across the Atlantic and on Teubner (1984). Furthermore, the analyses of J. Habermas (1975), N. Luhman (1981) and H. Willke (1983) were helpful in trying to understand this very Inrteresting line of theoretical development.
44) G. Teubner (1983), p. 268.

Regarding the market system, some similarities to von Hayek's "theory of complex phenomena" and its policy implications are recognized from a perspective based on an autopoietic concept of systems theory whereas his related views on the rôle which the state should play in a modern society are not shared at all.[45)]

Legal evolution - so it seems according to this theory - is about to enter a new stage. The present social-engineering capacity of law is considered to be insufficient in view of the degree of functional differentation of society reflected by subsystems like unions, public associations and groupings within the educational and cultural sector. The rôle of a new type of "reflexive law" would be "to structure and restructure semi-autonomous systems, by shaping both their procedures of internal discourse and their methods of coordination with other social systems." Thereby a general objective would still be something like social justice, namely "to guide human action by redefining and redistributing property rights."[46)]

Assuming for a moment that "reflexive law" would be adequate to a neo-corporatist structure of society and leaving the distributional objective unquestioned which is considered to provide the (normative) legitimation of this type of law, there remains a crucial perception problem. The political concept of neo-corporatism as well as its counterpart in the theory of law reveal an image of society which seems at least significantly distorted with respet to the economic system. Its description as "organized capitalism" and the emphasis placed on a "growth of monopoly power"[47)] besides state intervention suggests that the market order is already largely converted into a bargaining system dominated if not controlled by a few big corporations, business associations, unions and the state. However, so far there exists no convincing evidence in favour of a concentration of economic power which would really meet the historicist anticipations of Marx and Schumpeter.

Admittedly, the perception of the economic system is easily dominated by big business, business associations and unions and by their interplay with the representatives of the state. Furthermore, many members of the legislature and of the public administration probably share this biased image; this is particularly likely if they have been recruited from large economic organizations or if they are hoping to joint them after their time in public offices. Hence the segment of the economy which lends itself most easily to a corporatist formation tends to be over-represented. This should also apply when it comes to the specification of economic and social legislation by the legislature and the public administration. As a consequence, the inadequacy of substantial law may not show so much in the performance of this segment of the economy. Its pernicious effects on the capacity to employ and to innovate are probably much larger on small and medium-sized economic units operating in a competitive environment.

45) E.g. G. Teubner (1984), pp. 331 ff.
46) G. Teubner (1983), p. 255.
47) G. Teubner (1983), p. 268.

If it must be seriously doubted that the economic system conforms predominantly to a corporatist pattern, a change-over to a structure of law corresponding to such a pattern would be no solution. It would not be able to meet the systemic needs of the market-oriented segment even if this segment would be properly represented in the corporatist discourse. Following the theory's own logic, the market-oriented segment would most likely be destroyed if the corporatist requirements would be fulfilled. An interesting evolutionary alternative would be that at least some parts of it would submerge into an unofficial market economy (section 13).

However, much more important than the implications of the perception problem discussed so far is to see that neo-corporatism and a corresponding theory of law do not supply a substitute of a market order capable to handle the economic problems of society. So far no concept appears to exist with respect to the requirement to coordinate, control and stimulate billions of ever-changing economic activities in an efficient way. And it requires too much speculation to hope that a new economic system between socialist planning and a market order would somehow envolve out of such a muddled configuration.

XIII. Limited hopes for self-correcting forces

Given the difficulties in attacking the economic and political causes of the atrophy of the market system and the dubious systemic qualities of neo-corporatism, it may be worth-while to ask, finally, whether there are any self-correcting forces at work. A first source of such forces can be seen in the openness of the economic system with respect to space and time:

- Regarding space, it can be hoped that international competition will find opportunities to make inroads into areas of the domestic economy sheltered by distributional legislation and that foreign trade and investment may provide an escape from some economically suffocating effects of internal protection. However, particularly the rapidly expanding non-tariff barriers to trade are not only privileges themselves. They frequently represent efforts to prevent already existing distributional rents from becoming swept away by foreign competition. And since the areas in which rents are provided are not identical between trading countries, the pressure to protect the interests of distributional coalitions by restraints of trade tends to accumulate across these countries.
- Regarding time, hopes can be set into change which may take privileges obsolete and open up new opportunities. A major source of such a change could be innovation. However, again it can be observed that a rising tide of legislation and of agreements mainly between labour-market organizations aims at softening the social effects of change in a way which ultimately makes this change economically less attractive to be carried out. And where change is considered desirable, the state finds itself in the position to have to compensate for self-erected and tolerated barriers to such a change. In the case of Germany, this appears to be one of the major although hardly reflected functions of innovation policy.[48)]

48) This is one of the results of an assessment attempted by the author (M.E. Streit, 1986 b).

A second source of self-correcting forces could be that old and new economic burdens produced by the welfare state are vetoed by a further growth of the shadow economy. This growth signals most clearly the rise in the shadow prices of maintaining inefficient welfare-state arrangements which ultimately might act as a brake upon the process of institutional sclerosis. Considering the various segments of the shadow economy in a wider sense,[49] the following examples may illustrate this point:

- An expansion of black or grey-market activities could act as a brake upon attempts to increase the politically attractive but notoriously costly social services. With the necessary rise of contributions the incentive to avoid a confiscation would become larger. Corresponding to the induced evasion, the fiscal and para-fiscal burden to the official economy would have to be further increased. As a first consequence, the cost-benefit ration of social services would deteriorate to those who pay and would probably add to the resentment which can already be found for the bureaucratic supply of many of these services. A second consequence would be that the competitive pressure of the shadow economy on at least some parts of the official economy would increase further which in turn could foster their resistance against a further expansion of social services.
- The growth of the grey and black labour markets but also of marketable household production could make it increasingly difficult to functionaries of the labour market organizations to maintain positions which mainly serve their organizational interests. The shadow economy does not only seem to demonstrate that the demand for labour is price-elastic. It also signals that the supply of labour can react in a much more differentiated and flexible way with respect to working time than is permitted or economical according to unimaginative working laws and collective agreements including retirement scheme. Equally, the shadow economy provides evidence that the employed and unemployed are capable to develop much more creativity and initiative than is possible and rewarding within the densely regulated and rigid structures of personnel and production of corporations which are hierarchically organized and highly centralized.
- The social network which develops on the basis of voluntary, nonprofit social services does not only reveal unavoidable gaps in the necessarily standardized and regulated supply of the public social service. It also indicates a silent protest against the displacement of the subsidiary principle in social affairs. And in some cases it may become a healthy competitive challenge to public services.

Taking the self-correcting forces together, there does not seem to be a need to end on a completely fatalistic note. However, there remains the provocation resulting from the losses of employment and output which are not widely recognized as consequences of a self-inflicted atrophy of the market-system. And there remains a democratic procedure which becomes increasingly discredited because of constitutional deficiencies which again are difficult to iden-

49) For a more detailed analysis of the shadow economy at large - comprising not only black or grey-market activities but also basically marketable household production and voluntary nonprofit social services - and its relation to the welfare state, compare a corresponding study of the author (M.E. Streit, 1984).

tify by a private citizen. Together the eonomic and public deficiencies represent a threat to welfare states which should not be ignored.

References

(1) Alchian, A.A. (1950),
Uncertainty, Evolution and Economic Theory, Journal of Political Economy, vol. 58, pp. 211-222.

(2) Bernholz, P. (1982),
Expanding Welfare State, Democracy and Free Market Economy: Are they Compatible; Zeitschrift für die gesamte Staatswissenschaft, vol. 138, pp. 583-598.

(3) Brennan, G. and J.M Buchanan (1977),
Towards a Tax Constitution for Leviathan, Journal of Political Economics, vol. 8, pp. 255-273.

(4) Brittan, S. (1975),
The Economic Contradictions of Democracy, British Journal of Politicl Science, vol. 5, pp. 129-159.

(5) Brittan, S. (1978),
How British is the British Sickness?, Journal of Law and Economics, vol. 21, pp. 245-268.

(6) Borchhardt, K. (1981),
Die Konzeption der Sozialen Marktwirtschaft in heutiger Sicht; in: O. Issing (ed.), Zukunftsprobleme der Sozialen Marktwirtschaft, Schriften des Vereins für Socialpolitik, new series, vol. 116, Berlin, pp. 33-53.

(7) Bronfenbrenner, M. and F.D. Holzman (1965),
A Survey of Inflation Theory; in: American Economic Association and Royal Economic Society (eds.), Surveys of Economic Theory, vol. 1, New York, pp. 46-107.

(8) Buchanan, J.M. (1974),
The Limits of Liberty - Between Anarchy and Leviathan, Chicago and London.

(9) Buchanan J.M. (1979),
Constitutional Constraints on Governmental Taxing Power, ORDO, vol. 30, pp. 349-359.

(10) Buchanan, J.M. (1980)
Rent Seeking and Profit Seeking; in: J.M. Buchanan, R.D. Tollison and G. Tullock (eds.), Toward a Theory of the Rent Seeking Society, College Station, Texas A & M, pp. 3-15.

(11) J.M Buchanan and R.E. Wagner (1977),
Democracy in Deficit - The Political Legacy of Lord Keynes, New York, San Francisco, London.

(12) Giersch, H. (1983),
Wie es zu schaffen ist - Agenda für die deutsche Wirtschaftspolitik, Stuttgart.

(13) Habermas, H. (1975),
Legitimation Crisis, Boston.

(14) Hayek, F.A. (1944),
The Road to Serfdom, London.

(15) Hayek, F.A. (1963),
Arten der Ordnung, ORDO, vol. 14, pp. 3-20.

(16) Hayek, F.A. (1964),
The Theory of Complex Phenomena; reprinted in F.A. Hayek, Studies in Philosophy, Politics and Economics, London and Henley 1967, pp. 22-42.

(17) Hayek, F.A. (1967a),
The Results of Human Action but not of Human Design; in: F.A. Hayek, Studies in Philosophy, Politics and Economics, London and Henley 1967, pp. 96-105.

(18) Hayek, F.A. (1967b),
Grundsätze einer liberalen Wirtschaftsordnung, ORDO, vol. 18, pp. 601-617.

(19) Hayek, F.A. (1968),
Competition as a Discovery Procedure; translated into English in: F.A. Hayek, New Studies in Philosophy, Politics, Economics and the History of Ideas, London and Henley 1978, pp. 179-190.

(20) Hayek, F.A. (1973),
Law, Legislation and Liberty, vol. 1: Rules and Order, Chicago and London.

(21) Hayek, F.A. (1976),
Law, Legislation and Liberty, vol. 2: The Mirage of Social Justice, Chicago and London.

(22) Hayek, F.A. (1979),
Law, Legislation and Liberty, vol. 3: The Political Order of a Free People, Chicago and London.

(23) Hume, D. (1786),
A Treatise of Human Nature; ed. by T.H. Green and T.H. Goose, Reprint of the new edition, vol. 2, Aalen 1964.

(24) Johansen, L. (1978),
The Bargaining Society and the Inefficiency of Bargaining,Kyklos, vol. 32, pp. 497-522.

(25) Kirsch, G. (1981),
Ordnungspolitik als Gegenstand politischer Auseinandersetzung; in: O. Issing (ed.), Zukunftprobleme der Sozialen Marktwirtschaft, Schriften des Vereins für Socialpolitik, new series, vol. 116, Berlin, pp. 255-275.

(26) Lehmbruch, G. und P.C. Schmitter, eds. (1982),
Patterns of Corporatist Policy-Making, London and Beverly Hills.

(27) Luhmann, N. (1981),
Politische Theorie im Wohlfahrtsstaat, Munich and Vienna.

(28) Mestmäcker, E.-J. (1978),
Die sichtbare Hand des Rechts - Über das Verhältnis von Rechtsordnung und Wirtschaftssystem, Baden-Baden.

(29) Mill, J.S. (1859),
On Liberty; in: J.S. Mill, Utilitarianism, On Liberty and Considerations on Representative Government, edt. by H.B. Acton, London 1972, pp. 63-170.

(30) Mueller, D.C., ed. (1982),
The Political Economy of Growth, New Haven and London.

(31) Niehans, V. (1982),
Persönliche Freiheit und moderne Demokratie - F.A. von Hayeks Demokratiekritik und sein Reformvorschlag eines Zweikammersystems, Tübingen.

(32) Olson, M. (1982a),
The Political Economy of Comparative Growth Rates; in: D.C. Mueller (1982), pp. 7-52.

(33) Olson, M. (1982b),
The Rise and Decline of Nations - Economic Growth, Stagflation and Social Rights, New Haven and London.

(34) Röpke, J. (1980),
Zur Stabilität und Evolution marktwirtschaftlicher Systeme aus klassischer Sicht; in: E. Streißler and Ch. Watrin, Zur Theorie marktwirtschaftlicher Ordnungen, Tübingen, pp. 124-154.

(35) Rupp, H.H. (1979),
Zweikammersystem und Bundesverfassungsgericht - Bemerkungen zu einem Reformvorschlag F.A. v. Hayeks, ORDO, vol. 30. pp. 95-104.

(36) Schmidt, M. (1982),
Does Corporatism Matter? Economic Crisis, Politics and Rates of Unemployment in Capitalistic Democracies in the 1970s; in: G. Lehmbruch and P.C. Schmitter (1982), pp. 237-258.

(37) Schmitter, P.C. (1982),
Reflections on Where the Theory of Neo-Corporatism Has Gone and Where the Praxis of Neo-Corporatism may Be Going; in: G. Lehmbruch and P.C. Schmitter (1982), pp. 259-279.

(38) Scitovsky, T. (1980),
Can Capitalism Survive? - An Old Question in a New Setting, American Economic Review, vol. 70, pp. 1-9.

(39) Streißler, E. (1980),
Kritik des neoklassischen Gleichgewichtsansatzes als Rechtfertigung marktwirtschaftlicher Ordnungen; in: E. Streißler and Ch. Watrin (eds.), Zur Theorie marktwirt schaftlicher Ordnungen, Tübingen, pp. 38-69.

(40) Streit, M.E. (1984),
The Shadow Economy: A Challenge to the Welfare State?, ORDO, vol. 35, pp. 109-119.

(41) Streit, M.E. (1986a),
Marktwirtschaftliche Ordnungspolitik im demokratischen Wohlfahrtsstaat; in: M. Kaase (ed.), Politische Wissenschaft und Politische Ordnung - Analysen zur Theorie und Empirie demokratischer Regierungsweise, Opladen, pp. 97-110.

(42) Streit, M.E. (1986b),
Industrial Policies for Technological Change - The Case of Germany; in: C.T. Saunders (ed.), Industrial Policies and Structural Change, London, forthcoming.

(43) Thurow, L.C. (1980),
The Zero-Sum Society - Distribution and the Possibilities for Economic Change, reprint 1983, Harmondsworth, Middlesex

(44) Teubner, G. (1983),
Substantive and Reflexive Elements in Modern Law, Law and Society Review, vol. 17, pp. 239-285.

(45) Teubner G. (1984),
Verrechtlichung - Begriffe, Merkmale, Grenzen, Auswege; in: H.F. Zacher et al (eds.), Verrechtlichung von Wirtschaft, Arbeit und sozialer Solidarität - Vergleichende Analysen, Baden-Baden, pp. 289-344.

(46) Usher, D. (1981),
The Economic Prerequisite to Democracy, New York.

(47) Weber, M. (1921),
Wirtschaft und Gesellschaft - Grundriß der verstehenden Soziologie, 5th rev. edition, Tübingen 1972.

(48) Weede, E. 1984),
Democracy, creeping socialism, and ideological socialism in rent-seeking societies, Public Choice, vol. 44, pp. 349-366.

(49) Wicksell, K. (1896),
Finanztheoretische Untersuchungen nebst Darstellung und Kritik des Steuerwesens Schwedens, Jena.

(50) Willke, H. (1983),
Entzauberung des Staates - Überlegungen zu einer sozietalen Steuerungstheorie, Königstein/Ts.

Comment on M.E. Streit: "Economic Order and Public Policy - Market, Constitution and the Welfare State"

by

Rupert Windisch

In commenting on a comprehensive paper by Prof. Streit, I would first like to say that I agree with many of the basic points of his paper. Therefore the following remarks aim rather at being a supplementary note than a criticism of some of his statements.

Among influential scholars of the past supporting his arguments Prof. Streit quotes John St. Mill, Knut Wicksell and Max Weber, but he does not mention Alexis de Tocqueville. The latter has been studied extensively in particular by sociologists, but deserves to be read carefully by political economists too. Especially the second volume of his *Democracy in America* (1840) contains an at that time most astonishing visionary reasoning that big government is inherent in representative politics[1): The age of "blind sacrifice and instinctive virtue" already having been long past de Tocqueville finds the average citizen being occupied by "the complicated little cares that are the excitement and joy of his life" and constitute the essence of individualism in an equalitarian age. Because unpaid political service can be performed only by the rich and privileged, democratization of power and mass equality have an accelerative influence upon bureaucracy, which means "the substitution of paid for unpaid functionaries", and by eroding social hierarchy and regionalism intensifies "administrative centralization". The affinity between mass equality and bureaucracy attracts "place-hunting" - that is "rent-seeking" in public choice theorists' parlance -, the propensity to "rush to the head of the state and ask for his help" as the often easiest and most expeditious means to increase (private) comfort at the expense of the public treasury. De Tocqueville was deeply alarmed about the "unproductive activity" which "unsettles the country without adding to its resources" and might well culminate in a political blizzard eventually destroying democratic desision making institutions. He thus ends in a pessimistic view of civilization not alien to at least some visions of contemporary institutional sclerosis hypotheses which also figure prominently in Professor Streit's paper.

The very term sclerosis has a definitely normative ring: The filter function of real competition does not work as promptly and as pervasively as it *should* work. Likewise property rights are more uncertain as they *should* be in order to give the *right* incentives to invest.

1) See L.L. Wade: "Toqueville and Public Choice", *Public Choice*, XLVII (1985), pp. 491-508 for more extensive quotations and interpretation.

The democratic procedure is overburdened with transaction cost enhancing processes of political bargaining which is riddled with a variety of *deficiencies*. From a *positive* point of view the theoretical and empirical foundation of the sclerosis hypothesis is far from being an accomplished, reliable and mainly undisputed body of knowledge. It has to be admitted that we do not know much at the present time about the quantitative importance of various effects looked upon by many as deficiencies of the build up of "high tax" welfare states. Therefore, "the assessment of the quantitative importance of (these) effects... is still to a considerable extent an issue of personal judgement in spite of much empirical research in recent years"[2]. Referring to the latter, I may mention endeavors to measure the marginal cost of public funds or to test for causality and quantitive impact of government activity on productivity growth (to say nothing about general welfare). There is evidence that "the accumulation of physical and human capital, as well as technological and organizational know-how, which is the basis for the present affluence of these (the scandinavian) nations, took place long before the establishment of present incentive system"[3]. In other words, there are presumably quite long lags of influence of the welfare state on productivity development. So there is little wonder that idelogical positions as well as predictions about what might happen in the future are given ample scope in discussions on the future of the welfare state.

Prof. Streit states (p. 8): "It is the relative anonymity of competitive calculatedness allowing to apply the principle of exit and the reduction of moral requirements to minimum which explain both, the high level of productivity of a market system as an allocation mechanism and its low level of conflict despite the pressures of scarcity." But she or he who is not able to amortize costs sunk in physical or human capital because of the "gale of competition" would as a rule not agree ex post that the conflict thrown upon her or him by the pecuniary externalities of "creative destruction" is low. In the end it is the central normative question whose interests are to count and why. An "efficiency" view is possible and of course congenial to the economist. The view, however, cannot be rationalized by asserting that implied consent to the losses has taken place embedded in a presumed ex ante compensation, as Posner has attempted to argue.[4] The problem of consent has to be transferred to another level: the area of social choice at the constitutional level. But, unfortunately, so far we do not have any theoretically convincing consensus requirements concerning collective actions and especially legal change of economic interests to be protected as legal rights.

Let me conclude with remarks on the poliotical economy of special interest groups. As is now well documented, industrialization and the accompanying division of labor multiplied seperate interests which might be the basis for a myriad of possible pressure groups. But actually - and furtunately - only some special interest groups gained political influence due

2) See A. Lindbeck: "Work Disincentives in the Welfare State", *Nationalökonomische Gesellschaft-Lecutres*, Vienna, 1981, pp. 60-61.
3) Lindbeck op.cit., p. 65.
4) R. Posner: *The Economics of Justice*, Cambridge, Mass., 1981, p. 94.

to the effort of political entrepreneurs who succeeded in forming politically viable groups, i.e. minimal winning coalitions. The new orthodoxy championed by public choice theorists is to view pressure group politics as a societal zero sum game or even worse as a negative sum game. This view is likely to lead to excessive condemnation of special interest groups. It has recently been somewhat corrected by G.S. Becker[5]. In Becker's model of competition among special interest groups for political influence each active group exerts pressure to affect its subsidies and taxes, both being related by an overall budget constraint equating total tax collections to total subsidy payments. Political influence is determined by the magnitude of gains (avoided losses) from the budget, relative ability to organize - that is, effectiveness in controlling free riding by members - , and relative efficiency at providing political support. The main argument of Becker runs that an increase in the deadweight cost of taxation (subsidization) encourages (discourages) pressure by taxpayers (recipients) because they are harmed more (benefit less) by the taxes paid (from the benefits received). These countervailing forces are modelled as a competitive Cournot-Nash-type political equilibrium. Becker concludes that if the gains to groups that benefit exceed the loss to groups that suffer, then the gainers would be able to exert more political pressure than loosers unless there is highly unequal access to political influence. Consequently, whether efficient policies would have a chance to be implemented without actual compensation paid to loosers depends on the access to political influence. Hence the central question remains what secures the openness to technological and organizational experiment, diversity of organizational form, and flexibility of institutional choice.

Not surprisingly Becker's approach is in the spirit of the wealth-maximization principle. That approach brings up a fundamental question not only of constitutional economics but also of the whole field of Law and Economics, a question without any easy solution in sight. Consider a certain institutional change of potential productivity recommended by an economist, which has not yet taken place within a given institutional framework. A neo-institutional equilibrium analysis then is led to infer that the proposed change was, at the for this institutional context specific transaction costs, not worthwhile for the parties potentially concerned; otherwise, by the logic of wealth- or utility maximizing behavior, those parties would have carried it out. The insistence of the external observer that the proposed change is *desirable* now leads to the *recommendation* to change the underlying institutional context and thus, the transaction cost structure governing the agents' decisions. However, if *this* change was not yet carried out by those agents who would be in a position to do so, then an analogous argument reads that it was apparently not to their advantage to carry out this change *within* the ruling *constitutional* framework. Hence, insisting that the proposed change should be carried out, now implies that the constitutional framework itself should have to be changed. As this has not yet happened, we can at the end of this chain of arguments finally only ascertain that the proposed change is *not* in actual fact, desirable. For

5) See G.S. Becker: "A Theory of Competition Among Pressure Groups for Political Influence", *Quaterly Journal of Economics*, XCVII (1983), S. 371-400.

the economist there remains here after only to explain that and why the world, as it presents itself, is the best of all worlds.

Even if, as STIGLER claims, " the role of the economist as preacher"[6] is more the exception in the case of the great economists, the origins of political economy in moral philosophy should not, whilst understandably striving for an objective analysis, slip into oblivion. Authors such as G.J. STIGLER, J.M. BUCHANAN and F.A. HAYEK are, despite their different analytic approaches to political-economic questions, united by a commonly shared normative postulate. As political economists they want to make a contribution, so that individual freedom can, within the framework of a restricted democracy, be maintained for the sake of the progress of civilized nations. The efforts by POSNER and others to establish the wealth maximization principle as an ethical maxim, indicate that even the positivistic attitude of an economic imperialism cannot deny a need for normative anchorage. A provocatively sharpened formulation of the problem such as "Economics *or* Ethics" is fruitful because it challenges other positions to an open ethical discourse. By this, we can reveal amongst things the utilitarian bias shown by the creation or normative doctrines in economics in comparison with doctrines which commit themselves to take individual rights seriously for their own sake. But the economist, looking at it from his point of view taught to think in opportunity costs, will raise the objection that "lexiographic orderings crumble in the face of scarcity"[7]. In an evolutionary perspective, this ethical discourse can be understood as a central element of socio-cultural speciation, that is to say as that element which serves the finding out or discovery of what is "right" and "wrong", without ever producing a definite solution, as is only achievable for purely technical problems.

6) G.J. Stigler: *The Economist as Preacher and Other Essays*, Chicago 1982, Chap. 1.
7) H. Demsetz: "Ethics and Efficiency in Property Rights Systems", in: M.J. Rizzo (ed.), *Time, Uncertainty and Ecquilibrium*, Lexington, 1979, p. 101.

Macroeconomic Policy, Rent seeking and Economic Order

by

Ulrich Schlieper

The "Economist" (May 31st, 1986) recently published an article with the sub-headline "Believe it or not, America's Senate is pondering a tax code that is fair, simple and efficient". Why is it that economists are amazed when they see an act of rational economic policy, when at the same time they propose a theory which relies on individual rationality and the "invisible hand" of the market yielding (Pareto-) optimal results?.

Politicians usually have no specific role in models of efficient market equilibria - except taking the blame of interfering with the market. We can construct models where the politician's interfering behaviour is rational from his point of view or according to his preferences. But if we have reason to believe that there are individuals (or groups) in the economy whose rational behaviour calls for tampering with the market mechanism we can no longer rely on this mechanism to yield optimal results which convinced advocates of the free market economy seem to believe in. As far as I know we do not have a satisfactory model or theory which could explain an economic order (be it a market economy or any other) as the result of rationally behaving individuals. The reason is fundamental: a stable economic order is unthinkable without some minimal amount of cooperative behaviour which is beneficial collectively but which also can offer high rewards for noncooperative behaviour. These rewards can be profits from restricting trade and competition by various means. Cooperative behaviour is necessary, e.g. to keep transaction costs (all costs of making and enforcing contracts) low. Prisonner's dilemma - models can be used to illustrate such situations. Axelrod's (1984) work on the evolution of cooperation is a very important step in developing a theory of emerging cooperation. It turns out that in prisoner's dilemma situations cooperative behaviour is likely only if the game is expected to be repeated for an unknown number of times.

One may ask why cooperative behaviour is important in a competitive market economy. This isobvious when we consider transaction costs. If traders honour contracts and do not try to cheat transaction costs of making contracts and enforcing them will be small. The gains from trade can be captured by traders. If, however, traders only honour contracts when being forced by legal action then transaction costs are high and part of the gains from trade

Pethig Schlieper (Eds.)
Efficiency, Institutions, and Economic Policy

will be lost to the traders. This kind of cooperative behaviour cannot be enforced by law or constitution, neither does if follow from individual rational behaviour in the sense of maximizing utility. "Certainly an individualistic calculus of costs and benefits would suggest that cheating, shirking, stealing, assault, and murder should be everywhere evident. We do observe all these kinds of behaviour, but side by side with them we also observe individuals obeying rules when they could be violated with impunity at considerable benefit. Indeed, "a neoclassical world would be a jungle and no society would be viable". (North, 1982, p. 11). Moral and ethical codes of behaviour and (or) ideological considerations have to be investigated in order to explain institutions and economic order - individual rational calculus of costs and benefits is not enough. To quote North again (p. 12): "Individuals may ignore such a calculus, in an attempt to change the structure, because of deep-seated ideological convictions that the system is unjust. Individuals may also obey customs, rules, and laws because of an equally deep-seated conviction that they are legitimate".

Of course, ideological convictions can be incorporated into the preference order of an individual so that observed behaviour is the result of a calculus of cost and benefits. But then we would have to explain the changes of preferences in this respect and there is still the problem of explaining the emergence of different ideological convictions. Whether we put these into the preference order or among the set of constraints is of secondary importance.

One may ask why these considerations are important in a macroeconomic context. I think they are important if we want to understand why opinions of macroeconomists differ so widely over questions of macroeconomic policy. While economists' opinions do not differ widely over microeconomic policy issues there is a wide variety of opinions when it comes to macroeconomic policy (Ch. Schultze, (1982), Nordhaus (1983)). This variety of opinions corresponds to a similar variety of macroeconomic theories (or models, or "schools"). Take, e.g. the fixed-price-cum-quantity-rationing-models and the new classical macroeconomics. The basic difference between both types of theoretical reasoning is the assumption about the market clearing process. If we assume market clearing then, of course, the only unemployment which the model can display is search unemployment of voluntary unemployment. Involuntary unemployment in the Keynesian sense can only occur if markets are not cleared, i.e. if some prices are prevented from assuming their equilibrium values. The existence of involuntary unemployment suggests that there is an unexploited potential of Pareto-improvements. Superficially this is a powerful argument against disequilibrium models of unemployment due to sticky wages and prices. Rational agents would soon carry out the mutually beneficial transactions.

However, this may prove to be rather difficult. The snag is that these mutually beneficial transactions may be - and quite often will be - infeasible because they imply lump sum transfers. Take the example of a new production process which is cost and labour saving and which destroys the value of existing capital (human and physical). To make the example more precise, assume unit costs of production of the new process c_1, while total average cost of the old process is $c_0>c_1$ and variable average cost of the old process is $c_v<c_1$. A firm equipped with the old type of machinery is not going to invest in the new process until existing equipment is worn out. New competitors however, will start with the new process and offer the product at lower prices. Producers operating the old process have to reduce their prices and are not able to recover all of their investment in machinery (a similar argument may apply to workers). The competitive market mechanism devalues existing assets, and the owners of these assets do have an incentive to resist the change - they engage in activities designed to obstruct the introduction of the new production process. The question is: Can the new firms pay compensation to the owners of existing assets and thus move to a Pareto superior situation? Two problems arise: First, even if some would be willing to do so there is still the free-rider-problem of newcomers who are not contributing to the compensation and thus being able to sell at lower prices. Second, the firms with the new production technique cannot capture all the benefits (which would enable them to pay compensation) if they sell at lower prices (which they must do to sell at all). The benefits would ultimately accrue to consumers, and here the free-rider-problem probably becomes unsurmountable.

The case is similar when we start from a situation of - say - classical unemployment where real wages are "too high". Exploiting the potential of Pareto improvement by moving to a corresponding full employment equilibrium would require a reduction of real wages for people already employed. Again, it is not possible for the unemployed to pay compensation to the employed for a reduction in wages. The benefits are widespread and difficult to capture by an agreement. Transaction costs are far too high for an agreement leading to a Pareto superior situation and compensating the losers.

One may put forward further arguments why such agreements are not even desirable because they change the incentive structure in a way which protects the status quo. But that is beside the point I want to make here: Pareto optimality of a competitive equilibrium cannot be taken as an argument that rationally behaving agents in a market economy will always end up in a situation of an efficient market equilibrium (or even competitive equilibrium). Individual rational behaviour may include activities designed to change or to bend existing rules of exchange, and models of competitive equilibria would be poor guides to understanding situations of sustained unemployment.

The paradigm of the "invisible hand" guiding self interested actions in a direction towards social objective rests on the assumption that the "rules of the game", i.e. the institutional framework and compliance with the stipulated rules is given. Individual rationality is not enough to explain economic or social *relations* among individuals, and from preferences and rationality alone it is impossible to predict the resulting framework of economic organisation, patterns of division of labour, institutions etc.

Macroeconomics in a decentralised market economy is the analysis of the whole system of interrelated markets whereas microeconomics deals with the analysis of individual firms of households and partial equilibria. Assumptions of optimising behaviour and market equilibrium are appropriate assumptions for *some* markets but certainly not for all, and while parts of the system do work like a perfect market there are other parts which behave differently. This in turn must have consequences for the behaviour of the system.

Obeying the rules of a competitive market mechanism implies that agents may suffer because their physical of human capital loses its value due to changes in production technique or changes in tastes. They would have to bear these losses up to the point where society provides some welfare "safety-net". The temptation is great (and the payoffs may be large) to resist the harsh winds of competitive change so that the system does not work as indicated by models of competitive equilibria.

Sometimes economists make a distinction between "utility maximisation" and "maximisation with guile" (or rent seeking, opportunism etc.) in the sense that the first variety is perfectly legitimate while the second one is frowned upon. In terms of individual rationality this distinction is difficult to defend. Basically this distinction is a consequence of the desirability of cooperative behaviour while it is difficult to explain cooperation by relying simply on self-interested rational agents. The fundamental problem can be formulated as follows: A competitive equilibrium assumes individual maximisation subject to the usual constraints. On the other hand, the system can only work if agents comply with the rules, honour contracts etc., i.e. if they display highly cooperative behaviour. This is a combination of competition and cooperation which may not be stable for two reasons: First, cooperative behaviour may be extended to form coalitions like cartels, etc. and secondly, competitive behaviour may induce cheating, shirking etc. which also leads to inefficiencies or (market disequilibria).

What is the consequence of special interest groups for macroeconomics? The consequences must be looked for in two directions. First, special interest groups seek to influence government decisions on regulation, subsidies, tax advantages etc. Second, they seek to protect their memebers against adverse consequences of the competitive process by means of barriers to entry, pricing policies etc.

These two kinds of activity impede the functioning of the competitive market mechanism, and - for macroeconomic analysis of great importance - can lead to more inflexible prices and market disequilibria. It is also possible that special interest groups increase the difficulties of executing the mutually beneficial exchanges which can be carried out in moving from unemployment to full employment. Olson (1982) suggests that coalitions of special interest groups are responsible for price rigidities and market inflexibilities which seem to characterise most industrialized economies in the last two decades. Superficially Olson seems to say that his proposed process of institutional sclerosis is irreverisble. This hypothesis, however, appears to be contradicted by the recent American policies of deregulation.

As to rent seeking it is usually argued that it is especially governmental action which provides opportunities for (wasteful) rent seeking activities. Subsidies, tax exemptions, monopoly rights and import restrictions are the usual examples. Macroeconomic policies do not normally count as interventions providing opportunities to rent seeking activities. Proponents of Keynesian stabilization policies even argued, that fiscal and monetary interventions are necessary to stabilize the market mechanism while the allocation problem is solved efficiently by decentralized decisions in a market system (Heller, 1966). Today it would be difficult to defend such a position. It is now common knowledge that fiscal and monetary policy measures will be taken into account by private decision makers, and the effect can be counterproductive.

If we are looking for rent seeking opportunities being opened up by macroeconomic policy measures we have to look for distributional consequences of these policies. It is difficult to construct policy measures which are distributionally strictly neutral - nearly every measure is likely to change the income and wealth distribution to some extent: government spending will favour the industries supplying the commodities in question. Increasing public employment in order to increase production of public services will benefit workers in the particular job market; restrictive monetary policies affect most adversely construction industries. The different distributional contents of macroeconomic stabilization policies induces corresponding lobbying activities - either to initiate certain policy measures or to avoid certain government actions.

Distributive aspects of macroeconomic policies are most pronounced in the realm of incomes policies, and here the rent seeking potential is most obvious. Incomes policies are usually understood as policies trying to modify the process of wage and price formation, and, of course, this will have direct distributional impacts. This kind of macroeconomic policy became prominent in the macroeconomist's tool kit when "ordinary" fiscal and monetary measures seemd to be incapable of curbing inflation and promoting employment, when the Phillips curve trade-off between unemployment and inflation disappeared.

But before we can investigate the rent seeking potential of macroeconomic policies a remark about the justification of stabilization policies seems to be necessary. A government may rely completely on the market mechanism to guide the economy on a stable path of economic development augmented by a set of policies which are designed to keep the competitive market mechanism alive and well. Such a philosophy does not call for any macroeconomic stabilization policy. Should occasional bouts of unemployment occur there is only the social safety net designed to guarantee a minimum standard of living (whatever that may be). But now let us assume that there is a major breakdown in the marginal efficiency of capital (to use Keynes' terms), investment demand is reduced drastically, and the market and price mechanism cannot cope with the problem of restoring full employment and redirecting resources fast enough. Some assets will lose their value, and redistribution of income and wealth may be large. Will the losers bear these losses patiently as a streak of bad luck and try to improve their situation by innovations, offering their services at lower prices etc. or will they blame it on "the system" and demand government help and lobby for it? Individual rationality is compatible with both; the crucial question is ideolgy (or moral and ethical values). The government will be confronted with the choice of either just sitting tight and hoping that the competitive market mechanism will correct things sooner or later (and this implies that those who are adversely affected by structural change bear the full consequences) or the government can try to redistribute the losses of value in human and physical capital. What the government can and will do does depend to a large extent on the ideologies, moral and ethical values prevailing in the society (North (1982), esp. ch. 5).

Given the set of moral and social values it is always possible to imagine a recession where the negative effects of the market mechanism are so severe that an inactive government will lose legitimacy, and existing economic and political institutions become endangered. Forces will be set in motion intending economic and political change. So there is a point where the government has to step in. If conditions are well defined under which employment schemes become effective then there is considerable potential for rent seeking. An obvious potential for rent-seeking is in the labour market for unions. here I am not referring to the case where unions push up the money wage, and the central bank tries to keep employment constant by letting money supply grow appropriately so that prices rise, real wages and employment stay constant, and the final result is cost push inflation augmented by an accommodating monetary policy. In this case there is hardly a benefit for the workers and unions to be seen - on the contrary, they probably are going to lose by accelerating inflation.

Aggressive wage policy only pays if real wages rise and the government pursues an accommodating fiscal policy. A simple calculation shows the effects of this policy. Total output is divided into marketable output X and output which is sold to the public (i.e. purchased by the government at cost-plus-prices). Denote GNP by Y and government spending by G, then

$$(1) \qquad Y = X + G$$

Production of X needs factor inputs K_1 and N_1 while production of the goods purchased by the government needs inputs K_2 and N_2. As G is being valued by its factor costs we have (all in terms of the "private" good X):

$$(2) \qquad Y = X(K_1, N_1) + qK_2 + wN_2$$

where q and w indicate the real factor prices. Let q, K_1, K_2 be fixed and assume the real wage rate w is equal to marginal productivity in the X-sector. Under these conditions a rise of the real wage rate and an accommodating fiscal policy keeping total employment constant results in an increase of total wages and in an increase of GNP. Let $N_1 + N_2 = N = \text{const.}$ and we obtain

$$(3) \qquad \frac{\partial Y}{\partial N_1} = \frac{\partial^2 X}{\partial N_1^2} (N - N_1) < 0.$$

The real wage increase induces the X industry to shed some of its labour force which will be employed in the government sector at the increased wage rate.

The question arises whether this policy is beneficial to the workers if government expenditure is financed by taxes. A uniform tax rate θ then must be equal to

$$(4) \qquad \theta = \frac{G}{Y} \; ; \qquad 1 - \theta = \frac{Y - G}{Y}$$

so that the sum of net wages L is

$$(5) \qquad L = wN(1-\theta) = \frac{\partial X}{\partial X_1} \cdot N\left(\frac{X(K_1, N_1)}{X(K_1, N_1) + qK_2 + w(N - N_1)}\right) .$$

For sake of simplicity assume $X = K_1^{\alpha} N_1^{\beta}$; $0 < \beta < 1$, so that

$$(6) \qquad L = \frac{\beta X^2 N}{N_1 (X + qK_2) + \beta X (N - N_1)} .$$

Differentiating with respect to N_1 yields the result

$$\frac{dL}{dN_1} \geq 0 \text{ if } \frac{N}{N_1} \geq \left(\frac{1-\beta}{\beta}\right)^2 + \frac{(1-2\beta)}{\beta^2} \frac{qK_2}{X} .$$

So, if $\beta < 0.5$ there is an optimal $N^*_1 < N$ which maximises the sum of net wages paid to the workers. Depending on the initial size of N_1 it may be optimal either to increase or decrease N_1. Empirical estimation of production functions usually show a value of β significantly larger than 0.5. But if we disaggregate the labour force and assume $X = K^{\alpha} N_1^{\beta_1} \cdots N_m^{\beta_m}$ then the above argument still holds, and we probably have $\beta_i < 0.5$. Proper disaggregation has to take into account production structure and organization of unions.

The short run consequences are: rising wages, rising GNP, and possibly price stability - these macroeconomic goals are achieved. In the medium term the decline of the "market sector" will have negative effects on investment and growth as less output is available for capital formation. Bacon and Eltis (1976) pursued a similar hypothesis for the British economy and claimed that the relative decline of the British economy is due to the decline of the market sector. They also refer to the works of Quesnay who analyzed the economy of the ancien regime and concluded that the productive sector (agriculture) was taxed too heavily, declined, and so the tax base diminished. Apparently here the rent seekers destroyed the source of their rents.

References

(1) Axelrod, R.M. (1984),
The Evolution of Cooperation, Basic Books, New York

(2) Bacon, R., Eltis, W., (1976),
Britain's Economic Problems: Too Few Producers, London

(3) Buchanan, J., Tollison, R., Tullock, G. (ed.) (1980),
Toward a Theory of the Rent-Seeking Society, Texas A &M University Press

(4) Flanagan, R., Soskice, D., Ulmann, L., (1983),
Unionism, Economic Stabilization, and Incomes Policies: European Experience, Washington, D.C..

(5) Heller, W., (1966),
New Dimensions of Political Economy, Cambridge, Mass..

(6) Nordhaus, W., (1983),
Macroconfusion: The Dilemmas of Economic Policy, in: Tobin, J. (ed.) Macroeconomics, Prices and Quantities, Oxford.

(7) North, Douglass, C., (1982),
Structure and Change in Economic History, New York, London.

(8) Olson, M. (1982),
The Rise and Decline of Nations, Yale University Press, New York

(9) Schultze, Ch. (1982),
The Role and Responsibilities of the Economist in Government AER, Papers and Proceedings

Comment on U. Schlieper: "Macroeconomic Policy, Rent Seeking and Economic Order"

by

Georg Ziemes

Most macroeconomic work does not deal explicitly with the issue of political power to execute stabilization policies. "Positive" work deals with the structure of economic relations while "normative" work generally takes the objectives as determined exogenously through a political process which is both outside professional economic competence and beyond professional economic concern. There does, however, appear to be a "consensus political theory" implicit in macroeconomic work. It is that the political process which generates monetary and fiscal decisions is reasonably "fair", "unbiased" and genuinely concerned with the public interest. In general, economists seem to subscribe to the implicit view that a national economic interest exists and that the government pursues that public interest to the best of its ability. But is the structure of the economy really to be characterized by an objective harmony or is it better depicted as a conflict of economic interests among economic classes? That is, are the monetary and fiscal policies which are optimal from the point of view of one class also optimal for all other classes?

In his paper Professor *Schlieper* enters into the wide-ranging question about the incentives that lead to macroeconomic stabilization policies. In the economic literature there are at least two approaches providing answers: the "electoral (or political business cycle) theory" and the "radical class theory".

The political process sometimes utilized by economists is the "electoral theory" or "voting model of government behavior". Stated quite simply this economic theory of politics postulates that governments choose their policies in order to maximize the probability of being reelected.

The "radical theory of the state" asserts: the economic class or classes which own or control the means of production dominate the state and determine its objectives. The radical class theory has always been an important part of Marxist political philosophy. One component of the analytical method of historical materialism is the relationship between the economic base or structure of society and the "super-structure" to which it gives rise and which influences its development. Part of the social superstructure is the entire set of state institutions (educational, legal, military, political, etc.). Since the superstructure if formed

Pethig Schlieper (Eds.)
Efficiency, Institutions, and Economic Policy

in harmony with the economic base it will represent the existing economic class and power relations. Thus, it is assumed that under capitalism the captialists will dominate the state and the state will pursue the interests of this class. Abstracting to a two class model (capital and labor) the approach assumes that capital controls state decision-making institutions and that the state will act in favor of capital interests whenever there is a conflict of interest among classes.

Even though SCHLIEPER puts forward his two class model only as an example, nevertheless he chooses the (opposite) case where *labor* exploits some of the stabilization potential. As in the "radical theory of the state" there is no explanation given about how the individual or class preferences are transmitted (e.g. via voting, logrolling, or bribing) to the state objective function. It is merely assumed that the government executes some kind of direct hiring financed by a proportional income tax.

The straightforward two-sector, two-factor general equilibrium model applied differs from the typical static full employment HARBERGER-type models with respect to the following aspects:

- substitution effects between capital and labor are assumed away by taking the sectoral capital stocks as given,

- explicit demand functions (commodity, labor supply, government action) are neglected, and

- labor in the public sector is paid above its marginal productivity.

The complete model is shown in the following diagram, where the labor supply functions (NS^0 and NS^1) are added. Besides the usual comments about HARBERGER-type models SCHLIEPER's divergencies require further questions:

Does the surprising result hold e.g. for more general production functions, for models where the number of production factors is greater than the number of goods, and for non-constant capital stocks? How does the inefficient production structure in the "G"-market affect factor prices and investment? It seems unrealistic to believe that changes in absolute or even relative factor incomes would not give rise to counteractions of capital owners to the rent seeking efforts of the labor unions. In the literature on this matter there is yet no clear cut answer to the question whether the actions by capitalists and unions would in fact countervail each other.

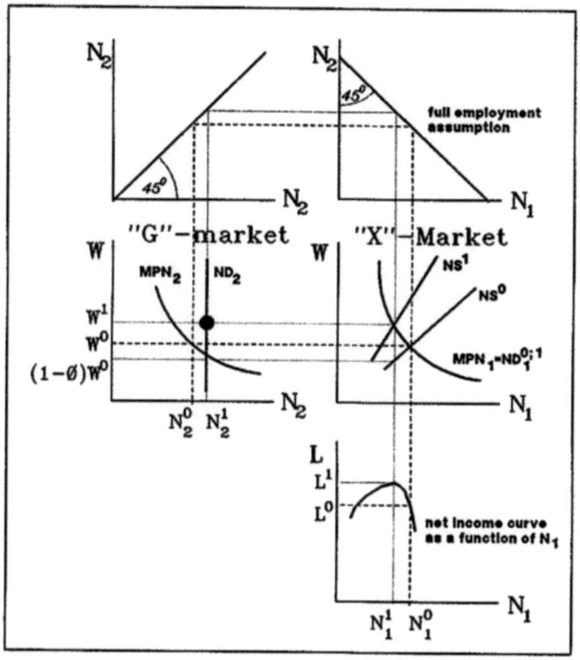

N2
45°
N2
N2
45°
full employment
assumption
N1
"G"-market
"X"-Market
W
MPN2
ND2
W1
W0
(1-ø)W0
N2
N2^0 N2^1
W
NS1
NS0
MPN1=ND1^0;1
N1
L
L1
L0
net income curve
as a function of N1
N1
N1^1 N1^0

The Growth of Government and the Rise of Pressure Groups

by

Bengt-Arne Wickström*

1. Introduction

Redistributional policy is often seen as an important factor in explaining the growth in the size of government that has been observed in this century.[1] Several factors explaining the expansion in redistributional activities, can be thought of. On the one extreme, one has pure altruism in combination with some ideologically motivated concept of justice leading to a redistribution in favor of the poor; on the other extreme, pure self-interest in combination with the prevailing politico-economical system leads to redistribution in favor of the strong and influential[2].

In this essay we study the redistributional effects of interest groups engaged in lobbying activities. Direct transfers from general revenues to organizations and representatives for special interests in the private sector of the economy, such as farmers and certain industries, have become common in many industrialized countries during the last decades[3]. The general hypothesis behind this essay is that these transfers only become possible if the government plays an active rôle in the economy. It is further hypothesized that the lobbying effort of the interest groups increases with increasing government involvement in the economy. Increased lobbying effort, in turn might lead to more government activity with an ever increasing volume of transfers as the end result.

* Institutt for økonomi, Universitetet i Bergen, Jonas Reinsgate 19, N-5000 Bergen, Norway.
This work is part of a research project, "Transfers, subsidies, and efficiency in the policy of redistribution", financed by the Norwegian Research Council for Social Sciences and the Humanities (NAVF). It was written while the author, with financial support in the form of a Ruhrgas stipend from the Stifterverband für die Deutsche Wissenschaft, was visiting the Sonderforschungsbereich 5, Fakultät für Volkswirtschaftslehre und Statistik, Universität Mannheim. This support from the Stifterverband and from the Sonderforschungsbereich 5 is gratefully acknowledged.
The essay has benefitted from comments from and discussions with R. Pethig, J.-M. Graf von der Schulenburg, and L. Thorlund-Petersen. Also this is acknowledged with gratitude.

1) For an extensive general review of the theories about the growth in government activities see Larkey, Stolp, and Winer (1981).
2) For an interesting discussion of these ideas, see Lindbeck (1985).
3) In Norway this type of subsidies increased by 14.3 per cent per annum in the period 1973-82. In the year 1982, 4.6 per cent of the Norwegian gross national product was redistributed in this manner; farming received 2.4 per cent, industry 1.5 per cent and fisheries .3 per cent of GNP in direkt subsidies (NOU, 1984). In addition, there are indirect subsidies in the form of import and other regulations, the value of which might be considerable.

Pethig Schlieper (Eds.)
Efficiency, Institutions, and Economic Policy

More specifically, "neutral", general government involvement in the private sector, such as counter-cyclical stabilization policy, creates incentives for interest groups to form, in order to influence the manner in which the public money is distributed in the private sector. These incentives are stronger the greater is the government involvement. The greater is the "cake", the better are the opportunities to secure a big piece.

The rise of interest groups and lobbying activities influences government policy. Ministries and bureaus are formed to deal with the sectors of the economy that are represented by the various groups. A bureau, in many ways, has interests similar to those of the interest group it is set to administer. A big budget makes the bureau and its bureaucrats influential. It will thus exert pressure on the government and the amount of transfers will increase[4)], making the "cake" larger and the lobbying incentives stronger. This might explain some of the growth in government activity.

In this essay we will not investigate this hypothesis in its entirety. We will rather limit ourselves to a comparative-statics analysis of the behavior of interest groups facing a given amount of transfers which is to be distributed. Each interest group will then engage in rent-seeking activities. This is modelled as a non-cooperative game. This game is of the prisoner's dilemma type. We study the properties of the Nash equilibrium of this game and derive several, in principle, testable propositions.

First, the behavior of an individual pressure group in response to the actions of the others is studied. Then, the existence and uniqueness of a Nash equilibrium is established, and its stability properties are investigated. Finally, the comparative-statics properties of the Nash equilibrium are discussed. For the latter purpose, also some examples are given.

Among other things, it is seen that the size of the potential subsidies determines the incentive to lobby and the lobbying effort, that is, the amount of resources used up on lobbying activities. Also the number of active pressure groups increases with the size of potential benefits.

The essay closes with some concluding remarks.

2. The model

We study an economy with I pressure groups indexed by $i \in \{1, ..., I\}$. Each group is characterized by its strength, or power, n_i. For convenience's sake we order the groups according to decreasing power: $n_1 \geq n_2 \geq ... \geq n_I$.

The number I can be arbitrarily large, and all potential pressure groups in the economy are listed. Whether a given group is active or not, will be determined within the model.

4) Compare Niskanen (1971).

The government gives out subsidies to the pressure groups. The total amount of subsidy, the "cake", is fixed and set equal to y. Each pressure group expends a certain amount of resources, x_i, in order to influence the government to give it a larger share of the cake. If $x_i = 0$, we say that group i is inactive.

The fraction of the cake that a certain group receives is denoted by β_i. Thus, the net benefit to a group of the lobbying activity is

(1) $$\pi_i := \beta_i y - x_i .$$

We assume that β_i is an increasing concave function of x_i and decreasing in all other x_j. We further assume that it takes the form $\beta_i = z_i / A$, where z_i only depends on x_i and A depends on all x_j. Normalization of the β_i implies that $A = \Sigma_i z_i$.

We also assume that z_i, and the resources expanded by a pressure group, x_i are related by a strictly concave increasing function of x_i, parametrized by the power of group i, n_i:

(2) $$z = g(x;n)$$

The concavity and monotonicity of g imply the same properties on β_i as a function of x_i. The function g is assumed to satisfy the conditions

(3a) $$g(0;n) = 0,$$

(3b) $$g(1;n_1) = 1$$

(3c) $$g(x;n) > g(x;n') \Leftrightarrow n > n',$$

and

(3d) $$g_x(x;n) > g_x(x;n') \Leftrightarrow n > n',$$

such that $x > 0$.

Condition (3a) says that without lobbying a group does not receive any cake. For completeness' sake, we define β_i to be $1/I$ whenever $x_j = 0$ for all j. That is, if all x_i were zero, the cake would be evenly distributed. As will be seen, this will never occur in equilibrium. There will always be at least two active pressure groups.

Condition (3b) insures that the function g is well-defined. The definition in terms of β only makes it unique up to a multiplicative constant. Condition (3b) will never be needed in the analysis, however.

The concept of power in the model is defined by conditions (3c) and (3d). They state that, for any two pressure groups expending the same amount of resources, given the total expenditures of all groups together, the more powerful of the two will get a larger share of the cake and, for a given increase in its lobbying effort, the more powerful group will receive a larger increase in its share of the cake than the less powerful one. In other words, both the total and the marginal impact from lobbying is greater, the more powerful is the pressure group.

In the following, we will refer to the variable z_i as the pressure from group i.[5)]

The behavioral assumption is that each group attempts to maximize its net benefits, π, from the lobbying activity. In doing so, it takes the action of all other groups as given. That is, the pressure groups play a non-cooperative game, the *lobbying game*. Defining the pressure of all groups but group i by $A_i := \Sigma_{j \neq i} z_j$, we can write the problem facing group i as

(4) $$\max_{x_i} \frac{g(x_i; n_i)}{A_i + g(x_i; n_i)} y - x_i .$$

3. Nash equilibrium

If the problem (4) has a solution for all groups at the same time, the lobbying game has a Nash equilibrium. It is convenient to rewrite (4) in a slightly different manner. Denoting the inverse of g with respect to x by g^{-1}, we find:

(4a) $$\max_{z_i \geq 0} \frac{z_i}{A_i + z_i} y - g^{-1}(z_i; n_i).$$

The solution to (4a), $z_i^M(A_i, y)$, exists for $A_i > 0$ and can be found from the expression

(5) $$\frac{A_i + z_i^M}{y} = \ell_i(z_i^M)\left(1 - \frac{z_i^M}{A_i + z_i^M}\right),$$

if the z_i^M solving (5) is non-negative; otherwise $z_i^M = 0$.

5) Our model is in essence a special case of that in Pethig (1984) and a generalization of that in Tullock (1980). Tullock's g is given by $g(x) = x^r$, and r can take all positive values. However, if $r > I/(I-1)$, the game has no Nash equilibrium (see Pethig, 1984). Hence, our requirement that g be concave, is not a very strong limitation in comparison with Tullock's model. Pethig only proves existence in the general model. The comparative-statics analysis is carried out in a two-player parametric version. Our analysis is thus to some extent more general in that it is carried through in the general model.

The function ℓ_i is defined by

(6) $$\ell_i(z_i) := \frac{1}{\partial g^{-1}(z_i; n_i)/\partial z_i} .$$

$\ell^i(z_i)$ is the marginal impact of lobbying expenditure on pressure, dz_i / dx_i, as a function of z_i. It is easily verified that ℓ_i, for $z > 0$, satisfied the inequalities

(7a) $$\ell_i(z) > 0,$$

(7b) $$\ell_i'(z) < 0,$$

and

(7c) $$\ell_i(z) > \ell_j(z) \Leftrightarrow n_i > n_j .$$

If $\ell_i(0)$ is bounded and y sufficiently small, then $z_i^M(A_i, y) = 0$.

3.1 The reaction function

The function $z_i^M(A_i, y)$ is the reaction function. It is defined for all $A_i > 0$ and $y \geq 0$. It is easily seen from (4a) that the limit of z_i^M, as A_i vanishes, is zero. We therefore define $z_i^M(0,y) = 0$. However, it is also readily seen that $z_i = 0$, for all i, is no equilibrium of the lobbying game, although satisfying the reaction function when it is extended in this manner.

To avoid the problem at zero, we assume that at least one group is bounded away from zero. We assume that this is the most powerful one. That is, in (4a) for $i = 1$, the restriction on the variable z is $z_1 \geq \varepsilon > 0$. Now, $z_1^M(0, y) = \varepsilon$. We will show that if ε is small enough, this restriction is not binding in a Nash equilibrium.

Before doing so, we investigate the form of the reaction function in general. It is evident that it is a continuous function of A_i and y. The critical value of y for which z_i^M becomes equal to zero is

(8) $$y^0(A_i) = \frac{A_i}{\ell_i(0)} .$$

For any $A_i > 0$ and $y > y^0(A_i)$ we can find the partial derivatives of z_i^M with respect to A_i and y. Differentiation of (5) yields

(9) $$\frac{\partial z_i^M}{\partial A_i} = - \frac{2(1-\beta_i^M)-1}{2(1-\beta_i^M) - y(1-\beta_i^M)^2 \ell_i'(z_i^M)}$$

and

(10) $$\frac{\partial z_i^M}{\partial y} = \frac{\ell_i(z_i^M)(1-\beta_i^M)}{2 - y(1-\beta_i^M)\ell_i'(z_i^M)},$$

such that $\beta_i^M := z_i^M / (A_i + z_i^M)$. The derivative of β_i^M with respect to A_i is found in the same manner:

(11) $$\frac{\partial \beta_i^M}{\partial A_i} = - \frac{1}{A} \frac{(1-\beta_i^M) - y(1-\beta_i^M)^2 \ell'(z_i^M)\beta_i^M}{2(1-\beta_i^M) - y(1-\beta_i^M)^2 \ell_i'(z_i^M)}.$$

If $y > y^0(A_i)$, we have the following results: β_i^M decreases with increasing values of A_i; z_i^M increases with increasing y; and z_i^M increases with increasing values of A_i as long as $\beta_i^M > \frac{1}{2}$ and it decreases with increasing values of A_i if $\beta_i^M < \frac{1}{2}$. The maximum value of z_i^M is reached for $\beta_i^M = \frac{1}{2}$, or $z_i^M = A_i$. It satisfies

(12) $$\ell_i(z_i) = \frac{4 z_i}{y}.$$

Since g is concave, $\ell_i(z_i) < z_i / x_i$, and the maximum value of x_i is thus less than $y/4$.

It is also seen that $z_i^M(A_i, y) > z_j^M(A_j, y)$ if $A_i = A_j$ and $n_i > n_j$. Finally, we note that $\partial z_i^M / \partial A_i > -\frac{1}{2}$. Figure 1 gives a diagram of the reaction function and the corresponding β_i^M for different values of n_i and y.

3.2 Existence of a Nash equilibrium

We have seen that z_i^M is a continuous function of A_i. Further, z_i^M will take on values between zero or, in the case of z_1^M, ε and some number less than $g(y/4; n_i)$. The function z^M defined by

(13) $$z^M(z, y) := (z_i^M(A_i, y))$$

is thus a continuous mapping from the set

(14) $$S := \{(z_i) | 0 \le z_i \le g(y/4; n_i), 0 < \varepsilon \le z_1\}$$

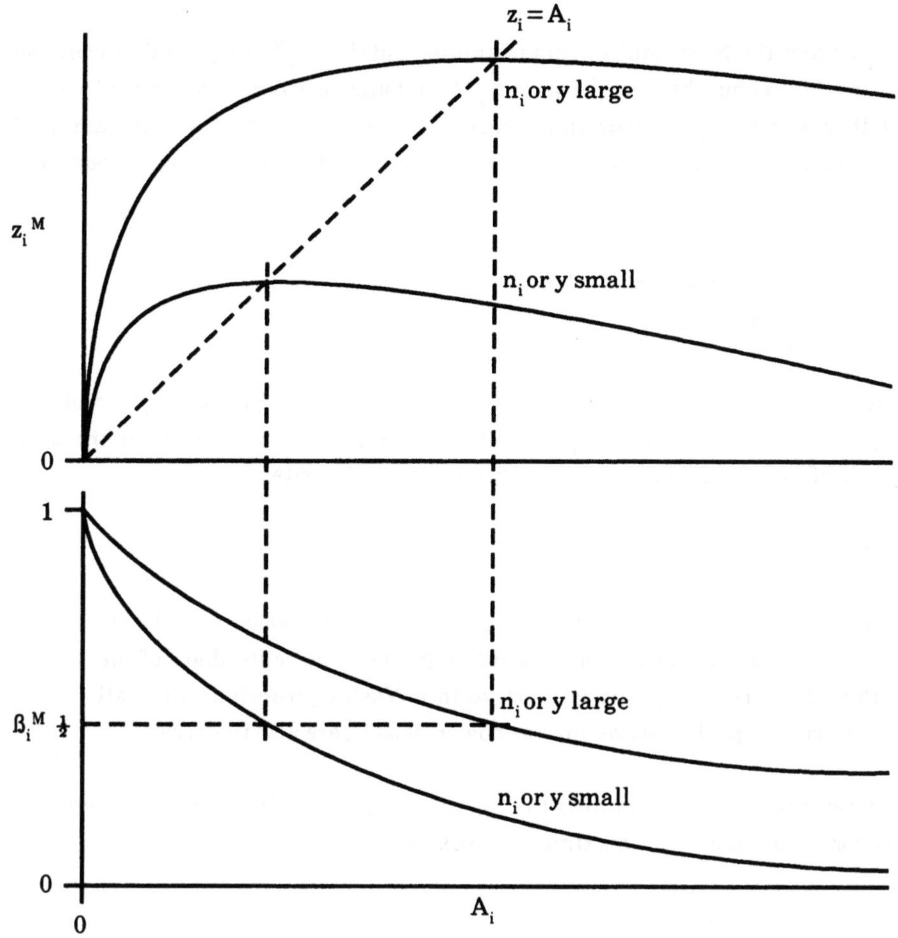

Figure 1: The reaction function

into itself. S is compact and convex. Thus, Brouwer's fixed-point theorem can be applied, and the function $z^M(z, y)$ has a fixed point $z^N(y)$. This function is the Nash equilibrium of the lobbying game (4a). We have

Proposition 1:

The lobbying game has a Nash equilibrium.

3.3 Uniqueness of the Nash equilibrium

In order to show that the Nash equilibrium is unique and that $z_1^N > \varepsilon$, it is first convenient to show that in a Nash equilibrium $z_i^N(y) > z_j^N(y)$ if and only if $n_i > n_j$, if $z_i^N(y) > 0$. If $z_i^N(y) = 0$, then also $z_j^N(y) = 0$ or, in the case $z_1^N(y) = \varepsilon$, $z_j^N(y) \leq \varepsilon$. Assuming that both $z_i^N(y)$ and $z_j^N(y)$ are positive, we find from (5) that they and the corresponding β's satisfy

$$(15) \qquad 1 = \frac{\ell_i(z_i^N)(1-\beta_i^N)}{\ell_j(z_j^N)(1-\beta_j^N)}$$

Now, assume that $n_i > n_j$ and $z_i^N \leq z_j^N$. We then find that $\ell_i(z_i^N) > \ell_j(z_j^N)$ and $\beta_i^N \leq \beta_j^N$, which contradicts (15). Hence, $n_i > n_j$ implies that $z_i^N > z_j^N$, which is the desired result. The case of a corner solution is similarly analysed. We write:

Proposition 2:

> The more powerful is an active pressure group, the greater will be its pressure in a Nash equilibrium and the greater will be its share of the cake[6]. If a pressure group is inactive in a Nash equilibrium, then all pressure groups that are at most as powerful as it, are also inactive.

Now, we assume that $z_1^N = \varepsilon$. According to Proposition 2, we then have that $z_i^N(y) \leq \varepsilon$ for all i. That is, for any i, some $z_i \leq \varepsilon$ maximizes the expression

$$(1b) \qquad \pi_i = \frac{z_i}{\varepsilon + (n-2)\delta\varepsilon + z_i}\, y - g^{-1}(z_i; n_i),$$

such that δ is some number between zero and one. On the range $0 \leq z_i \leq \varepsilon$, π_i is bounded from above by $y/2$. Now, let $z_i = 2(n-1)\varepsilon$. Then, π_i is bounded from below by $2y/3 - g^{-1}(2(n-1)\varepsilon; n_i)$. By making ε sufficiently small, the last term can be made arbitrarily small.We thus find that for small enough ε, some $z_i > \varepsilon$ maximizes π_i. This contradicts Proposition 2. Hence, the assumption that $z_1^N(y) = \varepsilon$ is contradicted, and the restriction on z_1 is not binding in a Nash equilibrium. We have

Lemma 1:

> If $\varepsilon > 0$ is chosen small enough, then $z_1^N(y) > \varepsilon$.

6) Compare Pethig (1984) and the following footnote 7.

In order to show that the Nash equilibrium is unique, we assume the existence of two Nash equilibria, z' and z" with corresponding β' and β'', and A' and A". We distinguish three cases: β'_1 and β''_1 both less than one half, both greater than one half, and one β greater than and one less than or equal to one half.

Case one: Both less than one half. If z' and z" differ, there must exist some group i such that z'_i and z''_i are different. Without loss of generality, assume that $z'_i > z''_i$. Hence, $A'_i < A''_i$, and there exists some group j such that $z'_j < z''_j$ and $A'_j > A''_j$. However, since $-\frac{1}{2} \leq \partial z_k^M / \partial A_k \leq 0$ for all k, $z'_i > z''_i$ implies that $A' < A''$, and $z'_j < z''_j$ implies that $A' > A''$. We have a contradiction.

Case two: β'_1 and β''_1 are both greater than one half. If z'_1 is equal to z''_1, case one applies. Thus, the only interesting case is when they differ. Assume that $z'_1 > z''_1$. This implies that $A'_1 > A''_1$ and, hence, $A' > A''$. However, $A'_1 > A''_1$ implies that there exists some group i such that $z'_i > z''_i$, which implies that $A' < A''$. Again, we have a contradiction.

Case three: One β_1 is greater than one half and one less than or equal to one half. Assume that $\beta'_1 > \frac{1}{2} \geq \beta''_1$. Hence, $A'_1 < A''_1$ and there exists some group i such that $z'_i < z''_i$. This implies that $A' > A''$. But $z_1 = A - A_1$. Thus, $z'_1 > z''_1$. Since $-\frac{1}{2} \leq \partial z_1^M / \partial A_1$, this implies that $A' < A''$, and we have a contradiction.

Thus, the two equilibria, z' and z" must be identical. We have:

Proposition 3:

The lobbying game has a unique Nash equilibrium.

3.4 Stability of the Nash equilibrium

The concept of stability in a static model is, of course, rather unclear. Here we will limit ourselves to a fairly strong form for stability. We will investigate when the function $z^M(z, y)$ is a contraction for a given value of y. That is, a sequential process where $(z_i)_{t+1}$ is given by $z^M((z_i)_t, y)$ converges as t grows.

The mapping z^M is a contraction if and only if

$$(16) \qquad \left| \frac{\partial z_i^M}{\partial z_j} \right| < \frac{1}{I-1}$$

for all i and j. From (9) we see that (16) is equivalent to

(17a) $$-\ell'_i(z_i^M) > \frac{1}{y}\,\frac{I-3-2\beta_i^M(I-2)}{(1-\beta_i^M)^2},$$

for $\beta_i^M \leq \frac{1}{2}$, and

(17b) $$-\ell'_i(z_i^M) > \frac{1}{y}\,\frac{I(2\beta_i^M-1)-1}{(1-\beta_i^M)^2},$$

if $\beta_i^M \geq \frac{1}{2}$.

Inequality (17a) will be satisfied if

(18a) $$I \leq 3$$

or if

(18b) $$-\ell'_i(z_i^M) > \frac{I-3}{y},$$

independently of the value of β_i^M. Inequality (17b) will be satisfied if

(19) $$\beta_i^M \leq \frac{I+1}{2I},$$

and will never be satisfied if β_i^M is sufficient large. If we assume that no group gains more than half the cake in the Nash equilibrium, that is, $\beta_i^N \leq \frac{1}{2}$, then inequalities (18a) and (18b) are sufficient to guarantee local stability of the Nash equilibrium. If $\beta_i^N \leq \frac{1}{2}$, we say that no group dominates the lobbying game. We can then rewrite (18b) in the following manner:

(20) $$\frac{y}{I-3} > -\frac{g_x(x_i^N;n_i)}{g_{xx}(x_i^N;n_i)}.$$

Hence, we can formulate:

Proposition 4:

> A lobbying game with three pressure groups has a stable Nash equilibrium if no group dominates the game. The greater is the cake and the smaller is the number of pressure groups, the more likely to be stable is the Nash equilibrium if there are more than three pressure groups.

4. Properties of the Nash equilibrium of the lobbying game

We have already seen in Proposition 2 that the pressure exerted and the share of the cake received by different pressure groups in a Nash equilibrium stand in a direct relationship to the power of the groups. This means that in any game, independently of the size of the cake and the number of players, the most powerful player will exert the strongest pressure and receive the largest piece of cake. This, however, does not say anything about the amount of resources used by the different groups, nor does it imply anything about the size of the net cake, π. It is easy to show, though, that the size of the net share of the cake is directly related to the power of the group. This is done in Section 4.1.

As was noted in the introduction, it is reasonable to assume that the size of the total cake in the long run depends on the amount of resources expended by the pressure groups. It is, therefore, of some interest to see how the total expenditure on lobbying and the size of the cake are related. Therefore, in Section 4.2, it is shown how the pressure and the expenditure of each pressure group depend on the size of the cake. The pressure groups that are observed, are the active ones in our terminology. In Section 4.3 it is shown that the number of active pressure groups increases with the size of the cake. That is, we develop some rudiments of a theory for how pressure groups are formed.

4.1 The distribution of net benefits

We write the net benefit of the lobbying game to group i as $\pi_i(A_i, z_i)$. We know that $\pi_i(A_i^N, z_i^N) \geq \pi_i(A_i^N, z_i)$ for all z_i. Assume that $n_i > n_j$. We have that

(21) $$\pi_i(A_i^N, z_j^N) = \frac{z_j^N}{A^N - z_i^N + z_j^N} y - g^{-1}(z_j^N; n_i).$$

But, $z_i^N > z_j^N$ and $n_i > n_j$. Hence, $\pi_i(A_i^N, z_j^N) > \pi_j(A_j^N, z_j^N)$. Consequently, $\pi_i(A_i^N, z_i^N) > \pi_j(A_j^N, z_j^N)$, which is the desired result:

Proposition 5:

> The more powerful is an active pressure group, the greater is its net benefit of the lobbying game.[7]

4.2 Lobbying effort and expenditure for different size cake

It is convenient to return to expression (5) and rewrite it as follows:

7) The corresponding result is obtained by Pethig (1984) in his two-player parametric model.

$$(22)\quad \begin{aligned} &\frac{A}{y} = \ell_i(\beta_i A)(1-\beta_i), \text{ if } \ell_i(0) > \frac{A(1-\beta_i)}{y};\\ &\beta_i = 0, \text{otherwise.}\end{aligned}$$

Expression (22) defines β_i as a function of A and y, β_i^A (A, y). It is seen that, for active groups, β_i^A is continuous and decreasing in A and continuous and increasing in y. The equilibrium condition now becomes

$$(23)\quad \sum_i \beta_i^A(A, y) = 1$$

Equation (23) defines A as an increasing and continuous function of y, $A^E(y)$.

Now, we define Ω by A / y and rewrite (22) as

$$(24)\quad \begin{aligned} &\Omega = \ell_i(\beta_i \Omega y)(1-\beta_i), \text{ if } \ell_i(0) > \Omega(1-\beta_i);\\ &\beta_i = 0, \text{otherwise.}\end{aligned}$$

Equation (24) defines β_i as a function of Ω and y, $\beta_i^B(\Omega, y)$. Again, it is seen that, for active groups, β_i^B is continuous and decreasing in both Ω and y. The equilibrium condition,

$$(25)\quad \sum_i \beta_i^B(\Omega, y) = 1$$

defines Ω as a decreasing and continuous function of y, $\Omega^E(y)$.

We have:

Proposition 6:

> The total pressure increases as the size of the cake increases, but the pressure per unit cake decreases.

Now, assume that the cake increases from y' to y" and that the pressure of some group decreases: $z'_i > z''_i$. Hence, $\ell_i(z'_i) < \ell_i(z''_i)$. From Proposition 6 we know that $A' < A''$ and $\Omega' > \Omega''$. Thus, $\beta'_i > \beta''_j$. This contradicts equation (24) and gives us:

Proposition 7:

> As the cake increases in size, the pressure of each active group also increases and, consequently, the lobbying expenditure of each active group increases.

Corollary:

As the cake increases in size, the total expenditures on lobbying in the economy also increase.

In other words, the greater is the total amount of public subsidies, the stronger will be the incentives for pressure groups to attempt to get part of the subsidies, and the greater will be the amount of resources used by each pressure group on lobbying efforts. Hence, the direct cost to society of the lobbying activities also increases as the cake grows.

On the other hand, the greater is the cake, the stronger is the pressure on the government to supply more cake which might lead to an ever increasing cake. However, the pressure per unit cake decreases, and this might stabilize the process. Of course, if the cake is variable, we have to take its financing into account, and pull those who pay for it into the game. We then have a new strategic situation. Our present short-run model is therefore, in a certain sense, a partial model. It tells us how great the pressure on the providers of the cake is, but tells us nothing about their counter-pressure.

4.3 Number of active pressure groups for different size cake

From equation (8) we deduce that if a pressure group i is inactive in Nash equilibrium, then

(26)
$$\ell_i(0) \le \frac{A}{y} = \Omega .$$

Ω is a decreasing function of y. It is thus reasonable to suspect that the number of pressure groups that are active, will increase as y increases. To show this, we will look at the limiting cases when y is close to zero and very large.

First, let y approach zero. Equation (24) no becomes

(24a)
$$\Omega_0 = \ell_i(0)(1-\beta_i),$$

since β_i and $\ell_i(0)$, and hence also Ω_0, are bounded. Now, assume that pressure groups i through k are active and k + 1 through I inactive From equation (25) we then obtain for Ω_0:

(27)
$$\Omega_0 = \frac{k-1}{\sum_{i=1}^{k} \frac{1}{\ell_i(0)}} .$$

Since group k + 1 is inactive, we have that $\ell_{k+1}(0) \le \Omega_0$. Further if $\ell_{k+1}(0) > \Omega_0$, group k + 1 would find it profitable to enter the game and our assumption of its inactivity would be false. Defining $\Omega^*_0(k)$ by the right-hand side of equation (27), we see that in a Nash equilibrium of a game with only the first j groups as players, the equilibrium value of Ω_0, $\Omega_0(j)$, is equal to $\Omega^*_0(j)$ if $j \le k$, and $\Omega^*_0(k)$ if $j > k$. This we use to determine which groups will enter the game. That is, we can start with group 2, continue with groups 3, 4 etc. and test whether the condition $\ell_i(0) \le \Omega^*_0(i-1)$ is met. The first i for which it is met, determines the first inactive group. From this group on, Ω_0, the equilibrium value of Ω, does not change although, of course, Ω^*_0, as a rule, will change. Since $\ell_{i+1}(0) \le \ell_i(0)$, all subsequent groups are also inactive. This clearly determines a Nash equilibrium. Since the Nash equilibrium is unique, this solves our problem of determining which pressure groups are active as the cake vanishes.

A straight-forward calculation shows that the condition $\ell_{i+1}(0) \le \Omega^*_0(i)$ implies that $\ell_{i+2}(0) \le \Omega^*_0(i+1)$. Thus, a group i is inactive if and only if $\ell_i(0) \le \Omega^*_0(i-1)$. We can find lower and upper bounds for $\Omega^*_0(k)$ by replacing $\ell_i(0)$ by $\ell_k(0)$ and $\ell_1(0)$, respectively:

(28) $$\frac{k-1}{k}\,\ell_k(0) \le \Omega^*_0(k) \le \frac{k-1}{k}\,\ell_1(0).$$

From this we see that group i would be active in the lobbying game in the limit of zero cake if

(29) $$\ell_i(0) > \frac{i-2}{i-1}\,\ell_1(0).$$

Of course, if group i is active, so is group i-1. This would also follow from applying condition (29). Further, group i would be inactive if

(30) $$\ell_i(0) \le \frac{i-2}{i-1}\,\ell_{i-1}(0).$$

If group i is inactive, so is then, of course, also group i+1. This would not necessarily be seen by directly applying condition (30). Therefore, the statement that i is inactive if there exists a group m, $m \le i$, such that m satisfies condition (30), is a stronger condition for deciding if a group is inactive. We finally note that expression (29) implies that there will be at least two active groups, even when the cake is small.

We now turn to the other extreme, $y \to \infty$. Assume that groups 1 through k are active in the limit, and k+1 through I inactive. For the active groups, equation (24) now takes the form

(24b) $$\Omega_\infty = \ell_i(\infty)(1-\beta\ )$$

if $\Omega_\infty > 0$. If the limit of $\ell_1(y)$, as y approaches infinity, is greater than zero, this is the case. If the limit of ℓ_1, and hence of all other ℓ_i, is zero, then also $\Omega_\infty = 0$.

For the first inactive group, group k+1, expression (26) implies that $\ell_{k+1}(0) \leq \Omega_\infty$. That is, in the case where the limit of ℓ_1 is zero, all groups with $\ell_i(0) > 0$, in other words all potential groups, will enter the game as y becomes large enough.

In the case where the limit of ℓ_1 is bounded away from zero, we can solve for Ω_∞ with the help of equation (25) and define $\Omega^*_\infty(k)$:

(31) $$\Omega^*_\infty(k) := \frac{k-1}{\sum_{i=1}^{k} \frac{1}{\ell_i(\infty)}}.$$

A discussion parallel to the one above, will give similar results to those in the case of zero cake. The difference is that, in this case, the condition $\ell_{i+1}(0) \leq \Omega^*_\infty(i)$ does not necessarily imply that $\ell_{i+2}(0) \leq \Omega^*_\infty(i+1)$.

Again, we can find bounds on $\Omega^*_\infty(k)$:

(32) $$\frac{k-1}{k}\ell_k(\infty) \leq \Omega^*_\infty(k) \leq \frac{k-1}{k}\ell_1(\infty).$$

That is, group i would be inactive in the lobbying game in the limit of infinite cake if there exists a group m, $m \leq i$, such that

(33) $$\ell_m(0) \leq \frac{m-2}{m-1}\ell_{m-1}(\infty),$$

and it would be active if

(34) $$\ell_i(0) > \frac{i-2}{i-1}\ell_1(\infty).$$

We see that also the case of $\ell_1(\infty) = 0$ is covered by (33) and (34).

We can now state one proposition and three corollaries:

Proposition 8:

> There will in all lobbying games be at least two pressure groups. Further, all pressure groups i, $i \geq 3$, such that $\ell_i(0) > \Omega^*_0(i\text{-}1)$, will always take part in the lobbying game in addition to groups 1 and 2, irrespective of the size of the cake. All pressure groups i for which there exists some $j \leq i$ such $\Omega^*_\infty(j\text{-}1) \geq \ell_j(0)$, will never enter the lobbying

game, irrespective of the size of the cake. All other pressure groups will enter the lobbying game as the cake grows from zero to infinity.

Corollary 1:

All pressure groups i, i ≥ 3, characterized by

$$\ell_i(0) > \frac{i-2}{i-1}\,\ell_1(0)$$

will, in addition to groups 1 and 2, be active in the lobbying game, irrespective of the size of the cake.

Corollary 2:

All pressure groups i which satisfy, or for which there exists a, at least as powerful, group m which satisfies,

$$\ell_m(0) \leq \frac{m-2}{m-1}\,\ell_{m-1}(\infty),$$

will never take part in the lobbying game, irrespective of the size of the cake.

Corollary 3:

All pressure groups i characterized by

$$\frac{i-2}{i-1}\,\ell_1(\infty) < \ell_i(0)$$

and which satisfy, or for which there exists a, at least as powerful, group m which satisfies,

$$\ell_m(0) \leq \frac{m-2}{m-1}\,\ell_{m-1}(0)$$

enter the lobbying game as active players as the size of the cake grows from zero to infinity.

Proposition 8 and Corollary 3 verify, in a precise manner, the statement at the beginning of this section that the number of active pressure groups increases as the cake grows. As a theory for how pressure groups are formed, this subsection tells us that the formation of interest groups is a consequence of increased government activity.

5. Some examples

In this section we will make some further simplifying assumptions in order to study some special cases. In section 5.1 we assume all groups to be of equal strength. Section 5.2 treats the case when there is a large number of active pressure groups, and in section 5.3 an example is given of how the number of active groups varies with y.

5.1 All pressure groups of equal strength

In this case β_i becomes equal to $1/I$ for all groups and equation (5) can be written as

$$(35) \qquad \frac{g_x(x)}{g(x)} = \frac{I^2}{(I-1)y}$$

where we have suppressed the index for each group and the dependence of g on n. The expression g_x / g is monotonly decreasing in x. Thus, x^N decreases as I increases and x^N increases as y increases.

The relative efficiency of the game can be defined as $\Sigma \pi_i / y$ which in this case becomes

$$(36) \qquad \frac{I\pi}{y} = 1 - \frac{I-1}{I} \frac{g_x(x)x}{g(x)} .$$

The expression $g_x x / g$ is always less than or equal to one, and it is decreasing in x for small values of x if $g_x(0) < \infty$. Thus, the relative efficiency of the game lies between $1/I$ and 1, and it is increasing as a function of the size of the cake, for small cakes at least, if the marginal impact of lobbying is finite for all efforts.

As the cake vanishes, the relative efficiency approaches the lower bound $1/I$.[8]

5.2 A large number of pressure groups

If we have a large number, k, of active pressure groups, the least powerful of them will each get a very small share of the cake, less than $1/k$. In the limit of a large k, equation (5) reduces to

$$(37) \qquad \ell_i(0) = \frac{A}{y}$$

for the least powerful groups, all of which have to be identical. For the powerful groups, equation (5) now becomes

$$(37b) \qquad \ell_i(\beta_i y \Gamma)(1 - \beta_i) = \Gamma,$$

where $\Gamma := \ell_k(0)$.

8) In Tullock's (1980) model with $g(x) = x^r$ and hence $g_x(0) = \infty$, equation (32) becomes $I\pi / y = 1 - (I-1) r / I$. The relative efficiency is here independent of the size of the cake and decreasing in the number of pressure groups, with the limit $1 - r$ as I becomes infinite (compare table 6.2 in Tullock, 1980). In the case that $g_x(0) < \infty$, of course, the limit of the relative efficiency as I becomes infinite will be zero. Tullock's case is thus unjustifiably optimistic in regard to the efficiency properties of rent seeking.

Equation (37b) defines β_i as a function only of y, since Γ is constant. It is readily seen that, for a powerful group, β_i decreases as the cake grows, This example seems to indicate that the least powerful groups have the largest relative increase in the share of subsidies as the total amount of lobbying activities increases as a result of a growing cake.

5.3 An example of how the number of active pressure groups varies

We let $\ell_i(z) = \ell_1(z)/i$ and $\ell_1(\infty) = \delta\,\ell_1(0)$. Substituting into equations (27) and (31), we obtain

(38) $$\Omega^*_0(k) = \ell_1(0)\,\frac{2(k-1)}{k(k+1)}$$

and

(39) $$\Omega^*_\infty(k) = \delta\,\ell_1(0)\,\frac{2(k-1)}{k(k+1)}\,.$$

Comparing Ω^*_0 and Ω^*_∞ with $\ell_{k+1}(0)$, we see, without any further ado, that in this case we will have two active groups when the cake vanishes. Furthermore, if $\delta \le \frac{1}{2}$, all groups will be active for sufficiently large cake. If $\delta > \frac{1}{2}$, the number of active groups for a large cake will be the smallest natural number at least as big as $2\delta/(2\delta - 1)$.

The condition $\delta \le \frac{1}{2}$ can hardly be viewed as unreasonable. If it is satisfied, the number of pressure groups will grow from two to all potential ones as the size of the cake is increased.

6. Concluding remarks

The growth of the public sector can have many causes. In this essay, we have focused on how a growing government sector influences the number of active pressure groups and the size of their activities. This is, however, only one side of the coin. The next step will be to look at the opposite causality: how pressure groups influence the size of government.

Also, how pressure groups affect the allocation of resources in the economy is a question meriting closer scrutiny. All to often one focuses on efficiency losses, due to the institutional structure of the eocnomy, in comparison with first-best solutions (see, for instance, the majority of the contributions in Buchanan, Tollison, and Tullock, 1980). Since, in reality, first-best worlds are scarce, this might not be the most interesting line of analysis.

Instead, one should perhaps concentrate more effort on comparative analysis of different institutional set-ups. If inefficiency through rent seeking is a necessary by-product of desirable redistributional policies, then it is valuable to know how the magnitude of this problem varies with different institutional structures. Pethig (1984) is a valuable contribution from this point of view. More are needed.

7. References

(1) Buchanan, J.M., R.D. Tollison, and G. Tullock, eds. (1980), Toward a theory of the rent-seeking society. College Station: Texas A & M University Press.

(2) Larkey, P.D., C. Stolp, and M. Winer (1981), Theorizing about the growth of government: A research assessment. Journal of public policy, 1: 157-200.

(3) Lindbeck, A. (1985), Redistribution policy and the expansion of the public sector. Journal of public economics, 28: 309-328.

(4) Niskanen, W.A. (1971), Bureaucracy and respresentative government. Chicago: University of Chicago Press.

(5) NOU (1984), Statlig næringstøtte i distriktene. NOU 1984:21. Oslo: Universitetsforlaget.

(6) Pethig, R. (1984) A basic model of rent seeking. Discussion Paper no. 74-84, Wirtschaftswissenschaftliche Diskussionsbeiträge, Universität Oldenburg.

(7) Tullock, G. (1980) Efficient rent seeking. In: Buchanan, J.M., R.D. Tollison, and G. Tullock, eds. (1980).

Comment on B.-A. Wickström: "The Growth of Government and the Rise of Pressure Groups"

by

J.-Matthias Graf v. d. Schulenburg

Bengt-Arne Wickström raises a very relevant topic, the competition among pressure groups to receive the biggest slice of the cake. The structure of the model, the 'lobbying game', is clear. The government distributes a given 'cake' (transfers, subsidies) according to the relative pressure of each interest group. Each interest group behaves as a Nash-competitor when it determines its lobbying efforts, i.e. takes the efforts of all other groups as given.

The results of Wickström's analysis are intuitively plausible:
(1) The lobbying efforts of a pressure group increases when the size of the cake also increases.
(2) The more powerful a pressure group, the greater are the net benefits from the lobbying game.

Although I found the mathematical presentation sometimes a little burdensome (because it is argued with a variable 1 which is one divided by the derivative of the inverse of the pressure function), the analysis is very well done. Sometimes, however, I would have preferred some more economic explanations concerning the definitions, assumptions, and results derived from the model and a broader discussion on how this model is related to the work of others, e.g. Gordon Tullock and Rüdiger Pethig. In my comments I will concentrate only on the assumptions of the model in relation to the results obtained.

It is assumed that the cake is exogenously given and that changes in the size of the cake are also exogenously determined. It is mentioned in the paper that "it is reasonable to assume that the size of the total cake ... depends on the pressure exerted by the pressure groups", however, this relationship is not analysed in the paper. In practice, the size of the cake distributed by the government is not given but the outcome of pressure group activities in the past.

The second main result of the analysis seems to be very plausible. However, it might be a tautology if power is not viewed as a exogenous variable. If power is a product of the lobbying efforts, and lobbying efforts are necessary to receive a larger slice of the cake, then the relative power of a group can be defined by the relative net benefits received in the lobbying game.

It is claimed that the results derived in the paper are in principle testable propositions. I have some doubt concerning the key variable 'pressure'. In (3d) it is implicitly assumed that pressure can be measured by a cardinal scale. In practice it will be difficult to find such a scale, and only an ordinal ordering of the pressure groups with respect to pressure and power might be possible.

Most results of the analysis presented in this paper depend on the assumptions introduced in (3c) and (3d). Assumption (3) can be accepted right away. Assumption (3d), however, can only be justified by mathematical requirements (see footnote 5). If we assume that pressure can be measured on a cardinal scale, I can still imagine other pressure functions than the one described in (3d). For instance that the marginal impact of the lobbying efforts on the pressure is the same for all groups or is even greater for less powerful groups. In Figure 1 the upper diagramme shows the pressure function assumed in Wickström's model. I believe, however, that in reality powerful pressure groups such as farmers, physicians, and unions, have built up a power-stock as a potential threat (see figure 1b). Even if they currently do invest only very little in lobbying efforts, they receive a big slice of the cake due to their potential ability to weaken the government. But in comparison with less powerful ones, these groups do not receive much more in addition if they increase their lobbying efforts. Very high lobbying efforts can be even counter-productive for very powerful groups, as we know from physician and dentist strikes or the Flick affair in Germany. German physician's associations, for instance, invested so much in the twenties that they have increased their power up to the point where only little efforts are needed to maintain their lobbying power.

To sum up, the paper is very stimulating and might serve as a basis for developing a more general theory on lobbying game. In a more general model the government should be included as a player. In addition, all characteristics of the cake should be included as targets of the lobbying efforts, i.e. the size of the cake and institutional arrangements how it is distributed. Lobbying power should be formulated as a function of the lobbying efforts in preceding periods. In addition power could for instance be handled as a stock which can be increased by lobbying efforts and which shrinks if no lobbying efforts are invested.

Figure 1: The pressure function

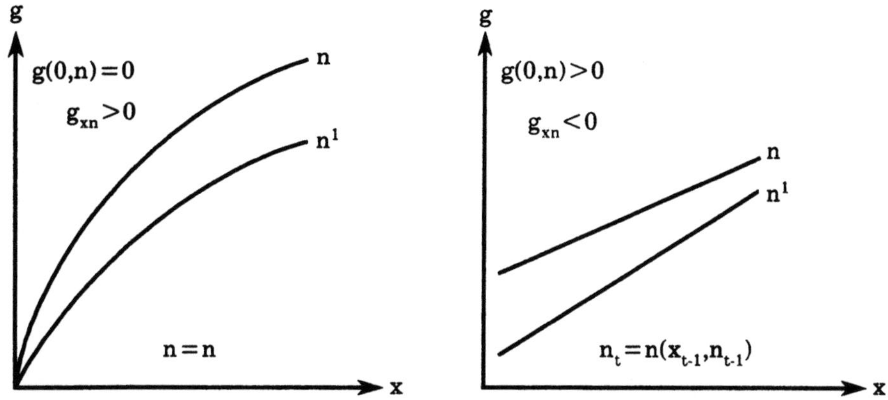

1a: Wickström's model **1b: Power as potential threat**

Family Structure and Intergenerational Transfers in Social Health Insurance: A Public Choice Model

by

Friedrich Breyer
J.-Matthias Graf v.d.Schulenburg*

1. Introduction

The key features of statutory pension funds are the so-called intergenerational contract and a pay-as-you-go financing. The first describes that employees pay contributions to finance the benefits for retired people. The pay-as-you-go financing requires that the current contributions of all insurees cover the total cost of the fund. Many papers have dealt with the implications of the intergenerational contract for economic efficiency, economic growth and the income distribution if demographic changes occur.[1] Recent papers address in addition the questions of equity among generations and the acceptability of intergenerational transfers via social institutions.[2]

Frey and *Leu* (1981) were the first to show empirically that not only pension funds but also social health insurance schemes are based on an intergenerational contract. For instance dependent children covered by the German statutory health insurance are non-contributory, and retired people pay only a reduced contribution of about 50 % of the regular contribution. It can be shown that if the demographics or the benefit structure change, those intergenerational transfers via social health insurance will lead to an unequal distribution of the cost and benefits among different cohorts. This generates two questions: First, do we receive more intergenerational equity by modifying the financing scheme of social health insurance? Second, will the unequal intergenerational distribution cause a threat for the further existence of social institutions based on an intergenerational contract?

*) Fernuniversität Hagen and International Institute of Management Berlin, respectively.
Valuable Comments by Michael Hutter, Gebhard Kirchgässner, Hans G. Monissen, Joachim Neipp, Jozef Ritzen, Alois Wenig and participants of the 1986 Meeting of the European Public Choice Society and the Workshop "Efficiency, Institutions and Economic Policy" in Mannheim, are gratefully acknowledged.

1) Cf. Samuelson (1959, 1975), Männer (1974), Arthur/McNicoll (1978), Hu (1979), Famulla/Spremann (1980), Balasko/Shell (1980, 1981), Willis (1983), Spremann (1984) and Dinkel (1986).

2) See Keyfitz (1984) and Kleindorfer/Schulenburg (1986). See also Sjoblom (1985) on the relationship between current acceptance and the beliefs concerning future existence of social security.

Pethig Schlieper (Eds.)
Efficiency, Institutions, and Economic Policy

This paper focusses on the second problem of acceptability of intergenerational transfer schemes. The analysis takes the example of social health insurance as it is organized in West-Germany rather than social pension funds. This is for the following reasons. First, in social health insurance there is not only a net-transfer from the working middle-aged to retired people but also a transfer to the children, who are non-contributory. Therefore we may call these transfers a three-generational contract, which is more general then the two-generational contract of pension funds.

Second, if the question of acceptability is raised, one has to describe the alternatives to the existing scheme and to examine whether the actual system might be at the voters' disposal. The alternative to social health insurance is obviously private health insurance, which already exists in most western countries. The attractiveness of a social health insurance scheme will always be measured relative to private health insurance.

Finally, for those covered by social pension funds appropriate retirement benefits can be seen as property rights more or less guaranteed by the constitution. Thus, even if a majority of the population favors the abolition of the social retirement insurance it will be difficult to liquidate it, because the minority in favor of the existing insurance scheme will assert their constitutional rights. This does not hold for social health insurance. Although it might be difficult to change the financing method of social health insurance or to abolish it totally, an arbitrary reduction of its coverage can be achieved by implementing co-payment of the patients. In principle, there is no limit to possible co-payment rates so that social health in surance can be eroded by legislation without violating any property rights guaranteed by the constitution.

In a recent paper *Schulenburg* and *Kleindorfer* (1986) discuss the acceptance of social health insurance if the demographic and cost structure changes. Their study is based on a life cycle analysis in an overlapping generations model. To model the acceptability problem the authors employ a public choice framework, where voters have rational expectations. They assume that a voter will favor the abolishment of the current mandatory social health insurance if his or her total discounted contributions to the social health insurance over his remaining life-time exceeds those to a private health insurer providing the same coverage. Taking this assumption on voting behaviour and employing projections on German demographic and health-care cost trends it can be demonstrated that in fifty to seventy years a majority of voters will object to a continuation of the current social health insurance scheme.[3)]

The approach mentioned above is based on the idea that each voter makes his voting decision dependent only upon his own personal net-benefits from the social health insurance system. If horizontal redistribution is ignored - for excample by assuming identical incomes across individuals within each generation - the result is a struggle among the different generations.

3) For these calculations see Schulenburg (1986).

This analysis, however, accounts for only one aspect of the impact of social security schemes on the net wealth of individuals. Persons do not live in isolation, but in the context of their families, and there are financial and moral links among members of the same family:

a) Parents have to pay for the present health care costs of their children, be it directly or through health insurance premiums or through contributions to a mandatory social insurance scheme.
b) Parents normally care for the future well-being of their children and allow for the expected future gains or losses of these, as well.
c) Adults with parents in the pensioners' generation will take the parents' financial well-being into account, both in their roles as potential heirs and because they have the legal or moral obligation to support their parents in case of impoverishment.

All these considerations show that intergenerational transfers within small segments of the society, called "families", act as substitutes for intergenerational transfers through a social security system. Furthermore, the latter system implies a redistribution of net wealth across families even in a world of equal incomes. Which of the two transfer systems is more advantageous for a voter, depends not only on his personal net benefits but on those for his or her family as a whole. This, in turn, will be influenced by the composition of the voter's family, i.e. the number of his siblings and his children as compared with the compositions of all other families.

According to this new hypothesis on voting behavior, the acceptance under majority rule of an intergenerational transfer system like the one described in the introduction depends critically on the prevailing family structure, i.e. the distribution of children across families. To give a simple example, compare two extreme cases: In society A, each family has two children, in society B, one-third of all families have six children while the others are childless. Although the average fertility and thus the age distribution is the same in both societies, the results of a popular vote on the survival of a social health insurance scheme may differ dramatically. An intuitively plausible outcome would be the following: the smaller the number of families with children, the more attractive is it for them to deal with the intergenerational transfer internally by opting against the mandatory social insurance contract.

It is the purpose of this paper to analyze the impact of the family structure on the acceptance of a social health insurance system within a simple majority voting model. Furthermore, we are going to examine the roles of other determinants such as the population growth rate and voters' time preferences on the majority decision.

The remainder of this paper is organized as follows. In Section 2, the assumptions of the model a represented, and the voting process is demonstrated by discussing a few illustrative examples. Section 3 contains a systematic analysis of the impact of the above mentioned determinants on the voting results, and in Section 4 we summarize our findings and give some suggestions for further research.

2. The Model

2.1 Basic Assumptions

The model is based on a set of extremely simplifying assumptions on the intergenerational composition of the society, the structure of families, health care expenditures and the characteristics of the social health insurance scheme.

(A1) Each person lives for three periods of equal length: in the first period ($\tau = 1$) as a "child", in the second ($\tau = 2$) as an "adult" and member of the work force and in the third ($\tau = 3$) as a pensioner.

Thus in each time period t, the society consists of members of three different generations aged 1, 2 and 3 periods, respectively. Compared to a life-expectancy of approximately 75 years, a period would correspond to 25 years. Thus, (A1) slightly understates the length of adult lifetime and exaggerates the lengths of the other two periods of life.

(A2) Each person can have up to two children, when he or she becomes an adult. The probability of having two children is p ($0 \leq p \leq 1$), and of having one child is q ($0 \leq q \leq 1-p$). These probabilities are constant over time.

This assumption is the simplest way of distinguishing between segments of the population with growing, constant and shrinking membership over the generations. The reproduction rate of the society as a whole is obviously given by $2p + q$ and the population growth rate, g, is

(1) $g = 2p + q - 1$.

Both rates refer to a period length of one generation. According to (A2), they are constant over time. By this we assume a population in steady-state growth (or, of course, decline).

Assumption (A2) also ignores the fact that two persons are needed for reproduction. The following definition of a "family" is in line with this simplification:

(D1) A **family** in period t is composed of one pensioner (of age $\tau = 3$ and born in t-2) and all his descendants already living in t.

The set of descendants consists of his adult children (born in t-1, now aged $\tau = 2$) and his grandchildren (born in t, now aged $\tau = 1$).

The next two assumptions refer to the characteristics of health care costs and their financing system:

(A3) Expected health care expenditures per person and per period are age-specific, but constant within each age group and constant over time:

$$k(\tau) = \begin{cases} 1 & \text{for} \quad \tau = 1 \\ 2 & \quad\quad\;\; \tau = 2 \\ 4 & \quad\quad\;\; \tau = 3 \; . \end{cases}$$

This assumption accounts for the strong and progressive relation between age and average health care costs. Studies on the health care cost of German and Swiss sickness fund members show that the cost incurred by elderly are about four times those of children and double those of middle-aged adults.[4] We ignore the observed increase of (age-specific) health care expenditures over time as well as differences in risk among persons of the same age group. (A3) implies, moreover, that the size of the expenditures is not influenced by the institutional features of the financing system.

(A4) Under the social health insurance system, everybody's health care expenditures are fully covered. Administrative costs are zero and total expenses are financed through age-related contributions $b(\tau)$:

$$b(\tau) = \begin{cases} 0 & \text{for} \quad \tau = 1 \\ b & \quad\quad\;\; \tau = 2 \\ 0.5b & \quad\quad\;\; \tau = 3 \, , \end{cases}$$

where the basic contribution b is calculated according to the pay-as-you-go system.

The contribution schedule conforms closely with the one prevailing in the GKV: children are insured free of charge and old-age pensioners pay a reduced rate.[5] The pay-as-you-go financing is typical for most social insurance systems. For the German GKV, it is prescribed by §§ 389 and 390 of the Reichsversicherungsordnung.

The next two assumptions refer to the decision on the retention or abolition of a social health insurance system on the political level:

4) See, e.g., the estimations given in Schmid (1980), Camphausen (1983) and Schulenburg/Kleindorfer (1986).

5) In 1981, the average contributions to the german statutory sickness funds amounted to DM 2986 per insured member of working age and DM 1458 per insured pensioner.

(A5) At the beginning of period t, there is a referendum on the social health insurance system. All adults and pensioners are entitled to vote. If a majority of the electorate votes for its abolition, then it is immediately dissolved. This decision is irreversible.

(A6) Private health insurance is available at actuarially fair premiums.

In the absence of risk differentiation, actuarial fairness means that the premium for each person of age group τ is $k(\tau)$. Obviously, this implies both the absence of intergenerational transfers and of piling up reserves for the age-related risk increase, which is a common feature of private health insurance contracts in Germany. Administrative costs and other loading factors are equally neglected.

2.2 Implications for the structure of insurance contributions

Assumptions (A1) and (A2) and definition (D1) imply that in each period t society is composed of families of nine different types. Table 1 lists for each family type j (j = 1, ..., 9)

- the number of pensioners, R_{jt}, of adults, A_{jt}, and of children, C_{jt},
- the total number of members, M_{jt}, and voters, V_{jt},
- the relative frequency of its occurrence, π_j,
- total health insurance contributions (or premia) under the social and the private system, respectively, in period t, S_{jt} and P_{jt},
- total expected health insurance contributions (or premia) in period t+1, $S_{j,t+1}$ and $P_{j,t+1}$, and in period t+2, $S_{j,t+2}$ and $P_{j,t+2}$.

The entries in the first seven columns of Table 1 need hardly any comment. Present social insurance contributions S_{jt} are derived from (A4) and the formula

$$S_{jt} = (0.5\,R_{jt} + A_{jt})\,b, \qquad j = 1, ..., 9. \tag{2}$$

Similarly (A3) and (A6) imply for the present private health insurance premiums

$$P_{jt} = 4\,R_{jt} + 2\,A_{jt} + C_{jt}, \qquad j = 1, ..., 9. \tag{3}$$

Because the numbers of adults and pensioners living in period t+1 are already known, social insurance contributions in t+1 can be computed as

$$S_{j,t+1} = (0.5\,R_{j,t+1} + A_{j,t+1})b = (0.5\,A_{jt} + C_{j,t})\,b, \qquad j = 1, ..., 9. \tag{4}$$

Table 1: Family type and expected health insurance expenditures

j	R_{jt}	A_{jt}	C_{jt}	M_{jt}	V_{jt}	π_j	S_{jt}	P_{jt}	$S_{j,t+1}$	$P_{j,t+1}$	$S_{j,t+2}$	$P_{j,t+2}$
1	1	2	4	7	3	p^3	2.5 b	12	5 b	20 + 4g	4b(1.5+g)	$4(7+4g+g^2)$
2	1	2	3	6	3	$2p^2q$	2.5 b	11	4 b	17 + 3g	3b(1.5+g)	$3(7+4g+g^2)$
3	1	2	2	5	3	$pq^2+2p^2(1-p-q)$	2.5 b	10	3 b	14 + 2g	2b(1.5+g)	$2(7+4g+g^2)$
4	1	2	1	4	3	2pq(1-p-q)	2.5 b	9	2 b	11 + g	b(1.5+g)	$7+4g+g^2$
5	1	2	0	3	3	$p(1-p-q)^2$	2.5 b	8	b	8	0	0
6	1	1	2	4	2	pq	1.5 b	8	2.5 b	10 + 2g	2b(1.5+g)	$2(7+4g+g^2)$
7	1	1	1	3	2	q^2	1.5 b	7	1.5 b	7+g	b(1.5+g)	$7+4g+g^2$
8	1	1	0	2	2	q(1-p-q)	1.5 b	6	0.5 b	4	0	0
9	1	0	0	1	1	1-p-q	0.5 b	4	0	0	0	0

j = family type
R_{jt} = pensioners
A_{jt} = adults
C_{jt} = children
M_{jt} = family members
V_{jt} = family members entitled to vote

π_j = relative frequency of family type j
S_{jt} = contributions of family type j to social health insurance in period t
P_{jt} = expenditures of family type j in period t if social health insurance is abolished
$S_{j,t+s}$ = expected contributions of family type j to social health insurance in period t+s (s=1,2)
$P_{j,t+s}$ = expected expenditures of family type j in period t+s (s=1,2) if social health insurance is abolished

In contrast, the number of children that the family members of age $\tau = 1$ will have in the next period, $t+1$, cannot be known in period t and thus has to be replaced by its expected value

$$(5) \qquad C_{j,t+1} = C_{jt}(2p+q) = (g+1)\,C_{jt}, \qquad j = 1, ..., 9.$$

Hence, the private insurance premiums in $t+1$ can be derived from

$$(6) \qquad P_{j,t+1} = 4\,R_{j,t+1} + 2\,A_{j,t+1} + C_{j,t+1} = 4\,A_{jt} + (3+g)\,C_{jt}, \qquad j = 1, ..., 9.$$

Analogously, the respective values of expected total family payments in period $t+2$ can be computed for both systems, where now the expected number of children

$$(7) \qquad 2p+q = g+1$$

has to be inserted for the two future periods:

$$(8) \qquad S_{j,t+2} = (0.5\,R_{j,t+2} + A_{j,t+2})b = (1.5+g)\,C_{j,t}\,b, \qquad j = 1, ..., 9.$$

$$(9) \qquad P_{j,t+2} = 4\,R_{j,t+2} + 2\,A_{j,t+2} + C_{j,t+2} = (7+4g+g^2)\,C_{jt}, \qquad j = 1, ..., 9.$$

According to (A3) and (A4), we derive the basic contribution to the social health insurance system from the formula

$$(10) \qquad b = b_t = \frac{\sum_j (4\,R_{jt} + 2\,A_{jt} + C_{jt})}{\sum_j (0.5\,R_{jt} + A_{jt})}, \qquad t = 1, 2, ...$$

Using assumption (A2) and (1), this reduces to

$$(11) \qquad b(g) = \frac{7+4g+g^2}{1.5+g} = g + 2.5 + 3.25\,(g+1.5)^{-1}.$$

Since

$$(12) \qquad \frac{\partial b(g)}{\partial g} = 1 - 3.25\,(1.5+g)^{-2} \quad 0 \quad \text{for} \quad g \quad .303,$$

b has a minimum when the society is growing at a rate of approximately 30 % per period. This result is due to the "three-generation-contract" nature of social health insurance in contrast to the "two-generation-contract" nature of general social security. There the basic contribution-benefit ratio is a monotonically declining function of the rate of population growth. Here, however, both a very low (or negative) and a very high population growth rate lead to high contribution-benefit ratios, the latter because of the transfers from the adults to the children, who are non-contributory.

2.3 The Voting Hypothesis

As we argued in the Introduction, each voter will judge the attractiveness of a social health insurance system not only by his or her own personal net benefits derived from the system but by the total net benefits for all members of his family. This idea is formulated in the following assumption:

(A7) At the referendum in period t, a member of a family of type j will reject the social health insurance system if total present and discounted future contributions to the system for all family members exceed the respective figure in a private insurance system, i.e. if

$$(13) \qquad \sum_{s=t}^{\infty} (1+\delta)^{-(s-t)} (S_{js} - P_{js}) > 0$$

is fulfilled, δ where is the discount rate pertaining to a standard period length.

From (8), (9) and (11),

$$(14) \qquad S_{j,t+2} = P_{j,t+2} \qquad j = 1, \ldots, 9$$

and the same is obviously true for all $s > t+2$ since nothing is known about the composition of the specific family three periods into the future. Therefore the expected values apply to all family types. Hence (13) can be simplified to

$$(15) \qquad S_{jt} - P_{jt} + (1+\delta)^{-1} (S_{j,t+1} - P_{j,t+1}) > 0, \qquad j = 1, \ldots, 9.$$

To illustrate the outcome of the voting process, let us consider a stationary population ($g = 0$). From (11), $b(0) = 14/3$. If the voters in period t are completely myopic ($\delta = \infty$), members of families of types 2, 3, 4, 5 and 8 will favor the abolition of the social insurance system. Under neutral time preference ($\delta = 0$), however, a negative vote will be cast by members of families of types 1 through 6. This example shows that the time discount rate is an important determinant of the acceptance of a social health insurance scheme and that there is no simple relationship between this acceptance and the number of descendants in the family.

The outcome of the referendum obviously depends upon the relative frequencies of the respective family types in the society. Let us denote the share of negative votes on the social insurance system by n. In the last mentioned case of $g = 0$, $\delta = 0$, this share, i.e. the proportion of voters belonging to a family of one of the first six types is

$$(16) \qquad n = \frac{\sum_{j=1}^{6} V_{jt} \pi_j}{\sum_{j=1}^{9} V_{jt} \pi_j} = \frac{3p + 2pq}{2} = \frac{p}{2}(5 - 4p),$$

where the last equality follows from (1). Since $g = 0$, the parameter p measuring the distribution of children can assume values between 0 and 0.5. According to (16), n is a monotone function of p in this range with $n(0) = 0$ and $n(0.5) = 0.75$. The critical value of $n^* = 0.5$ is reached at $p = 0.25$, $q = 0.5$. This example shows that with given average fertility $(g + 1)$ and given time preferences, the distribution of children as measured by the parameter p can have a considerable impact on the persistence of social health insurance schemes in democratic societies.

3. Comparative Statics of the Voting Model

3.1 Population Growth Rate, Family Structure and Time Preference

In the previous section it was indicated that the level of acceptance of a social health insurance system depends on the demographic characteristics (number and distribution of children) and on the time discount rate. More specifically, the share of negative votes, n, is a function of the parameters g, p and δ:

$$(17) \qquad n = n(g, p, \delta).$$

As the analytic form of this function will be very complicated, we shall attempt a systematic analysis using the technique of simulation. In Tables 2 and 3, the values of n are printed for a large number of conceivable pairs (g, p) in the range of $-0.5 < g < 0.5$, i.e. for population growth rates between minus 50 per cent and plus 50 per cent in the course of one generation. In Table 2, δ is set equal to 0 (neutral time preference) and in Table 3, δ is set equal to 1. This latter value corresponds to a 2.8 per cent annual discount rate over a period of 25 years.[6)]

6) $(1 + 1)^{-1} = (1 + 0.028)^{-25}$.

Table 2: Percentage of voters favoring the abolition of mandatory social health insurance (n), if δ = 0

g \ p	0.000	.050	.100	.150	.200	.250	.300	.350	.400	.450	.500	.550	.600	.650	.700	.750
-.50	.667	.663	.600	.567	.533	.500										
-.45	.710	.677	.645	.613	.518	.548										
-.40	.750	719	.688	.656	.625	.594	.563									
-.35	.512	.491	.482	.485	.500	.527	567									
-.30	.576	.547	.529	.524	.529	.547	.576	.618								
-.25	.643	.606	.580	.566	.563	.571	.591	.623								
-.20	.711	.667	.633	.611	.600	.600	.611	.633	.667							
-.15	.781	.730	.689	.659	.641	.632	.635	.649	.673							
-.10	.853	.795	.747	.711	.684	.668	.663	.668	.684	.711						
-.05	.926	.862	.808	.764	.731	.708	.695	.692	.700	.718						
0	0.000	.120	.230	.330	.420	.500	.570	.630	.680	.720	.750					
.05		.120	.229	.329	.420	.500	.571	.632	.683	.724	.756					
.10				.329	.419	.500	.571	.633	.686	.729	.762	.786				
.15				.328	.419	.500	.572	.635	.688	.733	.767	.793				
.20						.500	.573	.636	.691	.736	.773	.800	.818			
.25						.333	.400	.467	.533	.600	.667	.733	.800			
.30								.457	.522	.587	.652	.717	.783	.848		
.35									.511	.574	.638	.702	.766	.830		
.40									.500	.563	.625	.688	.750	.813	.875	
.45											.612	.673	.735	.796	.857	
.50											.600	.660	.720	.780	.840	.900

Table 3: Percentage of voters favoring the aboliton of mandatory social health insurance (n), if $\delta = 1$ or $\delta = g + 1$

g \ p	0.000	.050	.100	.150	.200	.250	.300	.350	.400	.450	.500	.550	.600	.650	.700	.750
-.50	.667	.663	.600	.567	.533	.500										
-.45	.710	.677	.645	.613	.581	.548										
-.40	.750	.719	.688	.656	.625	.594	.563									
-.35	.788	.758	.727	.697	.667	.636	.606									
-.30	.824	.794	.765	.735	.706	.676	.647	.618								
-.25	.857	.829	.800	.771	.743	.714	.686	.657								
-.20	.889	.861	.833	.806	.778	.750	.722	.694	.667							
-.15	.919	.892	.865	.838	.811	.784	.757	.730	.703							
-.10	.947	.921	.895	.868	.842	.816	.789	.763	.737	.711						
-.05	.974	.905	.846	.797	.759	.731	.713	.705	.708	.721						
0	0.000	.120	.230	.330	.420	.500	.570	.630	.680	.720	.750					
.05		.073	.188	.293	.388	.437	.549	.615	.671	.717	.754					
.10				.252	.352	.443	.524	.595	.657	.710	.752	.786				
.15				.209	.314	.409	.495	.572	.640	.698	.747	786				
.20						.373	.464	.545	.618	.682	.736	.782	.818			
.25						.333	.429	.516	.593	.662	.722	.773	.816			
.30								.483	.565	.639	.704	.761	.809	.848		
.35									.534	.613	.683	.745	.798	.843		
.40									.500	.583	.658	.725	.783	.833	.875	
.45											.631	.702	.765	.820	.867	
.50											.600	.676	.744	.804	.856	.900

We first turn to the results in Table 2. The results are graphically represented in Figure 1, where the vertically shaded region denotes parameter combinations with n > 0.5. The most striking result is that for a wide range of slowly shrinking societies (-0.33 < g < 0), mandatory social health insurance is always rejected by a majority of voters, no matter how the descendants are distributed. The same is true for very rapidly shrinking or growing societies (g < - 0,37 or > 0.4). Where the distribution of children does play a role, opposition to the mandatory system is - with few exceptions - strongest when children are most unevenly distributed (high p). However, only for a stationary or growing population (g ≥ 0) is n a monotone increasing function of p, otherwise it is U-shaped.

Figure 1: Majority Opposition to mandatory social health insurance as a function of p and g

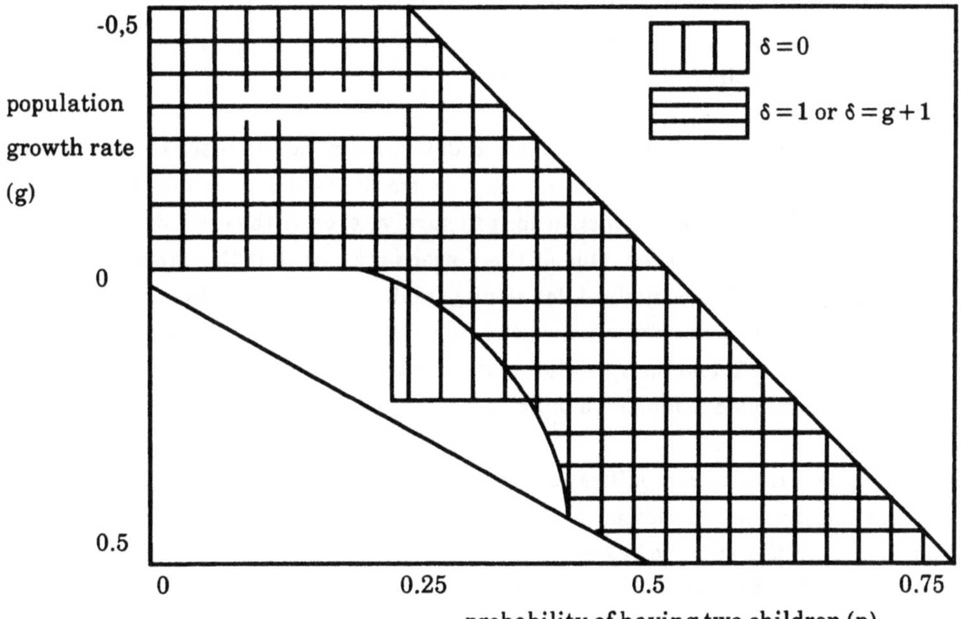

We now turn to a positive time discount rate of δ = 1. Table 3 shows that in most cases the share of negative votes on social health insurance is the same or slightly higher than in the absence of time discounting. However, in the region of small positive population growth (0 ≤ g ≤ 0.21), there is now less opposition to mandatory social insurance. The reason is that with positive discounting the future costs incurred by the generation of child age in period t is for some family types not big enough to outweigh the present benefits. Figure 1 shows that for growing societies the set of parameter combinations with majority opposition to the social insurance system (i.e. the horizontally shaded region) shrinks if the discount rate rises from

0 to 1. We conclude that even a large change in the time discount rate has only very limited impact on the survival chances of social health insurance under majority voting. Moreover, the direction of this impact is contrary to the results of the traditional social security literature where time discounting works unambiguously against the acceptance of mandatory social security plans. In our model where the decision unit is the familiy just the opposite result emerges if posulation growth is positive.

In the literature on economic growth models it has been shown that the interest rate or discount rate (δ) depends on the growth rate of the population (g) and the rate of technical progress (w). In a steady state economy the equality $p = g + w$ is fulfilled.[7] Assuming for simplicity $w = 1$, we receive $\delta = g + 1$. As Table 2 shows, identical results are received for the cases $\delta = 1$ and $\delta = g + 1$. This underscores the above finding that the discount rate has only a very limited impact on the acceptance of social health insurance if the voters take into consideration all costs and benefits to members of their families.

3.2 The Impact of the Size of Net Losses

So far it was assumed that every voter rejects mandatory social health insurance if his family incurs net losses under the system no matter how small these losses may be. Empirical evidence shows that the ability of institutions to survive even if they are detrimental to a majority of voters is quite marked. One of the reasons may be that the expected losses for many voters are too small to be noticed, let alone to make it worthwhile to organize political lobby against the institution. This observation is particulary relevant for societies where there is no recurrent referendum on social health insurance at regular intervals, but some political pressure is needed to make it a topic on the political agenda.

Therefore we now examine a modification of our model, where the new voting hypothesis requires that the expected net losses from the social insurance system have to exceed some threshold to induce the voter to reject the system. More specifically we shall assume that total (discounted) family contributions to social health insurance have to be more than x per cent higher than total (discounted) family payments toward private health insurance in order to lead to a negative vote. Thus equation (15) is replaced by

$$(19) \qquad S_{jt} + (1+\delta)^{-1} S_{j,t+1} > \left(1 + \frac{x}{100}\right)[P_{jt} + (1+\delta)^{-1} P_{j,t+1}], \qquad j = 1, ..., 9.$$

The result of this analysis for several values of x are represented graphically in Figure 2. Taking $\delta = 1$ as given, the demarcation lines of the regions with majority opposition ($n > .5$) are drawn for alternative values of x. The line for $x = 0$ corresponds, of course, to the lower boundary of the horizontally shaded area in Figure 1. It is seen at once that the set of values

7) See for instance Solow (1970). w denotes the rate of labour-augmenting technical progress, which is equal to the change of the wage-rate over time.

for g and p leading to a majority opposition against the system shrinks rapidly as x increases. If x exceeds 9 percent, opposition to the system never reaches majority for growing populations.

We conclude that the results of the previous section have to be interpreted with caution: Although the system of intergenerational transfers through social health insurance may harm a large enough share of families to comprise a majority of all voters, for many of them the net losses owing to the transfers constitute only a very small fraction of total expenditures for health insurance. If net losses have to amount to some minimum level in order to attract voters' attention, then the persistence of a social health insurance system is considerably increased.

Again, however, we find that the danger of abolition of the system is greatest when the population is shrinking and the children are very unevenly distributed among families.

Figure 2: Majority Opposition to mandatory social health insurance as a function of p and g if net losses must exceed x per cent of cost ($\delta = 1$)

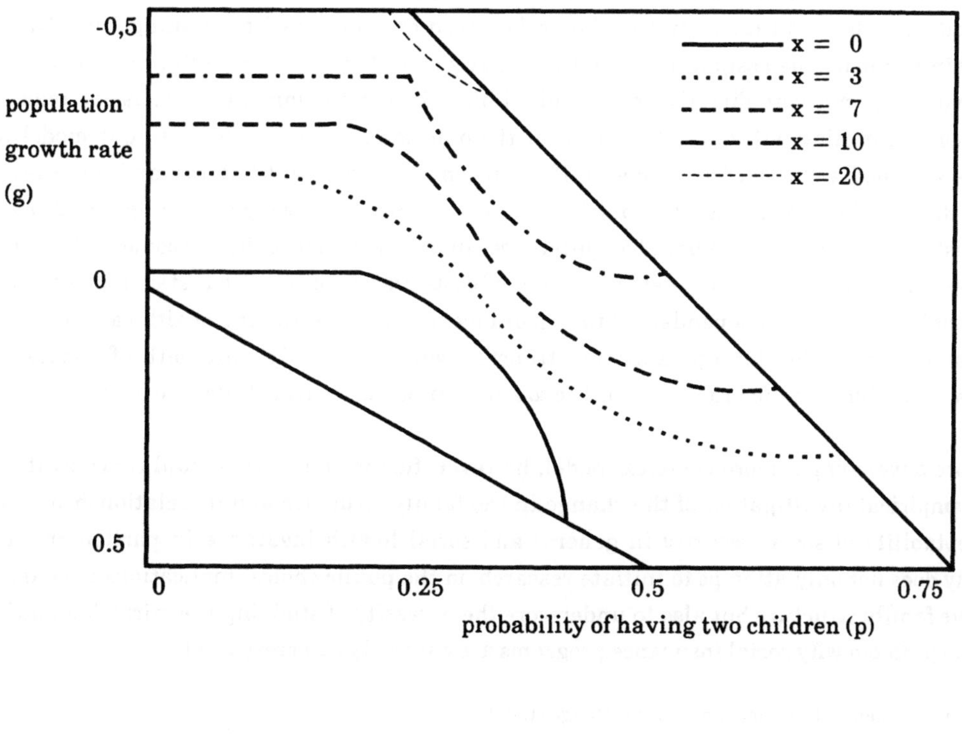

4. Summary

In this paper we have argued that family structure in addition to the growth rate of the population, the time preference and cost trends have an effect on the acceptability of social insurance schemes. This is because there exist intergenerational ties and transfers within families. A voter with rational expectations will, therefore, also consider these intra-family relations when it comes to a decision about inter-family transfers via social insurance. Our analysis shows that widespread beliefs concerning the acceptability of intergenerational transfers via social insurance have to be modified. For example, one can not generally conclude that the acceptability of an intergenerational contract decreases if the population grows at a lower rate or if the time-preference rate increases. The reverse is shown to be true for certain distributions of children across families.

In addition, the analysis presented in this paper suggests that as the distribution of children becomes more uneven the likelihood also increases that a majority of the voters favor an abolition of the social health insurance. Demographic data show that a tremendous change in the family structure took place during the past decade[8], which might explain partly the decline of the acceptance of social insurance programs.

Although our analysis has taken the example of German social health insurance, the framework may be adopted to the acceptability of other intergenerational transfer schemes in Germany or other countries. However, the framework of the model employed in this paper is quite simple, and future studies should be based on more realistic assumptions. This is certainly true for the assumption about the voting procedure. In representative democracies the voter can not vote directly on individual bills. In the parliamentary decisison-making process, log-rolling will take place, so that the outcome is undetermined. In our model we have assumed a standard life-time, uniform income and constant fertility and health-care cost distributions over time. In addition, those variables were exogenously given. A more realistic approach would be based on differences in mortality, morbidity, income and fertility as well as on an endogenous determination of costs and benefits. For instance health-care expenditures are not independent of the insurance scheme covering the health-care cost risk. Finally we modelled intergenerational transfers within a steady-state path of population growth and ignored the problems specific to a transition period from higher to lower fertility.

Before developing a more complex model, however, further research should concentrate on the empirical investigation of the change in the family structure and its relationship to the acceptability of social security in general and social health insurance in particular. This study does not only attempt to initiate research on the public choice implications of changes in the family structure but also to underscore the necessity of studying the micro-foundation of the problem why social insurance programs are currently at a cross-road.

8) See the quantitative survey by Bucher/Runge (1984).

References

(1) Arthur, W. Brian and McNicoll, Geoffrey (1978),
Samuelson, Population and Intergenerational Transfers, in: International Economic Review, Vol. 19, 241-246.

(2) Balasko, Yves and Shell, Karl (1980, 1981),
The Overlapping-Generations Model, I., II., III., in: Journal of Economic Theory, Vol. 23, 281-304 and Vol. 24, 112-152.

(3) ucher, Hansjörg and Runge, Ludwig (1984),
Regionalisierte Prognose der privaten Haushalte in der Bundesrepublik Deutschland bis zum Jahr 2000, in: Informationen zur Raumentwicklung, 1984, No. 12, 1181-1202.

(4) Camphausen, Bernd (1983),
Auswirkungen demographischer Prozesse auf die Berufe und die Kosten im Gesundheitswesen, Berlin, Heidelberg: Springer.

(5) Diamond, Peter A. (1965),
National Debt in a Neoclassical Growth Model, in: American Economic Review, Vol. 55, 1126-1150.

(6) Dinkel, Reiner (1986),
Social Security and Intergenerational Equity, in: Schulenburg, J.-M. Gf (Ed.), Essays in Social Security Economics, Heidelberg, Berlin, New York: Springer, 77-107.

(7) Famulla, Rainer and Spremann, Klaus (1980),
Generationenverträge und Rentenversicherung als Ponzi GmbH, in: Zeitschrift für öffentliche und gemeinwirtschaftliche Unternehmen, Vol. 3, 379-403.

(8) Frey, René L. and Leu, Robert E. (1981),
Demographie und Inzidenz öffentlicher Ausgaben im Gesundheitswesen, in: Schweizerische Zeitschrift für Volkswirtschaft und Statistik, Vol. 117, 319-336.

(9) Hu, Sheng Cheng (1979),
Social Security, the Supply of Labor, and Capital Accumulation, in: American Economic Review, Vol. 69, 274-283.

(10) Keyfitz, Nathan (1984),
Some Demographic Properties of Transfer Schemes: How to Achieve Equity between Generations, International Institute for Applied System Analysis, Laxenburg (mimeo).

(11) Kleindorfer, Paul R. and Schulenburg, J.-Matthias Gf. (1986),
Intergenerational Equity and Fund Balance for Statutory Health Insurance, forthcoming in: Schulenburg, J.-M. Gf. (ed.), Essays in Social Security Eocnomics, Berlin, Heidelberg, New York: Springer, 108-129.

(12) Männer, Leonhard (1974),
Überlegungen zum optimalen Finanzierungsverfahren in der gesetzlichen Rentenversicherung, in: Finanzarchiv, Vol. 32, 244-257.

(13) Samelson, Paul A. (1958),
An Excact Consumption-Loan Model of Interest with or without the Social Contrivance of Money, in: Journal of Political Economy, Vol. 66, 467-482.

(14) Samuelson, Paul A. (1975),
Optimum Social Security in a Life-Cycle Growth Model, in: International Economic Review, Vol. 16, 539-544.

(15) Schmid, Heinz (1980),
Die Morbiditätsstatistiken der Krankenkasse KKB, in: Blätter der Deutschen Gesellschaft für Versicherungsmathematik, Vol. 14, 497-553.

(16) Schulenburg, J.-Matthias Gf. (1986),
Solidaritätsprinzip und Verteilungsgerechtigkeit, forthcoming in: Hauser, H., Schulenburg, J.-Matthias Gf. (eds.), Health Maintenance Organisations - eine Reformkonzeption für die Gesetzliche Krankenversicherung, Gerlingen: Bleicher.

(17) Schulenburg, J.-Matthias Gf. and Kleindorfer, Paul R. (1986),
Wie stabil ist der Generationsvertrag in der sozialen Krankenversicherung? Zum Problem der Gerechtigkeit und Akzeptanz intergenerativer Umverteilung, forthcoming in: Gäfgen, G, (ed.), Ökonomie des Gesundheitswesens, Berlin: Duncker und Humblot.

(18) Sjoblom, Kjell (1985),
Voting for Social Security, in: Public Choice, Vol. 45, 225-240.

(19) Solow, Robert M. (1970),
Growth Theory. An Exposition, New York: Oxford University Press.

(20) Spremann, Klaus (1984),
Intergenerational Contracts and their Decomposition, in: Zeitschrift für Nationalökonomie, Vol. 44, 237-253.

(21) Willis, Robert J. (1983),
Life Cycles, Institutions, and Population Growth: a Theory of the Equilibrium Interest Rate in an Overlapping Generations Model, Working Papers in Economics No. E-83-75, The Hoover Institution, Standford University.

Comment on Breyer and von der Schulenburg: "Family Structure and Intergenerational Transfers in Social Health Insurance."

by

Michael Hutter

Breyer and von der Schulenburg introduce two structural features which clearly increase the applicability of theoretical results to real life insurance institutions: (1) Intergenerational distribution of costs and benefits takes place between three generations. Thus, the entire life span is taken into consideration. (2) Costs are minimized for the family unit. Thus, the function of the family as redistributive institution in its own right is recognized.

Within this mode, the authors show that, when it comes to a decision between alternative insurance schemes, family structures and their distribution matter, large differences in time-preferance rates matter, and proportional costs of transaction matter.

The model's possibilities make it tempting to think about applications and extensions. I will limit my discussion to two points which may be of specific interest with respect to the issue of efficient institutions: Point (1) refers to changes in the acceptability of insurance schemes due to changes in the ratio of pensioners to adults, and point (2) refers to implications of positive transaction costs.

Breyer and von der Schulenburg reduce their task to manageable proportions through the assumption of steady-state growth. In such a world, the ratio of pensioners to adults to children remains always the same. Real societies, however, are characterized by continual fluctuations of these ratios. Therefore, periods with a majority of pensioner voters are followed by periods with a majority of adult voters. Intuitively, one would guess that in pensioner majority periods there is a stronger tendency to favor redistributive social insurance schemes than in adult majority periods. The twenty-five year time periods assumed are long enough to make even frequent oscillations between two schemes plausible. In such an extended model, we are faced not only with a once and for all decision for or against a specific insurance scheme, but with the problems caused by a sequence of such decisions.

In order to allow the effects of such shifts to be analyzed, the family maximization assumption, which gives the model its original flavour, does not have to be discarded. It would be sufficient to assume a discount rate of $\delta = \infty$ for pensioners and $\delta = 1$ for adults in order to come up with different patterns of opposition to mandatory social health insurance.

It remains an open question whether such periodic reversals constitute an efficiency loss, or whether they are efficient adaptations to a cyclical shift in time preferences.

Related to the issue of alternating institutions is the discussion of positive transaction costs. Transaction costs are essentially costs of information and communication. Lobbying efforts are costs of informing law makers as well as voters about the consequences of alternate schemes, and ways of getting there. Net losses do not "attract voters' attention" by themselves, someone has to spend resources in detecting such losses and informing others about it. In a model with constant population and linear technical progress, one can hypothesize that specialization of services permits a prompt introduction of the insurance acceptability issue after a shift of the voter ratio and it provides an efficient process of navigating a proposed change through the legislature. If we open the model to fluctuations in the rates of growth and technical progress, the optimal amount of resources for producing efficient institutional changes will increase due to the rise in uncertainty. Given the well-known public good effects of investment in information, there will be a tendency to underinvest in such activities. Moreover, devices which reduce costs of communication or which increase performance at constant costs are institutions in themselves and must be analyzed accordingly. Proportional cost coefficients, as they are used in the paper, are not sufficient to capture such effects. In the contrary, they hide the peculiarities which distinguish transaction costs from conventional production costs.

Of course, changing voter ratios and underinvestment in communication producing institutional change are just two additions to the list of further research directions indicated by Breyer and von der Schulenburg. They demonstrate, however, the applicability of the approach to a wide range of institutional phenomena beyond the issue of alternative health insurance schemes.

The Demsetz-Hypothesis on the Emergence of Property Rights Reconsidered

by

Ulrich Witt*

I. Introduction

Although a whole literature on the economic theory of property rights exists and can be considered as an important institutional addendum to the abstract neoclassical equilibrium approach (see Albert 1977), comparatively little attention has been paid to an explanation of the conditions under which property rights actually emerge. Early contributions (in German) have gone virtually unnoticed (for a survey see Meyer 1983) and it is a hypothesis suggested by Demsetz (1967) that has been most influential up to now. According to this hypothesis, new, private or state, property rights in a resource emerge if, under changing environmental conditions, the gains that can be internalized from exercising the new rights are larger than the costs of internalization. In particular, if a regime of unrestricted individual access to the resource results in large externalities and thus in the inefficient use of the resource concerned, individual incentives to establish private property rights (a ppr-regime henceforth) arise.

The alternative would be a regime based on a perhaps implicit or tacit agreement among the members of the community so that externalities are prevented by internal regulation (a regulated community right or rcr-regime henceforth). Such a regime fails, it is asserted, because of the costs of reaching and policing the agreement. In order to highlight the significance of his hypothesis Demsetz draws on an example reported by Leacock (1954). That report is concerned with the historical process of acculturation of the Montagnais, an Indian tribe living on the Labrador Peninsula. During the process rights in land which is scattered with beaver colonies gradually emerged apparently coinciding with the development of the commercial fur trade at the turn of the sixteenth/seventeenth century.

The hypothesis suggested by Demsetz has been taken up, e.g., by Furubotn and Pejovich (1972), Pejovich (1972), North and Thomas (1973), Alchian and Demsetz (1973), Anderson and Hill (1975), Fredlund (1976), Libecap (1978), Baden, Stroup, and Thurman (1981), and Hesse (1983) without much query. However, thorough rereading of Leacock (1954) raises doubts with respect to whether Demsetz' case is well taken, if compared with the results of more recent comparative studies of property rights regimes e.g. in Ault and Rutman (1979)

* I wish to thank Michael Hutter, Juli Irving-Lessmann, and Cento Veljanovski for valueable remarks on an earlier draft.

Pethig Schlieper (Eds.)
Efficiency, Institutions, and Economic Policy

and Posner (1980). As will be shown in this paper, the example refered to by Demsetz is one of a rcr-regime rather than one of a ppr-regime. Correspondingly, the reasons for an adoption of the latter regime can neither be discussed on the basis of the example nor does it become clear from the suggested hypothesis why it was possible for an rcr-regime to succeed in this case.

These contentions are substantiated in what follows. First, a more precise restatement of the basic notions underlying Demsetz' hypothesis is given in Section II. Section III elaborates on the difference between the two alternative regimes and, in the light of the distinctions being made, looks more closely to the historical example referred to by Demsetz. In Section IV a critique of a misconstruction which, it is argued, biases the whole approach follows and a correction of the basic hypothesis is suggested. The conclusions are summarized in Section V.

II. The Demsetz-Hypothesis Restated

Consider a resource such as the beaver population in Demsetz' example which is self-regenating as long as a threshold value V of exploitation per period is not exeeded. Furthermore consider a measure $\alpha \in [0,1]$ indicating to what degree one individual is able to exclude other from the utilization of that resource, where $\alpha = 0$ indicates no exclusion and $\alpha = 1$ perfect exclusion. The first extreme can be identified with an unregulated communal rights or free access regime, the second with a ppr-regime in its perfect form[1]. Image a scenario in which there are several hunters in an area and the optimal individual utilizations of the resource per period sum up to a value less than V. Let the present value of the discounted stream of individual gains or benefits accruing to hunter i from the utilization of the resource be measured in utility terms as a function $U_i = U_i(\alpha)$. In this scenario we then have $dU_i/d\alpha = 0$, that is, a case of non-rival consumption. Nothing can be gained by excluding others from the resource. In fact, since exclusion, in general, is costly, any attempt to exclude others would impose losses on the excluders. The optimal value is $\alpha^* = 0$ and the optimal property rights structure is a free access regime.

Now imagine a situation in which new trading opportunities emerge. Assume that due to changing relative prices and/or preferences, the optimal individual utilizations of the resource per period sum up to a value greater than V. If everyone realized the individual short run optimum, the resource would thus be overutilized and spoiled so that $U_i(\alpha = 0)$ is drastically reduced to some small non-negative value. An individual attempt to reduce the short run utilization to preserve the resource would yield an even lower utility if free riding by

1) Actually α is to be interpreted as an expected value which can also be defined as the tail value of the expectation $E(\Pi) : \alpha = 1 - E(\Pi)$ where the random variable Π, $0 \leq \Pi \leq 1$, indicates to which degree others have access to the resource and take away what would otherwise be available to the owner ($\Pi = 1$: unrestricted access and complete exploitation by others; $\Pi = 0$: completely restricted access except by the proprietor).

others nevertheless overutilizes the resource. The crucial point thus is to somehow exclude free riding if overutilization of the resource is to be prevented.

One way to do so - and apparently the one Demsetz has in mind - is by a ppr-regime: everyone claims exclusive personal rights in a certain fraction of the resource, e.g. a fixed hunting area. In doing so others are excluded from exploiting the fraction one intends to preserve. Assume for that fraction a regeneration threshold value v_i and consider the utility

(1) $U_i = U_i(\alpha | v_i)$

that would result from excluding others, i.e. for $\alpha > 0$. Obviously, it increases as α increases since infringenments by others have to be less and less compensated for by renouncing use, until a point is reached where $\alpha = 1$ and the individual fraction of the resource can, up to v_i, be utilized by the proprietor alone. With respect to (1) we therefore get, in this scenario, $dU_i/d\alpha > 0$. Lacking more specific information, it will be assumed in addition, as the simplest case, that $d^2U_i/d\alpha^2 = 0$.

Let the present value of the discounted stream of costs which are connected with the exclusion of others from access to a resource also be measured in utility terms as given by the function

(2) $C_i = C_i(\alpha | v_i)$,

with $dC_i/d\alpha > 0$. Common experience says that there is a non-linear relationship between enforcement costs and the degree with which others are prevented from interfering with one's own claim of exclusive resource utilization. An increasing α requires a more than proportionately increasing effort, that means: $d^2C_i/d\alpha^2 > 0$.[2)]

Under the chosen assumptions, three cases can be distinguished. These are exemplified in figure 1 with the cost curve being turned down successively to the right for cases I through III. Obviously, the situation in case I is such that enforcement of exclusion does not pay; for all $\alpha > 0$ it is found that $C_i > U_i$. For case II optimization yields the well-known equation of marginal utility with marginal cost at some α^*, $0 < \alpha^* < 1$, that is a situation where it is optimal to put up with a positive expectation of others interfering with one's own utilization of the resource. Eventually, for still lower enforcement costs, a situation results as in case III with $\alpha^* = 1$. These considerations based on the example of a self-regenerating resource, can similarly be carried out for the case of resources that need cultivation/maintenance work in order to retain value over time. In any case, the net gain, that results from the ppr-regime, can for given v_i be defined as

2) For instance, the probability of burglary can be reduced to small values with rather cheap methods. But then a further increase in safety requires more and more refined and costly methods. Note that the arguments developed below do not depend on these particular specifications of (1) and (2).

Figure 1: Benefits and Costs as a Function of the Degree of Exclusion

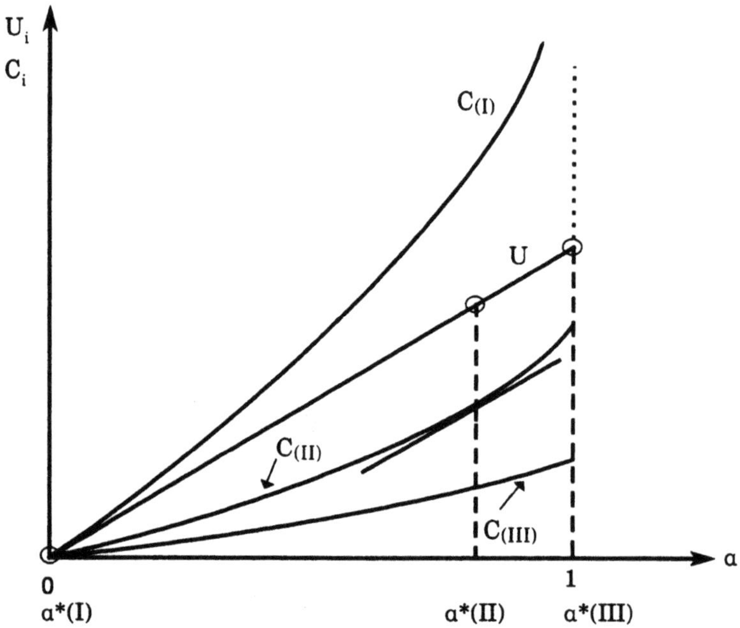

(3) $G_iP = U_i(\alpha^*) - C_i(\alpha^*),\ \alpha^* > 0.$

So far we have been concerned with exclusion of free riding by appropriating and enforcing private property rights. Other forms of overcoming the free riding problem, which are based on a community ownership, can, of course, also be imagined. As Demsetz (1967, 354) puts it:

"It is conceivable that (under communal right, U.W.) those who own these rights, i.e. the members of the community, can agree to curtail the rate at which they work the lands if negotiating and policing costs are zero. Each can agree to abridge his rights. It is obvious that the costs of reaching such an agreement will not be zero... Negotiating costs will be large because it is difficult for many persons to reach a mutually satisfactory agreement, especially when each hold-out has the right to work the land as fast as he pleases. But, even if an agreement among all can be reached, we must yet take account of the costs of policing the agreement and these may be large also."

In order to include the gains and costs of such an alternative property rights structure in a comparison we have thus to define the individual net gain under the rcr-regime (i.e. community ownership with a rationing/maintenance commitment imposed on every member of the community). Let these be denoted by

(4) $G_iC = W_i - K_i$

where under otherwise identical conditions W_i and K_i give the present values of the discounted streams of gains and negotiating and policing costs (including the costs of preventing non-community members from non-allowed access) in utility terms respectively.

As long as the possibility of a rcr-regime being adopted is not denied, the condition $G_i^P > 0$ in (3) could hardly claim more than being a necessary condition for a transition from a situation of open access to a ppr-regime.[3] But, Demsetz takes it for granted that always $G_i^P > G_i^C$ holds, that is the crucial relation

(5) $U_i(\alpha^*) - C_i(\alpha^*) > W_i - K_i, \qquad \alpha^* > 0.$

This is the decisive (tacit) assumption underlying the hypothesis then suggested to explain the emergence of private property rights:

D-Hypothesis: In a situation of unrestricted access to a resource private property rights in that resource emerge if $G_i^P > 0$.

The hypothesis clearly is an empirical assertion which can easily be tested: the first observation for which $G_i^P > 0$ is satisfied but private property rights do not emerge would yield a falsification of the hypothesis. In contrast to Demsetz' own assessment, unfortunately, his example already provides such an observation as the next section will show.

III. Communal vs. Private Rights

In order to evaluate the D-Hypothesis on the emergence of private property rights it is necessary to get the relations clear between the three different property rights structures under discussion: unregulated communal rights (open access-regime), internally regulated communal rights (rcr-regime), and private property rights (ppr-regime). Open access to a resource where everyone can take it up temporarily is a limiting case under a ppr-regime where $\alpha^* = 0$ as discussed in the previous section. It is no less a limiting case under a rcr-regime where a well-defined collection of individuals, the community, as a whole claims exclusive rights against any individual(s) not belonging to that community. Clearly, the enforcement of such a claim against the demands of individuals belonging to other communities - families, bands, tribes, nations, races, say - can be more or less effective, a fact that could be expressed just as in the private property case by a measure α. Thus, as far as the external exclusion problem is concerned the ppr-regime and the rcr-regime do not differ in principle. The decisive differ-

3) As mentioned by Demsetz the condition is necessary for a transition from a free access system to one of private *or* state property rights. However, the possibility of state ownership requires a discussion of its own. It is therefore neglected here as it is in Demsetz (1967).

ence is that under a rcr-regime, in contrast to the ppr-regime there is also an *internal* rationing/maintenance problem. The individual entitlements of the group members must somehow be regulated.

How do such internal schemes of assigning resources, in particular land, look under a rcr-regime? In the literature (see Hogbin and Lawrence 1967, Pryor 1977, Ault and Rutman 1979, Posner 1980, Baden, Stroup, and Thurman 1981) a lot of examples of arrangements can be found which have mostly been observed in precolonial tribal economies. Usually, a native authority within the community, e.g. a board of the eldest, a chief, the assembly of the adult men, etc., regulates access to land by granting exclusive rights of (i) *usus* and (ii) *usus fructus* to smaller subgroups, e.g. families, or their heads. These rights are enforced by tight social control and by making families responsible for any infrigements by their members (for a detailed description see in particular Posner 1980). Some rationing/maintenance commitments must, of course, in turn be imposed within the subgroups. The rules by which this is achieved usually are again governed by authority relations, e.g. the head of a family regulating family members, etc.

Thus, under rcr-regimes rights in a resource like land are usually granted to subgroups as, e.g., families and what is granted does not include the rights of (iii) *abusus* and (iv) *transfer* of the resource. It is often reported that tribesmen hold occupancy rights in land (that is essentially rights (i) and (ii), and may even be allowed to pass these occupancy rights to their heirs. However, abusus, that means here establishing claims in land that is not actually worked by members of the family, and free exchange of land are not allowed. Occupancy rights are lost once the tribesman abandons the land for a certain time. (Authorities can then allocate rights (i) and (ii) in the land to other members of the community.)

In the light of these reports the example of the Montagnais' land appropriation, as described by Leacock (1954), does not seem exceptional. Apparently, the transition from an unlimited access regime to one in which native families held occupancy rights in some sections of land has mainly taken place on a spontaneous basis (although first the Hudson Bay Company and later on the Canadian government seem to have propagated the idea in line with conservation plans developed by these institutions). As repeatedly pointed out by Leacock the result have been patterns of hunting practices and property right structures which strongly varied in the course of time as well as between the various bands in the different regions of Labrador. In any case, however, it was not more than the rights (i) and (ii) that were effectively appropriated. Moreover, they were excercised by families and bands, i.e. collections of individuals, so that an internal rationing/maintenance commitment must also have been established within the family groups. These two facts indicate that the features of a rcr-regime prevailed actually after the Montagnais had distributed the land among their families so as to internalize the benefits of controlled hunting of beavers.

A ppr-regime, in contrast, grants rights (iii) and (iv) in addition to (i) and (ii) to the individual (Pejovich 1976), a case not observed by Leacock (1954). Quite differently from Demsetz' argument one thus ends up with the result that in the case of the Montagnais most probably $G_i^P > 0$ (effectively, it can, of course, only be concluded that $G_i^C > 0$) but, nevertheless, instead of a ppr-regime a rcr-regime has been adopted. The Montagnais' case contradicts rather than supports the Demsetz-Hypothesis. With the unconditional presumption that always $G_i^P > G_i^C$ at its basis, this hypothesis raises more questions than it actually answers. In order to make progress we therefore have to pay more attention to the alleged superiority of a ppr-regime in comparison with a rcr-regime as it is expressed in relation (5).

IV. A Critique

One of the problems with the D-Hypothesis and the underlying relation (5) is the difference which is made with respect to the alternative property rights regimes in acknowledging costs of collective actions. In the case of the rcr-regime, costs of collectively negotiating and policing the regulations within the community are explicitly recognized. In the case of the ppr-regime, comparable collective policing and/or punishing activities of the community (or of its specialized institutions), by which the enforcement of private rights of the individual is supported, are neglected. However, they are no less important here as can be demonstrated by figure 1.

The position of the exclusion costs curve, that is whether case I, II, or III obtains for a given utility curve, certainly depends on individual factors such as personal skills, power, and exclusion technology. But besides these factors it is the support which the individual gets from the social environment, i.e. the community it is integrated into, that determines the actual costs of enforcing private rights. (It is instructive to see that enforcement of one's rights while dependent on oneself alone is a disturbing fiction which is often used in novels and movies in order to create excitement). Furthermore, the specific standards of conduct prevailing in the community as a consequence of (tacit) collective action play a role in the position of the cost curve, since by preaching norms and supervising their observance, the number and the behavior of potential offender is affected.

In view of the fact that a community provides what helps the C_i (α)-curve to shift downwards to the right so that a ppr-regime becomes more attractive, it seems highly questionable that the same community should not be able to enforce claims other than private ones, e.g. rationing and/or maintenance commitments based on communal rights in the same way, that is with similar costs. Notice that in *collectively* establishing and enforcing any law (private or communal) the problem of free riding, already met with in the internal regulation of access to scarce resources within a community, turns up again. Once this analogy between the problem of collectively enforcing private rights on the one hand and rationing/maintenance commitments under community rights on the other hand is acknowledged, it seems a misconstruction to emphasize the costs of collective community actions for the rcr-regime and to include them in eq. (4). while passing over them for the ppr-regime and omitting a corresponding term in eq. (3).

Thus, the following correction of eq. (3) is straightforward:

$$(3') \quad G_i^{P'} = U_i(\alpha^*) - C_i(\alpha^*) - k_i(\alpha^*), \qquad \alpha^* > 0,$$

where $k_i(\alpha^*)$ is the present value of the discounted stream of the individually born share of the costs of collective action in utility terms. For the function $k_i(\alpha)$ similar properties are assumed as for $C_i(\alpha)$, namely $k_i(0) = 0$, $dk_i / d\alpha > 0$, and $d^2k_i / d\alpha^2 \geqq 0$. Inserting (3') instead of (3) into eq. (5) we get

$$(5') \quad U_i(\alpha^*) - C_i(\alpha^*) - k_i(\alpha^*) > W_i - K_i, \qquad \alpha^* > 0.$$

In the light of the preceeding discussion, this modified relation should be interpreted as a necessary condition for the emergence of a ppr-regime. Moreover, since a ppr-regime can replace an open access regime as well as a rcr-regime a more general formulation is needed. A corrected form of the hypothesis suggested in Section II for explaining the emergence of a ppr-regime hence is:

D'-Hypothesis: Private property rights in a resource emerge if $G_i^{P'} > 0$ *and* $G_i^{P'} > G_i^C$.

The revised D'-Hypothesis is not only based on a corrected cost account but includes also the additional condition (5'). If this condition is fulfilled, it is expected that a transition from free access to a ppr-regime occurs or that a previously prevailing rcr-regime is superseded by a ppr-regime in a community. Condition (5') thus gives a starting point for investigating the reasons for thé historical emergence of private property rights. As outlined in the previous section, the example of the Montagnais which was discussed by Demsetz, unfortunately, does not allow such a discussion to be entered into simply because it is an example of a rcr-regime, i. e. (5') is far from being satisfied here. Why this is so, then, must of course be beyond Demsetz' argumentation and, in fact, requires quite complex hypotheses (see Witt 1986).

However, one idea of that argumentation can be carried over, by analogously formulating a necessary condition $G_i^C = W_i - K_i > 0$, to explain the transition from an open access regime to the rcr-regime with respect to hunting areas among the Montagnais. In a gradually evolving process this condition seems to have been satisfied first in the western parts of the Labrador peninsula and then extended to the east. From the detailed report given by Leacock (1954) it can be learnt that the shift in the benefits/costs relation resulted from the interplay of essentially two factors.

First, there was an increasing population size caused by other Indian bands which, evading the white settlers, immigrated into the Labrador area form the West. Like the Labrador bands they covered their nutrition needs mainly by hunting deer so that the deer population diminished continually. Since, for whatever reasons, it was not possible to organize deer-hunting on the basis of a rcr-regime (not to speak of a ppr-regime) the ultimate consequence was a depletion of the stock so that already by the nineteenth century hunting for large game had ceased to satisfy the nutrition needs of the Indians. To acquire imported substitute food from the Hudson Bay Company and other traders in exchange for furs the Indians had to rely more and more on trapping small fur-bearing animals. Thus, depletion of the traditional source of nutrition induced the Indian bands to engage in fur trade which in turn increased the benefits that could be gained by appropriating beaver hunting territories.

The second factor supporting the transition from the free access to the rcr-regime was a change in preference patterns, a factor that can be argued to play a key role in economic evolution in general (see Witt 1987, ch.4). The introduction of European equipment and materials by the trading posts created exchange opportunities for the Indians which had not been there before. They were not adopted, however, before the Indians gradually learned to appreciate the consumption of the new goods. What has been described by Leacock (1954) thus is an interesting case study of preference change which coincided with the diffusion of consumption innovations. The trade posts of the Hudson Bay Company and others, in their interest in acquiring furs, actively supported and tried to accelerate the process by offering commodities on credit. Along with this process a necessity for earning exchange values emerged which, as with the first factor, amplified the tendency to substitute deer hunting for trapping small fur- bearing animals. The increasing trapping efforts called for conservation measures so that the gains from establishing a regulated community ownership in beaver hunting territories by the Indian bands and families increased.

V. Conclusions

In the present inquiry the hypothesis suggested by Demsetz (1967) to explain the emergence of property right regimes has been critically discussed together with the historical example he chose to support his explanation. Roughly, the explanation holds that private property rights emerge whenever the gains which can be internalized individually by exerting private rights exceed the costs of enforcing such a claim. However, in this generality, the explanation neither gives information on the reasons why the crucial relation between gains and costs are satisfied, nor does it contribute much to an understanding of institutional developments, in which community instead of private rights in a resource supplemented by internal rationing/maintenance schemes, emerge. Contrary to Demsetz' assessment of his example such a regime - not to be confused with a regime of open access to the resource by everyone - prevails, in effect, in the case of the Labrador Indians he is concerned with.

The criticism brought forward here on the basis of a more precise restatement of Demsetz' hypothesis concentrates on the unequal treatment of costs resulting from the alternative regimes of private vs. regulated community rights in that approach. In comparing the enforcement costs of private rights on the one hand and the cost of negotiating and policing community agreements on the other hand, it has been argued that a neglect of the social costs of private right enforcement would be a fallacy. Where private rights are effective the community usually provides essential protection and enforcement services and they cause a cost to the community. Building on this criticism a correction of Demsetz' hypothesis has been suggested. Furthermore, in the light of that modification, an explanation which maintains the basic idea of the approach is sketched for what is actually left unexplained in the original argumentation: the emergence of regulated community property rights in the example of the Labrador Indians.

References

(1) Albert, H. (1977),
"Individuelles Handeln und soziale Steuerung: Die ökonomische Tradition und ihr Erkenntnisprogramm", in: H. Lenk (ed.), Handlungstheorien - interdisziplinär, Bd. IV, München.

(2) Alchian, A.A. and Demsetz, H. (1973),
"The Property Rights Paradigm", Journal of Economic History, 33, 16-27.

(3) Anderson, T. and Hill, P.J. (1975),
"The Evolution of Property Rights: A Study of the American West", Journal of Law and Economics, 18, 163-179.

(4) Ault, D.E. and Rutman, G.L. (1979),
"The Development of Individual Rights to Property in Tribal Africa", Journal of Law and Economics, 22, 163-182.

(5) Baden, J., Stroup, R., and Thurman, W. (1981),
"Myths, Admonitions, and Rationality: The American Indian as a Resource Manager", Economic Inquiry, 19, 132-143.

(6) Demsetz, H. (1967),
"Toward a Theory of Property Rights", American Economic Review, 57, Papers & Proceedings, 347-359.

(7) Fredlund, M.C. (1976)
"Wolves, Chimps, and Demsetz", Economic Inquiry, 14, 279-290.

(8) Furubotn, E.G. and Pejovich, S. (1972),
"Property Rights and Economic Theory: A Survey of Recent Literature", Journal of Economic Literature, 10, 1137-1162.

(9) Hesse, G. (1983),
"Zur Erklärung der Änderung von Handlungsrechten mit Hilfe ökonomischer Theorie", in: A. Schüller (Hrsg.), Property Rights und ökonomische Theorie, München: Vahlen.

(10) Hogbin L. and Lawrence, P., eds. (1967),
Studies in New Guinea Land Tenure, Sydney: Sydney University Press.

(11) Leacock, E. (1954),
"The Montagnais 'Hunting Territory' and the Fur Trade", American Anthropologist, 56 (Part 2).

(12) Libecap, G.D. (1978),
"Economic Variables and the Development of Law: The Case of Western Mineral Rights", Journal of Economic History, 38, 338-362.

(13) Meyer, W. (1983),
"Entwicklung und Bedeutung des Property Rights-Ansatzes in der Nationalökonomie", in: A. Schüller (Hrsg.), Property Rights und ökonomische Theorie, München: Vahlen.

(14) North, D.C. and Thomas, R.P. (1973),
The Rise of the Western World - A New Economic History, Cambridge: Cambridge Univ. Press.

(15) Pejovich, S. (1972),
"Towards an Economic Theory of the Creation and Specification of Property Rights", Review of Social Economy, 30.

(16) Pejovich, S. (1976) ,
"The Capitalist Corporation and the Socialist Firm; a Study of Comparative Efficiency", Schweizerische Zeitschrift für Volkswirtschaftslehre und Statistik, 112, 1-24.

(17) Posner, R.A. (1980),
"A Theory of Primitive Society, with Special Reference to Primitive Law", Journal of Law and Economics, 23, 1-53.

(18) Pryor, F.L. (1977),
The Origines of the Economy - A Comparative Study of the Distribution in Primitive and Peasant Economies, New York, Academic Press.

(19) Witt, U. (1986),
"Why do private Property Rights Emerge", Discussion paper # 322-86 (rev.), Institut für Volkswirtschaftslehre und Statistik der Universität Mannheim.

(20) Witt, U. (1987),
Individualistische Grundlagen der Evolutorischen Oekonomik, Tübingen: Mohr Siebeck.

Comment on U. Witt: "The Demsetz-Hypothesis on the Emergence of Property Rights Reconsidered"

by

Cento Veljanovski

The analysis of property rights has gradually entered the corpus of economic theory. The approach was largely founded by Alchian, Demsetz and others, although some of the issues which have become the central concern of the approach were already being discussed by economic historians and economists interested in the effects of different agricultural land tenure systems. The property rights theorists have contributed to our understanding of institutions by bringing a more systematic, theoretical and rigorous analysis to bear on different property rights systems. Although the literature has generated many insights and led to a reorientation of the way some economists think about markets, it still has many gaps. In this comment I want to use Professor Witt's paper to explore in more detail the strengths and weaknesses of the property rights approach.

I. The Property Rights Approach

The property rights approach brings to centre stage the institutions surrounding exchange and production in the economy. Even in essentially market economies the institutional arrangements governing economic activity vary markedly from industry to industry, between different individuals and for different commodities. This was all but ignored by neoclassical economic theory although this is not to say that one cannot find examples of ad hoc discussions of the importance and effects of different types of property arrangements. For the most part the institutions of the market were either taken as given, as part of the unstated background assumptions of the economists models, or else regarded with some bewilderment as irrational and inefficient obstacles to the sensible management of economic activity. In fact, as has been pointed out many times before, economists did not until very recently have a well thought out explanation for the existence of the firm as an economic institution (Coase, 1937; Alchian & Demsetz, 1972; Williamson, 1975). Economists were prone to regard institutions as beyond the scope of their discipline and the subject to have, at least to American economists, unsavory connotations with the now defunct Institutionalist School.

Yet traditional market analysis did contain an implicit albeit restrictive assumption about the underlying structure of property rights. The rights underlying the market were assumed to be private and could be costless defined, enforced and traded. That is, private property with zero transaction costs.

These omissions and deficiencies of standard economic theory became increasingly evident to those who tried to explain differences in institutional arrangements. In order to broaden the scope of microeconomic theory, the property rights approach both redefined the nature of exchange and the economic factors which were important in determining its efficiency. This was done by altering several of the key assumptions of the neoclassical model without abandoning the axiom of individual maximising behaviour. First, the *bundle* of property rights governing resources was made the central focus of analysis. This was coupled with an explicit recognition that there was a rich variety of different property right structures and, most importantly, that the concept of property rights was a multi-faceted one. Secondly, it redefined exchange as trade in bundles of property rights rather than the physical commodity or service. It was the nature of these property rights which both gave value to the commodity and affected the behaviour of buyers and sellers in and outside the marketplace. Thirdly, it replaced the behavioral assumption of wealth maximization with that of utility maximization. Individuals are assumed to maximise utility subject to resource constraints. Fourthly, it accorded transactions costs an important analytical role. These are the costs of defining, exchanging, policing and enforcing property rights. It is argued that property rights develop to economise on transactions costs (Williamson, 1975 & 1985). Thus we see trade in commodities evolving from autonomous trading in spot markets to forward markets and then future markets because these different ways of dealing or rather in transferring specific property rights in the physical commodities are cost efficient and generate enhanced benefits to the traders. Fifthly, the evolution of property rights is seen to be governed by economic factors. Property rights develop "to internalise externalities when the gains from internalization become larger than the costs of internalization. Increased internalization, in the main, results from changes in economic values ... stem(ming) from the development of new technology and the opening of new markets" (Demsetz, 1967 p. 350). Change and development of property rights are seen as the outcome of the interaction between individual utility maximization and changes in the cost-benefit configuration which make existing property rights poorly attuned to economic realities. The central theme of property rights theory is that property rights arise from the scarcity of resources.

The property rights approach thus constitutes a substantial revision of the nature and scope of economics. As Alchian (1967, p. 213) states '(I)n essence, economics is the study of property rights over resources'. The methods employed by the approach are, however, little more than the application of neoclassical techniques to a new subject matter which previous economists had taken as the datum for their models. In this regard it contrasts with Oliver Williamson's more taxonomical approach to institutional analysis which attempts to develop a different language and to highlight different factors as explanations for the institutional arrangements observed in capitalist economies. The key issue is not which one offers a more intuitively plausible description of property rights, but which better satisfies two requirements. Namely,

1. that the theory predicts how different property rights effects the allocation of resources and;

2. that it can explain the long-term development of property rights.

The work undertaken so far provides some justification for accepting that property rights theory has established itself on the first point (De Alessi, 1980). Although it should be noted in passing that the property rights approach has yet to offer a convincing explanation for either the nationalisation and subsequent privatisation movements in Western Europe, and that the evidence on the superior performance of private firms is at best equivocal. It must be said in fairness that this may be the result of the difficulty of devising acceptable tests of the predictions of property rights theory. As the Witt paper indicates there is more unease about the ability of the approach to convincingly explaining the evolution of property right systems. For the remainder of this paper I propose to examine some of the ambiguities of the property rights apporach on this count.

II. The Nature of Property

One of the difficulties with the property rights approach is the way it defines a property right. It is an all embracing definition that effectively captures any legal, institutional, customary and/or moral constraint on individual activity. Furubotn and Pejovich (1974, p. 3.) define property rights 'as the sanctioned behavioral relations among men that arise from the existence of goods and pertain to their use ... (they are) the set of economic and social relations defining the position of each individual with respect to the utilization of scarce resources.' A good is defined as anything that yields utility.

Economists are notoriously bad at definitions but one must really question whether such a broad definition is really meaningful other than as an ambitious way of reorienting economists attention away from the physical production process to institutions.

The broadness of this definition is, however, misleading. Property rights theorist do lay great stress on the qualitative differences in specific bundles of property rights governing resources. This is seen principally as a function of their 'exclusiveness' or privateness. Rights which are shared equally by a subset of individuals and for which there is an absence of exclusive use, either because of legal restrictions or the costs of policing and protecting exclusiveness, are called common property rights. At the other extreme there is the most attentuated form of property right, the private property right. The essential characteristic of a private property right is exclusiveness in the right of use (though not unrestricted use), its transferability and the ability of buyer and seller to negotiate the terms of trade. The important point to note, and the one that the Witt paper tends to confuse, is that these rights are polar extremes designed to bring into sharp relief the behavioral and economic consequences of two very different rights - the costlessly enforce private property right which results in allocative efficiency and the common property right which leads to over-exploitation of resources and the dissipation of rents.

However, even these rights are in fact a composite of other more specific rights. The private property right requires that it be exclusive, transferable and negotiable. It has at least three characteristics. These characteristics are also ill-defined because they can vary in degree. For example, private property is assumed to be synonymous with exclusive rights to the use and disposition of property. In Blackstone's *Commentaries* it is defined as 'that sole and despotic domain which one man claims and exercises over the external things of the world, in total exclusion of the rights of any other individual in the universe'. The definition of private property solely in terms of the ability to exclude others and transfer title is, obviously, much too simplistic. The legal protection of the right to exclude cannot reasonably be an absolute one because this would necessarily limit other individual's rights to the use and enjoyment of their property. A balance must be drawn between the incompatible and conflicting uses of property that will inevitably arise. Exclusiveness is therefore a fluid concept, as are all the other characteristics of private property. This is because apart from problems of definition, the nature of private property is fashioned to the particular needs of the contracting parties and/or imposed on them by the legal system in order to achieve collective aims. Thus while a right may be private along some dimensions, along others it will have more collective features. That is why the property rights approach tends to see exchange and production as involving *bundles* of property rights. This recognises both that actual property rights vary along the private-public continuum and that the concept of property is itself a multi-facted one.

If, as I have said, property rights vary dramatically according to the industry or commodity being exchanged, then a proper analysis must investigate very carefully the nature of the actual property rights existing in the industry. This was one of the important propositions advanced by Coase (1960) and later by Harold Demsetz (1969) article on the comparative institutions approach which has been developed and refined by Williamson (1975 & 1985). The property rights approach proceeds through a case-by-case analysis of the nature and effects of different property right structures. In this respect it is more microanalytical than orthodox theory.

It is for this reason that I find Witt's criticism of Demsetz somewhat misguided. Demsetz's original paper, like most innovative attempts to extend the boundaries of economics, propably suffers from overstatement, a certain crudeness and some inaccuracies in historical interpretation. But these deficiencies should not detract from the core proposition he is advancing - that economics can explain the evolution of property rights - and it is this which should be critically examined.

III. The Robustness of the Theory.

This brings us the critical issue in any evaluation of a theory. Does it successfully explain the data?

The property rights approach attempts to do two things as stated above. It is a theory of the effects and impact of different property rights and it is a theory of the development of property rights. These can be treated separately and much of the criticisms of the approach seem to be direct at the second application. In both these tasks, but more so for the second because of the qualitative nature of the data, the approach is susceptible to rationalising rather than predicting outcomes. This is so for two reasons: the use of the utility maximization hypothesis and the role that transaction costs play in its theoretical structure.

Property rights theorists replace the wealth maximization hypothesis with that of utility maximization. This has the effect of weakening its predictive power. The potentially subjective and untestable nature of utility maximization can turn the approach into an open construct which does no more than rationalise observe outcomes. This is why it is crucially important that the arguments which enter into the utility function be specified ex ante and that the evidence that is marshalled to support the predictions of the theory be treated with care. Much of the evidence used to support the evolutionary component of the property rights theory is historical interpretation. It is relatively easy by a selective choice of historical facts to find at least some evidence in support of the proposition that new property rights emerge in response to economic forces. But this is not the same as establishing that an economic theory can predict not only the nature but the form of new property rights. Quite simply, unless the theorist begins with a clearly specified utility function and states clearly what evidence constitutes an acceptable test (that is, would falsify the property rights theory) then there is a great danger that the approach while seeming to explain much in fact generates very few new insight on the process of institutional change.

This difficulty is compounded by the central role played by transaction costs in some areas of the property rights literature. It is only a slight exaggeration to claim that the bridge between law and economics has been built on the concept of transaction costs. In Ronald Coase's (1960) 'The Problem of Social Costs' it was argued that property rights do not have allocative or incentive effects in the absence of transaction costs. The transaction cost notion appeals to many law-and-economics scholars because it appears to resolve the tension between simplicity and descriptive realism, by giving a central role to the problems that beset individual decision-making and action (such as ignorance, lack of information, uncertainty etc.) which are generally ignored by economists. Like utility maximization this seemingly innocuous concession runs a great danger of robbing the theory of its predictive and explanatory content.

To repeat the above point in a different and slightly more strident way, if the axioms of utility maximization and transaction cost economising are used as descriptive propositions to interpret historical evidence and qualitative data, then property rights theory, like much of the new law-and-economics, runs a high risk of becoming tautological. Obviously, if individuals are constantly economising transaction costs the idea of inefficiency is a contradiction in terms. If all human behaviour is rational then individual actions and institutions must be the result of economising over all costs (including transaction costs) and can be explained as optimization of those costs. We are then forced to conclude that we are always in the best viz most efficient of all possible worlds. Yet if this conclusion is accepted then many of the time honored policy prescriptions of economists no longer stand. The economist can no longer argue that free trade is better than monopoly and that private property is better than communal property ownership. If protection, monopoly and communal property exist it is because of a rational process of economising over all costs associated with the economic and institutional systems.

Obviously one does not want to push this argument too far since the study of information costs, bargaining strategies and enforcement costs are of great importance to understanding how our legal system works and to evaluating its economic performance and efficiency. It is only that an economic theory built on utility maximization and transaction costs when applied as a tool of historical analysis is an incoherent structure.

Relating these points to Witt's analysis I am not convinced that Demsetz got it wrong, since neither Demsetz nor Witt have provided a robust test of their respective hypotheses.

IV. The Efficiency of Private Property.

The final area which requires some comment is one of central implications of the property rights approach - the relative efficiency of private property.

Property rights theorists are fond of claiming that private property is more efficient than any other property arrangement. The foremost exponents of the approach (Alchian, Demsetz, Furubotn) hold an admitted 'unsubstantiated proposition' (Furubotn & Pejovich, 1974, p. XIV) that the more private property rights are, the more efficient will be the allocation of resources. The logic behind these claims is perhaps most clearly stated by Cheung (1970, p. 64):

> Competition for and transferability of the ownership right in the market place thus perform two main functions for contracting. First, competition conglomerates know-

> ledge from all potential owners - the knowledge of alternative contractual arrangements and uses of the resources; and transferability of property rights ensures (via flexible relative prices) that the most valuable will be utilized. Second, competition among potential contract participants and a resource owner's ability to transfer the right to use his resource reduce the cost of enforcing the stipulated terms in a contract ... because competing parties will stand by to offer or accept similar terms.

However as the quotation itself indicates it is not privateness per se that leads to efficiency but privateness plus several other factors. The rhetorical use of economics (Mc Closkey, 1986), rather than the more sensitive and painstaking analyses of actual property rights systems, tends to omit discussion of these other equally important factors. In particular, private property must be coupled with competition. A monopolist has the most private of all property rights but his use of it is far from efficient. Secondly, it must also be assumed that transaction costs are relatively low. Some types of transaction costs are reduced by private property, such as monitoring costs, but others are unaffected or increase. One could give individuals rights to part of the environment but this would be an empty gesture and would not generate an efficient solution. The mere enactment of this private right would be defeated by the costs of bargaining and the free rider problems endemic in any collective action designed to improve the environment. In this situation collective action and hence non-private rights emerge as the only response because it is impossible to meaningfully enforcenment and trade private property rights. Thus the case for private property rights boils down to the as yet unsubstantiated assertion that where one can define and enforce such rights they are better than any other ownership arrangement. But one must be clear on the limited nature of this claim. First, it is a generalisation and does not tell us what the content of the bundle of property rights is. There can be efficient and inefficient definitions of private rights. And secondly, it still leaves room for a whole range of collective property rights which are potentially efficient.

The Efficiency of the Common Law: A New Institutional Economics Perspective

by

Charles K. Rowley and Wayne Brough

1. Introduction

Throughout the decade of the 1970s, Richard E. Posner (now Judge) mounted a major research program in the economic analysis of law designed to demonstrate that the common law is efficient, viewed from the perspective of wealth (even perhaps more generally of utility) maximization. Further, Posner urged, against an impressive array of dissenters, that such efficiency was an appropriate objective for the common law to pursue. The success of Posner's initiative, both in its normative and in its positive dimensions, is yet uncertain, perhaps incapable of any ultimate resolution. The contribution to jurisprudence, however, cannot be denied. For the first time since Blackstone's Commentaries, written two centuries earlier, Posner presented a novel, internally consistent and highly persuasive jurisprudence of the anglo-saxon common law. Legal scholarship has been non-trivially re-oriented by this contribution. Legal training has been significantly broadened to encompass the techniques prerequisite for an understanding of the new law and economics.

In this paper, we evaluate the positive assertion that the common law is efficient from the perspective of the new institutional economics. We demonstrate just how elusive the efficiency concept becomes within a subjectivist, contractarian comparative institutions context. We probe the robustness of Posner's hypothesis by outlining the origins of the common law and by evaluating the modern institutions of the common law for efficiency-generating impulses. We conclude that there is good a priori reason to have some confidence in the efficiency of the laws of property and of contract. The law of tort is a quite separate and much more suspect institution from the efficiency perspective.

2. Efficiency and the Common Law

The law can be conveniently subdivided into two categories - the statute and the common law - though this distinction becomes blurred in many areas where judge-made law and statutes are inextricably inter-related. The statute law is a derivative of society's political institutions and, as such, is amenable to public choice analysis. No-one claims efficiency for statute law, at least in any generalized sense. The common law, on the other hand, is judge-made law, buffered to a considerable extent from interests not directly involved. Judges are

Pethig Schlieper (Eds.)
Efficiency, Institutions, and Economic Policy

perceived to be non-partisan, devoid of any vested interest in the cases that they adjudicate. It is within this institutional environment that Posner's claims concerning efficiency have been advanced.

There are three main branches of common law: property, contract and tort. Property law deals with ownership and rights, including the alienability of rights, and as such plays a pivotal role in resource allocation. Evidently, an inefficient law of property would impose severe wealth losses upon society. Contract law also plays an important role, determining how the owners of property engage in mutually advantageous trade. In Posner's view, contract law has three functions. First, it maintains proper incentives for exchange to take place, protecting the parties from non-performance and fraud, minimizing the transaction costs of trade. Second, it reduces the complexity associated with trade, by establishing a systematic set of rules. Third, it forewarns individuals of the likely impediments to effective exchange, allowing them to plan exchanges more effectively in the future. Each such function has a dominant efficiency objective. Tort law is more suspect, from the viewpoint of Posner's hypothesis, since it deals with externalities and not with the exchange relationship. Nevertheless, Posner has argued that tort law is efficent, even where third party effects must enter into the calculus of the judicial decision. The developed system of liability and the rules concerning compensation are viewed as wealth maximizing for society.

Posner's concept of efficiency oscillates uneasily between wealth and utility, and he has been justly critized on this ground. It is unequivocally objective and ends-related, thus falling well within the conventional approach of welfare economics, even though is emphasizes the comparative institutions approach. The common law, as it has evolved, is viewed as the new benefit maximizing institution available to society in the areas of property, contract and tort. This judgment is not based on process efficiency, for example in the sense of Hayek's 'spontaneous order'. The ends are absolute and the actual achievements are amenable to objective evaluation.

Efficiency is viewed differently through the subjectivist-contractarian perspective of Virginian political economy. In such a perspective, the only source of valuation of assets or resource claims is the revealed choice behavior of parties to exchange. External observers cannot determine whether or not observed trades fall short of or exceed some idealized efficiency norm. Given the institutions, efficiency is ensured as long as all relevant parties are free to engage or not in the exchange mechanism. Even in the absence of coercion and/or fraud, however, the efficiency concept is refutable and, therefore, is not tautologous.

The appropriate test for efficiency, in this view, is that of consensus over the higher level choice between alternative institutions, much in the way that consensus over the constitution indicates efficiency even though conflict may be evident throughout the lower level behavior of in-period political institutions. At the lower level, rational utility maximizing individuals must be presumed to behave efficiently, given the institutional constraints that confront them, though, of course, efficient outcomes will not be defined uniquely on initial endowments, given the availability of alternative institutions. In the absence of transaction costs in higher level decision-making, whatever exists is efficient. Given transaction costs, evidence of dissent, in the form of individuals exercising the options available to them of exit and/or voice, constitutes prima facie evidence of higher level inefficiency. Even then, however, such evidence is far from conclusive. Voice may be an option at zero cost, utilized to satiation. In a comparative institutions environment, a solution is inefficient only if an alternative of a more consensual nature is available.

If transaction cost impediments to institutional reform are suspected, the political economist, in principle, has an important entrepreneurial role as depicted by *Buchanan* in his important 1959 paper. His task, as Buchanan then saw it, is that of 'locating possible flaws in the existing social structure and in presenting possible "improvements"'. His specific hypothesis is that *mutual* gains do, in fact, exist as a result of possible changes. The test, is the behavior of individuals in society in response to suggested alternatives. Consensus or unanimity is the only test which can ensure that a change is beneficial. Thus, the political economist in no sense is the Arrow social decision-maker. He does not claim omniscience; and he does not massage preferences. He interprets preferences and subjects his hypothesis to the full falsification test.

Reviewed from the perspective of 1986, Buchanan's solution appears to be over-optimistic. It is now recognized that public good problems make it likely that information will be underprovided by market forces; that political economists of Buchanan's category could not privatize the benefits of successful entrepreneurship. It is also recognized that government intervention is vulnerable to all the distortions chronicled in the burgeoning literature of public choice; that consensus is not a relevant criterion for interest group dominated democracies and that Arrow decision-makers do not exist in such environments. More seriously, from Buchanan's perspective, is the vulnerability of political economists to rent seeking pressures. If economic advisers are employed by special interests, they will reflect their paymaker's interests, distorting the higher level test to accommodate the dominant interest group's preferences. If they are employed by the state, they will reflect the short-term interests of the in-period government.

In such circumstances, a serious problem of incoherence threatens the consensus test. If everything within the political process is treated as endogenous, then the system is fully explained, and there is *no* effective route to change the political equilibrium, however non-consensual that equilibrium may be. This does not imply that independent research will not exist or that economic ideas will not from time to time direct the political process. Scholars working independently, sheltered by the quadrangles of their academies, periodically may fulfill Buchanan's task. Insodoing, they are the true exogenous entrepreneurs of political change, uncaptured by the existing political equilibrium. It has to be said, however, that such creatures are rare and that their contributions, however independent, are by no means guaranteed political success even if they satisfy the test of consensus. The impartial spectator certainly requires guidelines to evaluate signals of institutional distress and to assess the relevance of political economic advice in systems where efficiency impulses are absent or are obstructed by cost impediments.

3. Efficiency Impulses in the Common Law

If efficiency is difficult to identify within a comparative institutions framework, the observer must rely more heavily than is ideal upon relevant indicators of efficiency impulses in the particular institution under review. Let us apply this approach to an understanding of anglo-saxon common law.

(i) The Origins of the Common Law

The common law of England, in the twelfth and thirteenth centuries, was that body of rules prescribing social conduct and justiciable in the royal courts. This law, which was common to all the realm of England, was in competition with concurrent rules enforced in other courts. Save when a matter of freehold was at issue, Englishmen were not compelled to present their causes before the king's courts. They could take their cases, instead, into the local courts of the counties, which administered local, customary law; or into the church courts, which administered the canon law, touching on such issues as wills and testaments, marriage and divorce, and contracts involving a pledge of faith. Feudal barons might accept jurisdiction of a baronial overlord, whose court applied rules of feudal custom. Townsmen might bring their causes before the court of a borough, which would judge them by rules of the law merchant.

By the end of the thirteenth century, the common law had absorbed much, if not all, of the judicial business of its competitors, borrowing heavily from them in the process of aggrandizement. Its victory, for the most part, was a competitive victory, achieved in an environment in which voice and exit were powerful weapons available to those disaffected by its judgments. For those able to have their cases adjudicated, the efficiency impulses of such a market would be strong, at least in the contractarian sense of efficiency emphasized in this paper. Whether or not the feudal-based common law carried over to modern times, and if so, whether or not it remained efficient is worthy of further consideration. Clearly, post-feudal developments in the common law, most especially those dealing with property interests, were the product of a more monopolistic legal system in which the competitive impulse to efficiency was much less strong.

In medieval England, the notion of permanence in the law was imparted by its connection with immemorial custom. Law was not 'made', but was 'declared' by those familiar with the custom of a certain territory. Legal rights thus were based on unwritten law which usage had approved. Inevitably, however, there was a tension between the pull toward permanence, which was especially strong in the law of property, and which became enshrined in the doctrine of stare decisis, the reliance on precedents in interpreting legal principle, and the pull toward adaptability which is always evident during periods of rapid economic and social adjustment. The eventual outcome of this tension was influenced by the character of the royal judges and the willingness of English kings to enforce their decisions as well as by the jurisdiction of the royal courts.

The foundation of the common law were established most especially in the years between 1154 and 1307, essentially via the writ system. A writ was an order from the king under the Great Seal founded on some principle of law, regular juris, which gave the right on which the action was founded and which stated the facts of the case. Appropriate writs were created for the protection of every private right or interest recognized by the royal courts, especially during the thirteenth century. Thereafter, the writ system hardened and set, forcing plaintiffs to seek remedies outside the common law, perhaps by means of a petition to the king's council, or to the chancellor. Catalogs of writs employed by the Chancery were collected and were known as registers. Until the nineteenth century, at least, the Register of Writs was one of the most valuable sources of legal remedies available at common law. Ultimately, the court before which a case was tried passed final judgment on the suitablity of any writ.

Even now, although many forms of action have been abolished by nineteenth century legislation, a knowledge of the old writs is still useful for understanding common law principles. As Maitland put it

> 'The forms of action we have buried, but they still rule us from their graves.'

The growth of the writ system was facilitated by the practical authority of the Crown. Although litigants were compelled to seek the king's justice only in matters touching on freehold, the inventiveness of the royal council drew business to the royal courts, by providing the best available justice. Undoubtedly, this justice must have been heavily imbued with efficiency in the contractarian sense, since the royal courts dominated without coercion in the development of English law; and did so despite two major rebellions by the feudal barons (1215 and 1258) which attempted to curtail the authority of the Crown.

Undoubtedly, the king in council, the royal judges and the Chancery clerks were influenced by thirteenth century social and business morality. Efficiency impulses thus exerted themselves in common law development to reflect the preferences of alien merchants and money lenders brought to England by the development of foreign trade. Most especially was this the case in the development of leasehold law protection for leaseholders against those who disturbed the possession of the lease.

(ii) From Medieval Law to Modern Law

Only England, among the nations of western Europe, successfully carried the essential elements of its medieval customary legal system into the modern world. It did so despite significant violence and disorder intent on disturbing the balance between the prerogative of the Crown, the privileges of Parliament and individual liberties. Its continuity through almost eight centuries, despite such periodic threats, is unique in the history of European legal systems.

The common law might well have disappeared in the fifteenth century, as a consequence of dynastic quarrels between the Houses of Lancaster and of York, which deteriorated into a new feudalism and an erosion of the rule of law. But it was restored to good order after 1485, with the emergence of the House of Tudor and the cessation of dynastic disputes. It might have succumbed to the re-emergence of Roman law in Europe during the sixteenth century, as indeed was the case in Scotland, but for the chauvinism of Henry VIII and his immediate sucessors. It was imperilled during the seventeenth century by disputes between the Crown and Parliament, which encouraged the re-development of competing legal systems. But it was preserved by the revolution of 1688 and the consequential consolidation of parliamentary authority. It was threatened during the eighteenth century by the emergence of legislative sovereignty in Parliament and with it the prospect of drastic legal change by means of statute. But, despite Blackstone's acknowledgment of parliamentary sovereignty, the common law doctrines of stare decisis and of established legal principles survived.

Thus, the essential elements of common law remain unchanged, albeit with adaptations to reflect new conditions. Two factors were largely responsible for such ongoing stability, namely the early maturity in England of the common law and the fact that the early common law was land law (now referred to as the law of property). Early maturity brought with it technical complexity well before the end of the thirteenth century, implying that laymen could not hope to litigate successfully without the professional assistance of pleaders and attorneys. Judges, pleaders, attorneys and students formed an interest group concerned to protect a legal system into which they had rent sought via expensive outlays. The Inns of Court were finely honed in rent protection even through revolution and civil war, were well-designed to preserve stare decisis to the extent feasible in a rapidly changing environment.

Rules of land law, first enforced in the reign of Henry II, were elaborated during the reign of Edward I to provide for the alientation of freehold and for the creation of long-term family property arrangements by means of conditional gifts. Land was the principle form of wealth until the commercial and industrial revolutions created alternative sources of personal property. Thus, for several centuries, a complete overthrow of common law rules and and of the courts administering them, would have frustrated the expectations of almost every property holder in England. From the eighteenth century onwards, such interests had a privileged access to Parliament to prevent significant changes in the law of property. Economic interests thus played a significant role first in preserving the law of property and subsequently, in developing contract law within an efficiency-ordinated perspective. The law of tort, was a later, economically perhaps more suspect, development.

(iii) Judical Incentives and Constraints

The efficiency hypothesis in its original form was essentially a descriptive or empirical assertion. Little effort was devoted to explaining why, and through what mechanism, the judiciary itself might have exerted an instrumental influence favorable to efficiency in the common law. For the most part, advocates relied upon a nineteenth century social consensus in favor of efficiency, presumably shared by members of the judiciary, and implemented by them within their tenured, and essentially discretionary, environment. Posner, as the most aggressive proponent of the efficiency hypothesis, inevitably confronted trenchant criticism for this lacuna in his analysis.

As early as 1973, Posner acknowleged this weakness and predicted its early resolution:

> 'There is growing dissatisfaction with attempts to answer the question why the common law is efficient with vague references to nineteenth-century ideology. I expect the development of an economic theory of judical notification and behavior to occupy a prominent place in the future work of law-and-economics scholars.'

By 1979, however, Posner had shifted his position to that of Chicago methodology, asserting an 'as-if'defense of the efficiency hypothesis:

> 'The positive branch of the theory hypothesizes that common law rules and decisions are best explained on the 'as if' assumption, not intended to be realistic, that judges are consciously trying to promote efficient resource allocation, where efficiency is defined as wealth maximization.'

This shift of ground, however, was by no means categorical, for in the same article Posner suggested three reasons why judge-based law might be efficient:

> (1) Wealth maximization is closely related to utilitarianism, and the formative period of the common law as we know it today, roughly 1800-1950, was a period when utilitarianism was the dominant political ideology in England and America; (2) judges lack effective tools for enriching an interest group or social class other than by increasing the society's wealth as a whole in which the favored group or class presumably will share, and (3) the process of common law adjudication itself leads to the survival of efficient rules.'

and admitted that the failure to develop such arguments formally had weakened the credibility of the efficiency hypothesis:

> 'efforts to explain why the common law is efficient (if it is) have been handicapped by the lack of an accepted economic model of judicial incentives'

Posner has recognized explicitly that the absence of any causal explanation of the behavior of judges weakens not just the credibility, but also the explanatory power of the efficiency hypothesis:

> 'The economic literature---which has sought to explain how the common law might come to consist largely of rules designed to promote efficiency, has tended to elide the issue of judicial incentives, preferences, behavior etc. by treating the judge as an essentially passive spectator of the combat between the litigants. There is no objection in principle to such an assumption. But the literature erected on it cannot claim such great explanatory power as to make uninteresting an attempt to develop a theory of the judicial process in which the behavior of judges is assumed to be an important factor in judicial rules and outcomes.'

In fact two attempts have been made to model the behavior of judges, the first by *Landes and Posner* (1975) and the second by *Higgins and Rubin* (1980). Neither attempt was successful. Landes and Posner, accepted without serious questioning, the notion of the independent judiciary, accepting Buchanan's conception of the law in general, and the Supreme Court in constitutional adjudication in particular, as standing apart from and limiting the scope and intensiveness of the political process. They noted that Article III of the U.S. Constitution provided for the appointment, rather than for the election, of federal judges, that they were to have life tenure, and that Congress could not reduce their salaries while they remained in office. To a lesser extent, the independence thus bestowed held also for state and municipal judges at all levels both in the U.S. and elsewhere.

For Landes and Posner, the independence thus granted to the judiciary was designed to consolidate legislative deals arising within an interest group dominated, pluralistic political system. If Congress is to be capable of appropriating the present value of long term legislative commitments to particular interest groups, the probability of subsequent legislative renegement must be suitably low. Procedural rules within Congress are designed to facilitate stability and continuity. But these must be insufficient, since the courts are necessary to enforce the law where otherwise it would be disobeyed. Thus a judiciary subservient to the current legislature could nullify the enactments of an earlier legislature. To avoid the long-term erosion of congressional contracts, therefore, the independence of the judiciary is enshrined in constitutional contract.

This interpretation, which was subjected to somewhat crude empirical evaluation, is dependent on the assumption that the sole motivation of judges is expected wealth maximation. Suppress any association between expected wealth and judgements, it is implied, and the latter will be, in some sense, unbiased. Such a view is absurd, a figment of the narrowed intellects of professional economists. Judges, like almost all others in society, have arguments additional to wealth in their utility functions. With the wealth argument isolated, the others will assume control. Those arguments may be efficiency orientated, though there is no reason to suppose that they will.

Lawyers trained in critical legal studies in New England or California law schools, or lawyers trained in 'public interest' law as it is construed in certain minority law schools throughout the country, if they achieve the bench, which they well may during the incumbency of liberal democrat presidents, will not allow efficiency to dominate their judgements, unless the reward/constraint system somehow dominates their ideologies. Some indeed may be imbued with the desire to destroy wealth as a prerequisite for perceived social 'advance.' A categorical in favor of the efficiency impulse of the judiciary is not credible in the unconstrained environment.

In part to take account of such problems, which are endemic in any theory which posits unlimited discretion for its actors, and in part as a response to the criticisms of Posners' institutional lacuna by legal scholars hostile to the efficiency hypothesis, *Higgins and Rubin* (1980) developed and tested a formal theory of judicial discretion incorporating constraints on judicial behavior, as well as recognizing the objective of ideology in the judges' utility functions. Specifically, judges were assumed to maximize

$$(1) \qquad U = U(D, W, A)$$

subject to

$$R = f(D, P)$$

and

$$(2) \qquad W = g(R, S)$$

where D is judicial discretion; W is wealth; A is the age of the judge; R is the rate of reversal; S is the seniority of the judge; and P is a political variable denoting whether the party of the judge is the same as that of the majority of the appellate court.

Thus, judges are assumed to benefit from imposing their values on society, which would be achieved by precedent-setting opinions. They also benefit from increased wealth, which is enhanced for lower level judges by the absence of reversals in their judgmental records. The ensuing trade-off between wealth and discretion thus provides the basis for the constraint set of the Higgins/Rubin model. However, empirical testing suggests that their model is an empty box. Judicial discretion appears to be an unconstrained objective; age and seniority do not matter; the role of precedent is nil; and discretionary behavior is not policed by appellate review. Thus, if constraints operate on judges, they must come from sources other than the prospect of reversal - perhaps via the initial selection process itself.

The selection processes for judges is an area not yet well charted in the literature of law and economics. For federal judges, the process is one of selection and not of election. Evidently where the President and the Senate are politically close the opportunity to stack the bench is high; and that opportunity is rarely missed. Where the Executive and the Senate are divided, compromise will emerge in the political complexion of newly appointed judges. In any event, early assessments may be falsified as the rising conservative hostility to Justice Sandra Day O'Connor clearly indicated following 1986 Supreme Court judgements. An incumbent of the Supreme Court has virtually unlimited discretion, tempered only by the desire to write leading majority judgements.

In certain states, judges are elected and are not tenured into their incumbencies. In such circumstances, public choice pressures, evidenced in the vote motive, special interest group pressures, and bureaus' preferences, will predominate not merely in the selection process, but through the duration of all but terminal incumbencies. Public choice theory does not predict wealth maximizing outcomes in such circumstances. Indeed, rent seeking in a transfer society may produce highly wealth destructive judgements.

In essence, therefore, the judiciary remains a black box in the economic analysis of law. Any efficiency impulse from this source at best is weak, dependent on the strength of precedents established in the early development of the common law, together with the coalescence of underlying interests of the litigants. Once again, in the cases of property law and contract law, there may be little reason to doubt the main thrust of the efficiency hypoothesis at least on a priori grounds. Tort law, once again, is the outlier, an area in which wealth destructive do-gooders are able to exert a powerful judicial influence, confident that their judgements will be applauded by interest groups concerned more with the achievement of transfers than with wealth enhancement.

(iv) The Process of Litigation

An important comparative institutions test of the efficiency of the common law is the extent to which potential litigants utilize the courts. A number of leading scholars of law and economics - notably Landes, Gould, and Tullock - have separately argued that, in general, parties in dispute will tend to settle out of court. Evidence in a variety of fields does not refute this hypothesis. From this perspective, the efficiency hypothesis is vulnerable to effective attack. For, if the common law is efficient, it should dominate the process of dispute settlement, if only by ensuring that outside settlements are concluded under 'the efficiency shadow of the law.' How could it ensure such outcomes, under changing conditions, in the absence of significant litigation on cases that reflect the efficiency conditions of contemporary society?

Recognizing this problem for the efficiency hypothesis, Rubin has suggested that the presumed efficiency of the common law and decisions to use the courts to settle disputes are closely related. The courts will be utilized more frequently where the legal rules relevant to the dispute are inefficient and less frequently where the rules are efficient. In this perspective, efficient rules evolve from in-court settlements, and by their existence reduce the incentive for future litigation, thus raising the probability that they will persist through time. The efficiency outcome, in this perspective, is the outcome of an evolutionary mechanism which is generated by the utility maximizing decisions of disputants rather than by any efficiency predilections of the judiciary. If Rubin is correct, the efficiency hypothesis is rendered much more credible a priori since Posner's lacuna is circumvented by other efficiency impulses. This substitution becomes most important, as will be demonstrated, in the law of tort, which has been fingered in this paper as the suspect area for the efficiency hypothesis. Rubin's analysis centers on the tort of accident liability, although he claims that property and contract law can be analysed within the same framework.

Rubin posits an accident which involves A and B, with the former defendants and the latter victims. Efficiency in this case requires that liability be placed on B, with the Coase theorem obstructed by transaction costs. Liability assignments, seen to depend in part on precedents, will determine who will expend on accident avoidance ex ante and in what amount. Litigation is rendered worthwhile where there is a prospect of changing current precedents and where the parties have a sufficient interest to challenge inefficient precedents.

Individuals typically manifest only a one-time interest in legal outcomes, and are unlikely to litigate specifically to change an inefficient legal precedent save under the pressure of ambulance-chasing lawyers anxious to try their luck with a contingent fee contract. Corporate bodies, such as firms, insurance companies, government agencies or labor unions, in contrast, may well be concerned for ongoing reasons to litigate against inefficient precedents as well as to win specific court settlements.

Rubin shows that both parties to a case must manifest ongoing interests for efficient court evolution to be a predictable consequence of the litigation process.

Suppose that an inefficient rule exists, with A held liable if accidents occur, with A spending S_A on accident avoidance and N_AX on damage payments for those accidents which still occur. An accident occurs; the parties must decide whether to settle or to litigate. If the case is litigated and B wins, he is paid X. If A wins, he does not pay X and in addition, saves T_A in the future, whereas B must begin to pay T_B. Court costs for each party are C. The value to A of a court settlement is

(3) $$V_A = R(-X) + (1-R)\,T_A - C$$

and to B:

(4) $$V_B = R\,(X) + (1-R)\,(-T_B) - C$$

The parties will settle out of court if

(5) $$-V_A > V_B$$

where the expected loss to A of going to court is greater than the expected gain to B. Litigation will occur if:

(6) $$(1-R)\,(T_A - T_B) > 2C$$

where $T_A - T_B$ is the cost of the inefficient legal rule, and where R is the probability of the precedent holding ($R > .5$).

If the parties decide to litigate, B will probably win ($R > .5$), but A will continue to litigate in future cases. Some court will find in favor of A in the large numbers situation. The law then becomes efficient, with precedent favoring A in comparable cases. Now there is no deadweight loss to party B, who bears the liability (no term comparable to $T_A - T_B$). B will not litigate, but will spend S_B on avoidance and N_BX on residual accidents. If both parties are insurance companies, equally likely to be on either side in future cases, equation (6) is unchanged so that the pressure in favor of efficiency will be maintained. The rule is efficient, not because of efficiency objectives within the judiciary, but as a consequence of rules evolution under the wealth maximizing pressures of litigants.

If only one party to a dispute is interested in the ongoing liability system, precedents will evolve in favor of that party, whether or not that party's interests coincide with the efficient rule. Such an outcome describes the evaluation of nuisance law in the nineteenth century, which favored large factories and firms to the disadvantage of individuals. If neither party has an ongoing interest there is no incentive to litigate against a clearly defined precedent, if the specific interest of contingent fee lawyers is ignored. In such circumstances, the status quo will tend to persist, whether efficient or not, irrespective of any deadweight losses imposed upon society, as a consequence of the free rider problem implicit in the publicness of the existing precedent.

Rubin relies on an explicit process generated by far-sighted self-interest on the part of certain litigants to drive out the efficient evolution of legal rules. Strictly, such an approach is not evolutionary in the biological sense. For, in its extreme form, the evolutionary model assumes on absence of foresight and a random generation of behavioral options, with unsuccessful behavior dying away and successful behavior living on. In this perspective, the concept of an evolutionarily stable strategy is similar to that of a Nash equilibrium in a non-cooperative game. This approach to the evolution of the common law was developed from Rubin's seminal contribution by *Terrebonne*.

Suppose that each individual can pursue either one of two strategies, say strategy I or J. A particular strategy is said to be evolutionarily stable, if, when commonly employed, it is more fit than any other strategy. Thus, I is evolutionarily stable if

$$(7) \qquad E(I/I) > E(J/I)$$

or if

$$(8) \qquad E(I/I) = E(J/I) \text{ and } E(I/J) > E(J/J).$$

where $E(J/I)$ is the average expected value of strategy J given that an opponent is pursuing strategy I, etc. The criterion for a Nash equilibrium corresponding to such a game would be

(9) $E(I/I) \geq E(J/I)$.

Since pairs of competitors are drawn from different populations in Terrebonne's model, (potential plaintiffs and potential defendants), the criterion in (9) simplifies to

(10) $E(I) > E(J)$

The results derived by Terrebonne support the thesis that selection favors common law rules that promote economic efficiency. In all cases except one, plaintiffs and defendants adopt strategies that result in a high rate of litigation when legal rules are inefficient and a low rate of litigation when they are efficient. The important exception is that litigation costs may prevent the litigation of some inefficient legal rules. As with Rubin, Terrebonne assumed away the Coase theorem as being obstructed by transaction cost considerations. He also assumed, without explanation, that legal rules that are litigated more frequently have a lower probability of survival than those that are litigated less frequently, Terrebonne does not attempt to deal with the public good problem in which many individuals must engage collectively in litigation designed to reverse a precedent imposed by courts in the law of tort.

Both Rubin and Terrebonne rely heavily on the assumption that inefficient rules will attract high rates of litigation as the prime moving force of their evolutionary models. This assumption is not self-evidently valid, as *Cooter and Kornhauser* have demonstrated, by modelling legal evolution as a Markov process. One of their conclusions is an impossibility theorem which states that blind evolution will not cause the legal system to reach the best state or even continually to improve itself. Eventually, the process will settle down to a stable state in which each legal rule prevails a fixed portion of the time. This stable state will be closer to efficiency, the higher the frequency of litigation of bad laws.

The probabilty that the existing rule will change depends on both the probability that it will be litigated and the probability that a judge will change it when litigated. Thus, the overall probability is a combination of the two. The result is a transition matrix for the legal system, which describes the probability that any existing rule i will change to rule j. This matrix takes into account both the probability of litigation occurring and its likely outcome. A characteristic of the Markov process is that long-term behavior is independent of the legal rule from which the process is generated. The system never settles down to a situation in which the best rule prevails forever, even when bad rules are litigated more frequently than good rules, and when judges are more likely to replace bad rules by good rules than vice versa.

Moreover, Cooter and Kornhauser query the assertion that bad rules indeed do attract differentially high rates of litigation; or at least they request that the assertion be put to the econometric test. Rubin's assertion is based on a group rationality notion that the potential litigants seek to minimize joint costs. Yet, much litigation is not motivated by group rationality, but by bargaining failures, vengefulness or strategic behavior, all of which may increase joint costs. Even though the absolute value of successful reversal of a bad precedent may be high for a potential litigant, the expected value will be low, where precedent is not easily disturbed. This may provide incentives to settle out of court - just the opposite reaction to that posited by Rubin and by Terrebonne. A priori, the reaction is indeterminate.

The litigation process alone, therefore, cannot be relied upon to drive efficient rules into the common law. Where other impulses are operative, as arguably is the case with property law and contract law, litigation may lever the law towards a 'good' stable structure, albeit not necessarily to full efficiency. Where such impulses are absent, as arguably is the case with the law of tort, there is no presumption of evolutionary efficiency. Indeed, once the role of the jury in such cases is associated with contingent fee attorney renumeration, Posner's hypothesis becomes extremely dubious for this important branch of the common law.

4. The U.S. Tort Crisis and the Efficiency Hypothesis

Tort law is presented in Posner's *Economic Analysis of Law* within a highly idealized framework. Tortious acts are clearly defined by the courts. Given the liability rule, damage awards are efficiently evaluated by judges well-versed in present-value accounting techniques. The only significant issues under debate concern the comparative efficacy of alternative liability rules: strict liability; negligence; contributory negligence; comparative negligence or no-fault. By stretching transaction cost assertions, it is not difficult for Posner to find existing tort law to be efficient, in such circumstances, especially when third party effects are ignored. Indeed, it would be difficult indeed to locate lower-level inefficiency in the sense of Buchanan in such a hypothetical system, at least in the absence of widespread avoidance of the litigation process.

The reality of contemporary U.S. tort law is sharply at odds with Posner's idealized model. Indeed, it is widely regarded as being in a state of crisis, posing a major threat to the U.S. gross national product in the absence of fundamental reforms. Working groups on the causes, extent and policy implications of the tort crisis within the U.S. are in the process of reporting to the federal government. State legislatures are invading the common law to impose caps on jury damage awards and to force insurance companies to roll back premium advances. Hospitals and medical practices are closing down or re-orienting their services away from high-risk medical services. Even the attorneys are hounding each other out of existence by legal malpractice suits that are winning millions of dollars in damages for their clients. Such events are not incompatible with economic efficiency; but they require considerable explanation on the part of those who press the generality of common law efficiency.

What then are the perceived problems in U.S. tort law, and why have they arisen? The answers take us far from the idealized environment of Posner's vision.

(i) The movement Toward No-Fault Liability

The movement toward no-fault liability began during the 1960s, but has accelerated dramatically during the 1980s in the USA. Its genesis is to be found in the invasion of the twin historic pillars of tort law-deterrence and compensation- by sociologically-based notions of societal insurance and risk spreading and by the undermining of fault as a moral and doctrinal justification for a limitation on tort liability.

As the tort system moves away from fault it exposes itself to capricious moral hazard as individuals seek remedies for damages to which they expose themselves, and as contingent fee renumerated attorneys 'ambulance-chase' to pressure potential plantiffs into proceeding with 'deep-pocket' law suits. The ultimate effect of such developments has been to shift liability for compensation to defendants endowed with resources to compensate generously, whether or not they are tortfeasors in the conventional sense, and irrespective of the negligence, absolute, comparative or contributory of the injured person.

Fault has not been openly or completely rejected as part of U.S. tort law. If it were, almost any kind of activity would be exposed to tortious action. The courts thus engage in amazing distortions of relevant facts or legal doctrines to find fault rather than simply to reject the principle of fault. The result is an increasingly common and perverse combination of fault-based levels of compensation based on no-fault liability.

(ii) The Undermining of Causation

Tort law traditionally sought to place liability only on those actors whose wrongful conduct actually caused an injury - the so-called concept of 'proximate cause,' which requires a reasonable relationship between a given cause and effect. This concept has been subjected to systematic attack via a range of questionable practices and doctrinal innovations.

On such development has been the increasing use of joint and several liability to shift the cost of compensation to 'deep pockets.' This doctrine has been manipulated to make a defendant with only a limited role in causing an injury bear the full cost of compensation, even when the plaintiff was largely responsible for his own injury. A related development is the way in which joint and several liability has been applied by some courts in the form of 'market share liability' for injuries covered by generic products even where not all relevant manufacturers are accounted for or where the product is not truly generic in nature. A third means that has been used to undermine causation - increasingly common in the case of toxic torts - is the use of burden-shifting techniques to force the defendant to prove lack of causation in order to avoid liability, and/or of the reliance by judges and juries on noncredible scientific or medical testimony (the so-called junk science invasion of the courts).

(iii) The Explosive Growth in Damage Awards

In 1975, the Torts Branch of the U.S. Department of Justice (as it became designated) contained 39 attorneys and handled some 4000 cases totalling approximately $1 billion in claims. In 1985, the Torts Branch had expanded to 124 attorneys and handled about 11,000 cases totalling approximately $ 200 billion in claims. In 1975, the average medical malpractice jury verdict awarded $ 220,028 damages. By 1985 this average had climbed to $ 1,017,716. Over the same time-span, the average product liability jury award advanced from $ 393,580 to $1,850,452, an increase of 370 percent. These increases were characterized by a significant rise in the number of jury awards in excess of $ 1 million - from three to nine in medical malpractice and from nine to seventy one in product liability suits. The explosion in damages has arisen largely at the high end of the awards scale. Large verdicts tend to be composed to a differentially high extent of non-economic damages, including non-pecuniary compensatory damages for pain and suffering and mental anguish as well as punitive damages.

(iv) High Transactions Costs

The tort system is characterized by extremely high transaction costs. A study by the Institute for Civil Justice of asbestos litigations established that 62 percent of all damages were lost in attorneys' fees and litigation expenses - a rent seeker's dream world. This did not include the transaction costs borne by the courts in adjudicating such claims. The study also established that successful plaintiffs alone lost 34 percent of their damage awards to legal fees and an additional 5 percent to legal expenses. The clear beneficiaries of such a system are lawyers. Ambulance-chasing in such circumstances is a predictable rent seeking phenomenon. The social waste from such activities has risen to non-trivial dimensions even for an economy as well-endowed as that of the U.S.

(v) The Explosion in Tort Suits

Even though the expected value of a tort suit to the plaintiff is diminished by attorney rent-seeking, the rent margins to the attorneys are high and their rent-seeking outlays, not least in advertising in favor of litigation, are high. The consequence is a substantial increase in the number of tort lawsuits and in the aggregate of awarded damages.

The number of product liability cases filed in federal district courts in the U.S. increased from 1,579 in 1974 to 13,554 in 1985, a 758 percent increase. The states courts witnessed a similar rate of increase. A similar trend is apparent in medical malpractice, with the number of claims filed against physician-owned companies increasing from 10,568 in 1979 to 23,545 in 1983, and with the number of medical malpractice lawsuits per 100 physicians more than doubling between 1976 and 1981. Inevitably, the outcome has been substantial increases in insurance premiums and, in certain high risk areas, the outright withdrawal of insurance facilities.

5. Conclusions

If the subjectivist, contractarian approach to efficiency is adopted, it is difficult to avoid the conclusion that efficiency prevails, given the institutions that exist and the constraints that influence the outcome of self-seeking behavior. Questions rightly remain concerning the efficiency of the institutions and their associated constraint systems at a higher, constitutional level of decision making. Answers to such questions essentially require a complex comparative institutions evaluation dependent upon transaction cost assessments that are themselves ultimately elusive within the subjectivist paradigm.

Three transaction cost constraints, which serve as potential impediments to efficiency-enhancing constitutional reform are to be determined in the contractarian approach, namely (i) those related to bounded rationality on the part of the relevant individuals, (ii) those related to free-riding in public good situations and (iii) those related to strategic behavior opportunities. Each of these conceivably might impact on all three branches of the common law, property and contract as well as tort. Superficially, therefore, there might seem to be no reason to select out tort law, ab initio, as the area of the law fingered for inefficiency.

Such, however, is not the case. Innovative research by Williamson has demonstrated that governance contracts, designed to handle just those issues in which bounded rationality, asset specificity and state-contingent conditions coincide and pose problems for efficient contracts, have become an important late twentieth century innovation. As such, they offer transaction cost reductions which auger well for higher level efficiency in the law of property and of contract. Torts, in stark contrast, offer no contract nexus, no governance opportunity to evade the high transaction cost impedient.

Where higher level efficiency adjustments appear to be obstructed by transaction costs, internal efficiency impulses assume differential importance. This paper has demonstrated, however, that precisely where such impulses are most required, namely the law of tort, they are in fact at their weakest. In such circumstances, rent seeking opportunities are likely to be high and are vulnerable to exploitation. The combination of juries and contingent fee lawyers in tort law, together with the invasion of certain benches by 'public interest' judges, ensures that rent seeking losses will be imposed upon society. In the U.S. a major insurance crisis is the outward manifestation of the inefficiency of the law of tort.

References

(1) Buchanan, J.M. (October 1959),
"Positive Economics, Welfare Economics and Political Economy" *Journal of Law and Economics II*, pp. 124-138.

(2) Buchanan, J.M. (1969),
"Cost and Choice" Markham 1969.

(3) Buchanan, J.M. (Spring 1974),
"Good Economics-Bad Law" *Virginia Law Review* 60 pp. 483-492.

(4) Buchanan, J.M. (1983),
"Rights, Efficiency and Exchange: The Irrelevance of Transaction Costs" *Arbeitstagung des Vereins für Socialpolitik*, Baul 1983, pp. 9-24.

(5) Cooter, R. (Jan. 1982),
"The Cost of Coase" *Journal of Legal Studies* XI pp. 1-34.

(6) Cooter, R. and Kornhauser, L. (Jan 1980),
"Can Litigation Improve the Law Without The Help of Judges?" *Journal of Legal Studies* IX pp. 139-163.

(7) Goodman, J.C. (June 1978),
"An Economic Theory of the Evolution of Common Law" *Journal of Legal Studies* VII pp. 393-406.

(8) Higgins, R.S. and Rubin, P.H.(Jan. 1980),
"Judical Discretion" *Journal of Legal Studies* IX pp. 129-139.

(9) Hogue, A.R. (1985),
"Origins of the Common Law" Liberty Press.

(10) Landes, W.M. and Posner R.A. (Dec. 1975),
"The Independent Judiciary in an Interest Group Perspective" *Journal of Law and Economics* XVIII pp. 875-902.

(11) Mercuro, N. and Ryan, T.P. (1984),
"Law, Economics and Public Policy" JAI Press.

(12) North, D.C. (March 1984),
"Transaction Costs Institutions and Economics History" *Journal of Institutional and Theoretical Economics* pp. 7-17.

(13) Posner, R.A.,(1977),
Economics Analysis of Law 2nd Ed. Little Brown.

(14) Posner, R.A. (Winter 1979),
Some Uses and Abuses of Economics in Law *University of Chicago Law Review* 46, pp. 281-306.

(15) Rowley, C.K.,
"Past and Future: The Temporal Dimension in the Law of Property" (H. Manne Ed.) Forthcoming.

(16) Rubin, P.H. (1977),
"Why is the Common Law Efficient?" *Journal of Legal Studies* pp. 51-63.

(17) Terrebonne, P. "A. (June 1981),
Strictly Evolutionary Model of Common Law" *Journal of Legal Studies* X pp. 397-407.

(18) Williamson, (Oct. 1979) O.E.,
"Transaction-Cost Economics: The Governance of Contractural Relations" *Journal of Law and Econommics* XXII pp. 233-262.

(19) Williamson, O.E. (Spring 1985),
"Assessing Contract" *Journal of Law, Economics and Organization* pp. 177-208.

(20) Tort Working Group (Feb. 1986),
"The Cases, Extent and Policy Implications of the Current Crisis in Insurance Availability and Affordability".

Comment on C. Rowley and W. Brough: "The Efficiency of the Common Law: A New Institutional Economics Perspective"

by

Rudolf Richter

Charles Rowley and Wayne Brough offered a paper on a subject which is quite unknown on the continent, i.e. the Common Law and the American Court Rules. It is certainly unknown to me. Therefore I have to restrict my comments to some general remarks on the economic analysis in this paper.

I. The authors argue that Posner's hypothesis of the efficiency of the Common Law (efficiency in the sense of wealth maximization) appears to be quite convincing with regard to property and contract law while it does not seem to apply to tort law. The reality of U.S. tort law is sharply at odds with Posner's idealized model. They ask themselves, which impulses did contribut to greater efficiency of the law and they discuss three impulses: competition in the law, judicial incentives and constraints, and the process of litigation. Competition in the law is of no importance today; the workings of judicial incentives and constraints remain unclear up to date. Fascinating for the economic theorist is the Cooter and Kornhauser model of the process of litigation viewed as a Markov process. Their research suggests that the law will never reach the best state and remain there forever. But if bad laws are litigated more frequently and if more money is spent on preparing the case against bad law than on defending this will have a moderate influence on the persistence of good rules in legal process without judicial insight. Cooter and Kornhauser (1980) conclude: for very simple legal processes, the legal system will tend towards a stable state in which good laws prevail a greater proportion of time than bad laws. Of course, the transition probabilities from one state to another (of the Markov chain) are of importance in this model. Professor Rowley assumes, if I understand him correctly, that the transition probabilities depend on "other impulses" (then the three mentioned above). He states that these "other impulses" work in the right direction in the cases of property law and contract law, while they are absent (or work in the wrong direction?) in the case of tort law. As far as tort law is concerned the legal system may never meander into the proximity of best legal rules.

II. What are these "other impulses"? The authors mention them only briefly on the last page of their paper: they are the outflow of the *contractual relations* which develop between individuals doing business with each other on a regular basis. To elaborate this point somewhat: "contractual relations" or "relational contracts" is one of the most important concepts of the New Institutional Economics (together with property rights and transaction costs). They develop due to transaction-specific investments (e.g. specialized commercial relationships, labor and family relationships). The idea is that, by establishing long-term relations, traders economize the *sum* of production and transaction cost (Williamson (1979)). The 'order' or 'governance structure becomes part of the optimizing process. The parties shift emphasis from a detailed specification of the terms of the agreement to a more general statement of the process of adjusting the terms of agreement over time, so to speak, of the 'order' or 'constitution' of their relationship (Goldberg 1976, 428). Clearly where contractual relations obtain and contracts tend to be self enforcing, third-party enforcement plays a minor role. But it plays some role and, if applied, will terminate a contractual relationship.

So, why should the plaintiff or his attorney in a contractual suit be less aggressive than in a tort suit? Furthermore, contractual relations are not necessarily relevant to property law and irrelevant to tort law. Take the common law of trespass or nuisance. The intruder of my property in land needs not to be my neighbour or any other person with whom I might have some contractual relationship. There exists no contract with potential intruders. On the other hand medical malpractice typically occures within a contractual relationship. This is true for other services as well, e.g. for the services of architects, lawyers etc. In such cases torts can be seen within a contractual nexus, contrary to the authors' opinion. It is the factual issue wich counts. The factual issue of tort may or may not be part of a contractual relationship. I therefore doubt that it is the concept of contractual relations which explains the efficiency or inefficiency of common law.

III. If it is not the absence of contractual relationship - what else may explain the U.S. tort crisis? Is it a crisis at all and if so, is it necessarily the expression of inefficiency of the common law?

First some remarks on the West German situation: an increasing number of medical malpractice suits has been observed here during the last years as well. But, I was told, this is simply the result of the colapse of the doctors' "wall of silence". Damages are not higher now than they were years ago. As before, they fully cover actual losses of wealth, while compensations for personal suffering remain rather low (e.g. in a case of paraplegia no more than about 80.000,-- DM). So far, all seems to be quiet at the German front. I don't think this proofs the superiority of the German statue law to American common law. In addition we have judge-made law ourselves (typically: decisions of higher courts), though probably the boundaries within which judge-made West German law may develop are narrower than the boundaries (if any) within which American common law may develop.

On the other hand, the statutory framework is not necessarily very stable. The opposite may be the case as Hayek claims. Hayek therefore prefers common law to statute law, though he warns that "the development of case-law is in some respect a sort of a one-way street: when it has already moved a considerable distance in one direction, it often cannot retrace its steps when some implications of earler decisions are seen to be clearly undesirable." (F.A. Hayek 1973, 88). The Cooter and Kornhauser paper illustrates this problem. In other word, even if we believe in the efficiency of judge-made law we would not be well advised to dispense with legislation altogether. Furthermore, today in a time with low costs of organizing interest groups, statue law may be as efficient as case law. Paul Rubin (1982, 213) points this out.

The main problem of the litigation crisis in the U.S. seems to be the procedural law not the common law itself: in particular the composition of the court, and the fee schedule or regulation of the trial lawyers. One might also ask, whether state legislation should put a cap on damage awards, but I don't think that this would be a step in the right direction. The high insurance premiums which go together with high damages provide strong incentives for doctors or firms to perform better and avoid medical malpractice or product liability suits. They may stimulate private regulations of doctors and other professionals or of firms organizing themselves to self regulating groups who run their own insurance companies at lower premiums. Entrepreuneurs may find it profitable to establish regulatory associations. Private regulation may be more effecitve than public regulation. No regulation may not be a good answer to the problems at hand. Together with regulation contractual relations would enter the picture, with the private regulatory agency providing the necessary governance structure. Thus, high damages may lead to efficient institutional solutions.

References

(1) R. Cooter and L. Kornhauser (1980),
'Can Litigation Improve the Law Without the Help of Judges?', *Journal of Legal Studies*, 9, 139-164.

(2) V.P. Goldberg (1976),
Regulation and Administered Contracts, *Bell Journal of Economics*, 7, 426-448.

(3) F.A. Hayek (1973),
'Law Legislation and Liberty', A new statement of the liberal principles of justice and political economy, Vol. I, 'Rules and Order', Routledge & Kegan Paul, London.

(3) P.H. Rubin (1982),
Common Law and Statue Law, *Journal of Legal Studies*, 11, 205-224.

(4) O.E. Williamson (1979),
Transaction-Cost Economics: The Governance of Contractual Relations, *Journal of Law and Economics*, 22, 233-262.

Specific Human Capital and Collective Codetermination Rights*

by

Hans G. Monissen
and Ekkehard Wenger**

Dedicated to Professor William H. Hutt, the seminal thinker in this field

I. The Problem

The different legal forms of codetermination or job rights imply the specific assignment of decision rights or controlling influence to the workers. There are, first of all, individual codetermination rights for those in the lower ranks of the hierarchy with respect to the content and the implementation of their labor contract. But more important are collective decision rights that are exercised by elected workers' representatives. In Germany, these rights take the form of representation either in the traditional organs of the business firm or in separate worker bodies "codetermining" with management (Monissen, H.G., 1978). These collective (group related) decision rights are the essence of what is typically referred to as labor's codetermination in the decision-making process of the capitalistic business firm.

Whether this form of codetermination will be justified on efficiency grounds depends on the labor contract and on the competitive structure of the labor market specifying the opportunity costs for the workers already hired. If labor markets were perfectly competitive and complete, workers would be unaffected by the decisions of management. Consequently, collective codetermination rights would not be substantiated in this economic environment. Usually, the point is made that workers, once hired, are confronted with imperfections and therefore submitted to adverse (or opportunistic) ex post decisions of the executive authorities because workers very often start their careers undertaking firm-specific human capital investments that they have prefinanced. Under current and future decisions such investments are past or sunk costs which materialize in so-called quasi-rents, because they have been recognized and allowed for in the ex ante contracting process. Their existence causes a divergence between labor's value in use and its market exchange value, which specifies its opportunity costs. According to the advocates of codetermination, quasi-rents constitute "legitimate interests" of the employees that are to be protected by integrating workers' representatives into the firm's board of directors. Codetermination is proposed as an appropriate institutional device to prevent an unjustified devaluation or destruction of employees' investment in specific hu-

* The present article includes major parts of a previous one published by the same authors (1987).

** The authors acknowledge helpful comments by Louis De Alessi, University of Miami, Coral Gables, and University of Würzburg.

Pethig Schlieper (Eds.)
Efficiency, Institutions, and Economic Policy

man capital and to guarantee and secure a sufficiently high degree of employment stability over the investment cycle.[1] Arguments for codetermination based on asset specificity will certainly strengthen the theoretical and empirical position of the traditional propagators of mandatory solutions as enshrined in the German legislature. Free market advocates are somewhat puzzled over the political implications and count on an evolutionary process developing the appropriate institutions "in an environment devoid of special governmental constraints on structure." "Ultimately, efficiency is served by institutional arrangements that evolve freely in response to competitive forces" (Furubotn, E.G., 1987), whereby the final result of a complex process is captured in a standard neo-classical equilibrium model.

It will be our conclusion that the necessary institutional input for the appearance and survival of a codetermination solution based on collective rights cannot be provided by competitive market forces, because the environmental description is inconsistent with a dynamic capitalistic market environment, where firms wax and wane and where their financial structure reflects imperfections, risk, and uncertainty. It is needless to emphazise that asset specificity is not a new phenomenon which bears on recently observed institutional arrangements.

A solution to the problem of asset specificity, however, presupposes the answers to some important economic questions, namely, whether, how and to what degree quasi-rents can be protected by special contractual arrangements, and how the efficient creation and use of specific human capital in a competitive capitalistic environment can be ensured without externally imposed restriction. In our paper, we develop an interpretation of a solution somewhat counter to conventional wisdom. Both economic theory and market-derived institutional arrangements lend strong support to our conception as a relevant alternative. The protection of specific human capital is thereby related to the notion of an "exploitation-free" wage path that is not imposed by law but which may broadly determine the institutional evolution under extended freedom of contract.

II. The Coase Theorem as a Useful Starting Point

According to the Coase Theorem (Coase, R., 1960; Monissen, H.G., 1976, 1983), it is not evident that specific human capital has to be protected by collective codetermination rights. If the theorem applies, then the creation, efficient use, and destruction of human capital are independent of collective codetermination rights. Moreover, questions of the optimal time schedule and the number of dismissals are completely separate from the issue of which con-

1) This argument is now partly accepted even among conservative economists (e.g. Furubotn, E.G., 1987). He presents a formal model of the "participatory" firm where codetermination rights are recognized as an institutional device to protect the firm-specific investments against entrepreneurial expropriation. It is interesting to note that the by now classical article by A.A. Alchian and H. Demsetz (1972) on the theory of the firm completely ignores problems related to the existence of specific capital. This omission was accounted for by Alchian and others on several later occasions, which emphazise asset specificity as a particular problem in the allocative market process (Klein, B., Crawford, R., and Alchian, A.A., 1978; Alchian, A.A., 1984; Alchian, A.A., and Woodward, S., 1986).

tracting party has prepaid the investment outlays. From a Coasian perspective, codetermination rights have no ex post allocative consequences but only affect the distribution of remaining rents if the business venture should prove unprofitable. If workers' representatives have the right to block dismissals under a guaranteed labor contract, the efficient adjustment of the number of employees will be combined with severance payments.

The ex ante or, more exactly, pre-contractual environment, however, may involve allocative effects if there is a change in the allocation of risk among the contracting parties such as would be the case with positive transactions costs. This environment invalidates the application of the theorem.

Because it seems economically desirable to release workers from the employment risk associated with individual wage contracts vis-à-vis the stockholders, who are in a much better position to diversify risk, it appears that codetermination rights increase allocative efficiency. Economic theory, however, reminds us that the prevailing wage rate will be lower than that existing under the alternative arrangement without collective codetermination rights. This comparison by itself, however, is biased, because there is no economic basis for the popular argument that the only efficient way to allocate risk is by establishing collective rights instead of relying on individual contracts that induce the employer to prefinance specific investments or to indemnify workers by severance payments.

Only if such stipulations are insufficient to induce Pareto-efficient contracting are there special reasons for analyzing problems related to the distribution of decision-making rights. The content and extent of codetermination rights are thereby conceptually determined by a dynamic process based on both ex ante contracted restrictions and decision rights that will be operative in the implementation phase. In a Coasian world, of course, decision rights are redundant because the actions of the members in a productive coalition will be fully specified, including contingent specification in an uncertain environment. With the conclusion of the employment contract the actions of its parties are limited to the execution of the optimal labor contract.

Since in a Coasian world there is no need for post-contractual decision rights, we may conclude that a prerequisite for effectively dealing with codetermination issues is to analyze how the underlying assumptions have to be modified and what empirical conclusions can be derived when we proceed to a non-Coasian environment.

III. Decision Rights, Contractual Restrictions, and Codetermination Rights

In general, labor contracts are characterized by the fact that at the time they are drawn up not all contingencies (and thereby the optimal actions of the coalition members) can be anticipated. What constitutes the implementation in concrete instances will be determined by decisions taken according to the decision rights agreed upon initially. This later implementation necessarily carries distributive risks or even the danger of open distributional struggle, but it has been accepted as a flexible tool for coping with unanticipated changes in environmental conditions.

The traditional (non-codetermined) labor contract is characterized by the reciprocal right of short-term cancellation and by the clear-cut authority of the employer. The employer's authority would be neutralized if the signing of labor contracts did not presuppose sunk costs and therefore require a longer pay-off period. Otherwise, labor services would be contracted in infinitesimal quantities on spot markets involving no transactions costs or need for the employer's discretionary authority. Thus, Coase's "nature of the firm" (1937) would remain unsubstantiated. But because sunk costs arise at the beginning of the employment contract and usually during the initial contract period as well, it is mutually advantageous for both contracting parties to continue employment during an implicitly stated minimum length of time. Nevertheless, the parties insist on the right of short-term termination and forgo the stipulation of a minimum contract period, a provision that reflects the difficulties of anticipating conditions under which a future continuation of the labor contract would be disadvantageous for either party. Free negotiation in the absence of transactions costs implies that the employment contract will be terminated only if both parties explicitly consent. Unilateral termination will not occur as long as the other party is prepared to make sufficient concessions so as to avert realizing less advantageous alternatives outside the firm. Under these circumstances all decisions to terminate employment will be Pareto-efficient and will never occur against the will of the dismissed party. Only if renegotiation of the contract is characterized by high information and transactions costs or legally imposed restraints, do efficiency aspects relating to the initial distribution of the rights to terminate the employment relation become significant. In all instances, the contractual right to terminate employment will have distributive consequences, because a unilateral right delimits the set of distributions under which the continuation of the employment relation is to be reconsidered.

If spot markets for fully specified, infinitesimal quantities of labor services existed, the set of relevant distributional alternatives either would contain only a single element or would be empty, which means that either a contract with a determinate distribution would be drawn or one of the parties would not enter into a contractual agreement. If markets are imperfect, the majority of existing employment relations leave room for redistributive activities, because under normal conditions both contracting parties are better off than they would be with pre- or post-contractual alternatives. Workers' decision rights and other rights affecting the employment relation are no longer void of importance, because they determine the distributional position of the workers. That by itself is not a sufficient justification for granting collective codetermination rights to counterbalance the employer's authority. The unilateral right to terminate the contract suggests that the employee is always able to secure at least the distributional position offered by the next best alternative. Consequently, without sunk costs workers would have no reason to refrain from team production yielding co-operative rents. With sunk costs to be borne by the workers, however, a mutually advantageous labor contract has to offer a wage differential over the next best post-contractual employment alternative. This quasi-rent is the financial source for the amortization of their proportionate sunk cost components. Here, the right to terminate the contract is inadequate protection for the employee, and therefore the contractual arrangement should prevent the employer from exercising his bargaining power to appropriate the employee's surplus over the next best alternative by extorting wage concessions or by excessive use of discretionary power. Under unrestricted entrepreneurial power to redistribute cooperative rents at the expense of incumbent employees, the latter could not be induced to take over sunk costs. Consequently, rents from team production that might be created under a superior contractual arrangement must be forgone.

Under the traditional labor contract, workers' quasi-rents are partly protected by restricting the employer's discretionary authority with respect to content and powers of decision. More important, the contracted wage level is agreed upon for a minimum contract duration with the further implicit or explicit stipulation that the wages are fixed from below and general wage reductions are only permissible if the firm faces "extraordinarily" poor business conditions. Though the employer's right to terminate the contract remains unaffected, it proves an ineffective means of redistribution as long as wage reductions are ruled out. But precisely because wage cuts must be made conditional upon credible signs of the employer's financial difficulties, it may happen that with high transactions and information costs Pareto-optimality will be suspended: wage reductions will now be made dependent on dismissals which, in retrospect, occur against the will of the employees. The inefficient destruction or the inefficient use of specific human capital could become an inevitable consequence (Hart, O.D., 1983, pp. 3ff).

The terms of the traditional labor contract, therefore, do not exclude the possibility that under certain, not necessarily unlikely, circumstances the quasi-rents of employees will be annihilated by the inefficient allocation of specific human capital following ex post involuntary dismissals. This may occur when the quasi-rents of the employer become negative as a consequence of unfavorable market conditions or labor-saving technical progress. In both cases one might expect that wage concessions could be negotiated to stabilize employment as long as the workers are still receiving positive rents under the initial provisions of the contract. This, however, presumes the existence of reliable information about both the total amount and the distribution of rents. Without this informational proviso, the employees are reluctant to accept wage cuts because these might be too large or unjustified.

Consequently, the participation of workers' representatives in the planning and decision-making process cannot simply be justified by the popular argument that a capitalistic management does not pay heed to the quasi-rents of the workers[2]; likewise a factory shut-

2) This line of reasoning is familiar from early German socialist ideas (e.g. Bauer, O., 1931, p. 863 et passim).

down cannot be denounced as socially inefficient because the management's investment calculus "does not include" the discounted stream of quasi-rents annihilated by dismissals of employees. Price theory reveals that "capital orientation" of management is at most a necessary condition for the inefficient destruction of specific human capital. To destroy specific capital can never be a rational management response to a change in market conditions unless contractual imperfections and information costs exist that impede the adequate protection and conservation of quasi-rents and the proper assessment of the private and social values of specific human capital.

A major problem in determining the magnitude and distribution of employees' quasi-rents lies in the high costs of continuously assessing employment alternatives outside the firm. Even more important is the fact that it is in the interest of employees to understate the surplus over the next best alternative before the notice of a pending dismissal. Obviously, if em ployees were to continuously reveal their true estimates to the employer, labor's distributive share would be endangered. There is, however, a willingness to reveal them if a labor-saving investment is up for decision, but the resulting flow of information will generally be too late if the decision has already required a longer gestation period. Costly pre-commitments prevent a reconsideration of the investment decision even if the adjusted wage rate is now part of a revised calculus.

If one could expect that codetermination arrangements would contribute to the solution of these and related problems, efficiency considerations might suggest employees' representation in the decision-making process of the firm, provided that workers' representatives have exactly the information at their disposal which a capitalistic management is not allowed to have because its misuse could adversely affect labor's share in the total distribution. But the proposal only works if it is possible to bind the representatives effectively to the interests of their clientele. Moreover, capitalists have strong incentives to redirect the decision-making authority of labor's representatives by granting pecuniary or nonpecuniary allotments at the cost of the represented employees. Even disregarding this opportunistic behavior, labor's influence in the decision-making process does not generally lead to economically desirable results. By "protecting" the quasi-rents of the employees in one specific firm, the quasi-rents in related firms are completely ignored. The correct social evaluation of all costs and benefits will only come about under profit maximization using the proper scarcity values for all kinds of specific capital. If specific human capital is generally protected by blocking labor-saving investments, it is in the first instance to the disadvantage of the related investment industry if the latter is characterized by a high degree of specific human and nonhuman capital. As specificity seems likely in investment industries, the protection of quasi-rents in customer firms would prevent quasi-rents from becoming operative in these industries. The argument in favor of protecting quasi-rents by collective codetermination rights automatically raises a dilemma: should all quasi-rents be protected by granting decision rights or can an economically justified criterion be presented in order to discriminate against quasi-rents of minor social importance which do not substantiate decision rights?

Protecting all quasi-rents over and above scarcity values by decision rights will finally endanger an economic system based on decentralized decision-making. Within a network of interrelated economic activities the result would be tantamount to the paradoxical situation where everyone decides on everything. The social costs of such an arrangement are certainly higher than the annihilation of quasi-rents by labor-saving investment projects.

Let us now take up the criterion problem of how to evaluate quasi-rents according to their social importance. Even if the "narrow" economic efficiency calculus of optimal allocation is ignored and income shares are emphasized, collective codetermination rights to protect particular rents seem at variance with distributive justice. If we relied, for example, on the popular criterion of ranking the degree of direct material disadvantage, we should draw attention to the fact that the annihilation of firm-specific human capital with the ensuing income losses is very often less important than the general economic consequences of a fall in local real estate values or the collapse or decline of smaller local business firms. Perhaps when a major factory shuts down, the terms of agreement should be negotiated not with workers' representatives but with authorities of the county or community affected. Efficiency considerations, however, are not fully reflected in such arrangements because optimal contracting and allocation require negotiation of the terms of these contingencies before a major firm settles down. Consequently, it is economically desirable not to rely on mandatory codetermination rights but to enforce competition among municipal or communal authorities in order to achieve an optimal spatial distribution of firms.

The workers' right to block labor-saving investments in order to preserve specific rents is questionable for another reason: it also distorts the allocative efficiency of newly founded firms. The protective measures only restrict entrepreneurial decision-making authority within the organization. Where market competition prevails, everybody has the right to appropriate or annihilate rents or to affect relative prices by marketing new products or introducing new means of production. In general, the legal systems in the Western world have very wisely refrained from protecting the market value of positions endangered by the intruding competitor: the Western world has resisted instituting a general property rule (Buchanan, J.M., and Faith, R.L., 1981).

IV. The Protection of Quasi-Rents under Mandatory Codetermination - Selected Experiences from Germany

As shown in the previous section, codetermination arrangements cannot improve the protection of workers' quasi-rents unless they reduce transactions costs incurred in renegotiations of wages or of other conditions of employment. Consequently, lower costs of information exchange might be an argument in favor of codetermination. Indeed, advocates of codetermination, by granting decision rights to the workers, expect a better flow of information which would prevent the inefficient use of human capital and the endangerment of rents due to informational barriers (Furubotn, E.G., and Wiggins, S.N., 1984; Schneider, H., 1983). Early consultation with workers' representatives, they argue, allows careful long-term planning of employment adjustments by disclosing efficient employment alternatives both within and outside the enterprise. Thus, one might expect that the workers' ex post employment alternatives could be more effectively allowed for under codetermination schemes than under the traditional labor contract.

The practice of codetermination in Germany offers no grounds for such expectations. Renegotiations of wages to prevent the inefficient destruction of quasi-rents in declining industries or firms under competitive pressure do not seem to be favored by the existing codetermination arrangements; relevant episodes pertain to large companies on the brink of bankruptcy, where wage reductions amount to cosmetic concessions signalling only mutual concern (Wenger, E., 1984, pp. 211-212). This evidence, however, may be biased since employees had reason to expect that the government would intervene to subsidize the further payment of wages or finance a generous severance arrangement. Indeed, codetermination in large business firms seems to be an important device to mobilize the voting power of workers in order to press for government aid.

But even in cases where government aid is not anticipated, there is no indication that codetermination leads to more informed choices among ex post employment alternatives. Where competitive pressure calls for a major reorganization, codetermination mainly materializes in negotiations over severance payments.[3] Although the laws governing these negotiations reflect the hope that due consideration will be given to the consequences that arise for employees from the closing of plants or major cuts in the workforce (Reuter, D., 1980; Gessner, V., and Plett, K., 1982, p. 127), the results achieved in practice are rather disappointing. As a consequence of plant-level codetermination, schematic severance obligation patterns have emerged which disregard individual cases. Indemnification to be paid is determined by formulae in which the most important variables are the worker's current wage, length of service and age (Vogt, A., 1981, pp. 150-167). This schematic treatment induces even members of the legal profession to complain that no consideration is given to differences in income between the current and next best employment (Beuthien, V., 1982, pp. 184-185; Grub, V., 1983, pp. 873-875). There are two possible explanations for the observed phenomenon. On the one hand, gathering information which is vital for Pareto-efficient dismissal and severance strategies may be so costly technically and administratively that, even with codetermination rights, it is not worth the effort. On the other hand, codetermination rights are exercised by elected representatives who have little interest in following Pareto-efficient strategies (Downs, A., 1957).

3) Cf. §§ 111-113 of the Plant Constitution Act (Betriebsverfassungsgesetz). Recently, however, the courts have tended to acknowledge the right of the works' council to interfere with entrepreneurial decisions through injunction. The hazardous consequences of such extended codetermination rights are not yet fully recognized by economists, as they have so far only been discussed within the law profession (Eich, R.A., 1983).

But even if individual cases are disregarded, advocates of codetermination may argue that codetermined severance payments improve at least the average allocation of specific human capital because they create pressure on employers to incorporate quasi-rents of incumbent employees into the decision calculus. It will be shown that severance payments in Germany result in just the opposite of a correct consideration of workers' quasi-rents. Let us look at firms in shrinking industries, where decisions are not related to conditions of further profitable employment but to the optimal timing of dismissals. In such cases contractual impediments to the lowering of wages will result in dismissals prior to the economically efficient point in time. An employer with unrestricted power to hire and fire will initiate employment adjustments if steadily decreasing revenues reduce his own quasi-rents to zero.

Figure 1

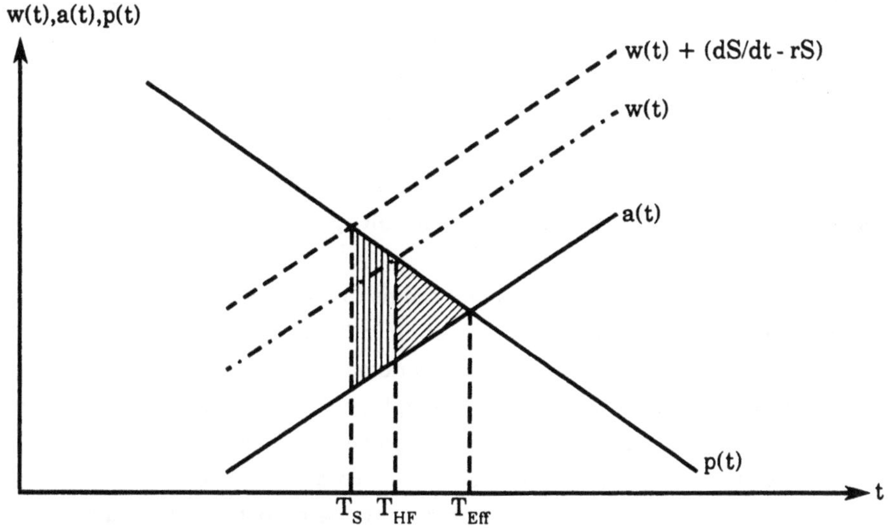

T_{Eff} : Efficient time of dismissal

T_{HF} : Dismissal under Hire- and Fire-Policy (without renegotiation)

T_S : Dismissal with severance payment obligation

In figure 1, the relevant point in time is T_{HF}, where the marginal value product p(t) falls below the current wage rate w(t). Given costless renegotiation of wages, T_{Eff} would be the efficient point in time for a dismissal; here the marginal value product falls below the worker's alternative wage a(t). Thus, informational and institutional impediments cause inefficient early dismissals, because temporarily postponed dismissals would still create cooperation rents for all the parties involved. In figure 1, the resulting efficiency loss corresponds to the shaded triangle.

Should the employer be faced with a severance pay obligation S, dismissals may be delayed or expedited, depending on whether the rate of interest r exceeds the growth rate of the potential severance payment. In a continuous representation the difference between the first derivative dS/dt and rS has to be added to the current wage in order to get the time of dismissal T_S, which is individually optimal to the employer.[4] If this difference is positive, an employer facing a severance pay obligation will dismiss earlier than an employer with unrestricted power to hire and fire: $T_S < T_{HF}$. The consequence is an additional efficiency loss corresponding to the shaded trapezoid in figure 1.

In Germany such an additional efficiency loss is very likely[5]. As severance payments are frequently calculated on the basis of half a month's pay for each year's service[6] and the monthly pay itself is raised by several percent each year as a result of industry-wide collective bargaining, the time of dismissal is very likely to be advanced.

Consequently, if prohibitive transactions costs exclude ex post agreements on wage reductions, the usual severance pay scheme is Pareto-inferior to a dismissal policy based on the employer's unrestricted power to hire and fire. Improved efficiency can only be achieved for workers close to retirement, so that dismissal can be postponed until the age limit is reached and a severance payment becomes unnecessary. The parties are, of course, quite at liberty to negotiate an ex post agreement to reduce wages. But why should severance pay obligations remove or even lower the barriers to such an agreement?

Neither economic theory nor empirical evidence seems to indicate, therefore, that the severance pay obligations emerging from codetermination in Germany are a suitable instrument for preserving quasi-rents. A Pareto-efficient postponement of dismissals would be possible if severance payments were to be lowered over the employment time. Obviously, this would be consistent with a situation in which newly hired employees finance firm-specific human capital. In practice, exactly the opposite can be observed. This increase of severance payments with age can be explained in large part by the fact that due to institutional barriers against

4) This follows from the first-order condition for a maximum of the employer's quasi-rent. Differentiation of the quasi-rent

$$\int_0^{T_s} [p(t) - w(t)] e^{-rt} dt - S(T_s) e^{-rT_s}$$ with respect to T_s yields

$$p(T_s) - w(T_s) - \left[\frac{dS}{dT_s} - rS\right] = 0.$$

5) Changes in p (t) and S (t) are usually discrete; this makes the analysis somewhat more complicated, but does not alter the main thrust of our argument.

6) This is a common practice accepted by German Courts (Vogt, A., 1981, p. 117). In many European States similar rules are effective (Gessner, V., and Plett, K., 1982, p. 125). Severance payments in case of major reorganizations or plant shutdowns are frequently governed by more complicated formulae which incorporate age in addition to seniority; but this tends to accelerate the growth of S and so our argument is reinforced. For further details see Wenger, E. (1986a, section 4.2.2.).

lowering wages, the wage differential of aging workers over their next best employment alternative tends to rise as their performance falls, and it is this group of workers that experience particularly high wage losses through dismissals. As long as it is impossible to divert the attention of labor representatives and the public from these visible losses to a comparison of workers' life-cycle income streams, severance obligations will distort dismissal decisions in such a way that quasi-rents are annihilated rather than preserved. In the next section we shall see that this distortion is a systematic consequence of interest representation by organized labor.

V. Quasi-Rents and Protective Rights - The Question of Cause and Effect

Up to now we have dealt with the question of whether codetermination might be an efficient protective device for quasi-rents of employees. This kind of reasoning suggests that the codetermination rights of employees are a consequence of the necessity to protect quasi-rents associated with firm-specific investments of workers. The crucial problem of modern labor markets, however, seems to be just the reverse: the rights of employees are not so much a consequence, but a cause of firm-specific investments which materialize in quasi-rents of workers. This not only applies to codetermination rights but also includes a much broader range of "protective" devices, especially the workers' rights to unionize and strike. As there is no reason to believe that any of these rights will only be exercised to maintain the status quo, it is indeed very likely that any potential increase in the market value of a firm dependent on decisions subject to workers' rights will be, in part at least, appropriated by the workers. The ultimate consequence will be that any change in business policy not initially anticipated has to be paid for by sufficiently large concessions to the workers.

Consequently, the more rights employees have, the higher are their quasi-rents. A strong ex-post-bargaining position enables them to capture above-average profits and forces employers to insist upon workers bearing a substantial share of the sunk costs of specialized investments. This will be reflected in a reduction of initial wages, which will, of course, grow over time as long as market conditions prove favorable. Otherwise, workers try to avoid income losses by defending the status quo. Any wage level once attained might be protected unless the firm faces the danger of going bankrupt, and, consequently, the probability of wage cuts for incumbent workers can be reduced in comparison to a system without protective rights. But human capital risk calculated over the potential employment cycle of a representative worker will certainly increase. The worker who happens to decide for a company experiencing unanticipated favorable results will enjoy steadily increasing wage levels. In contrast, a worker starting his employment career with a firm which goes bankrupt after some time will lose a substantial part of the expected value of his life-time income. Thus, the eventual lowering of the "risk" of wage reductions in consequence of protective rights has to be traded off against a sizable increase in the risk of human capital as related to a worker's life-cycle. The intensified exposure to firm-specific (unsystematic) risk brought about by protective rights is certainly not in the interest of a representative worker entering the labor market at the beginning of his worklife.

The pressure to take unsystematic risks will be increased by the fact that the continual forcing of concessions from company owners creates contract-specific risks which reduce the incentive for stockholders to finance firm-specific investments. Because their quasi-rents are permanently endangered by exploitation, the only protective device is to charge labor with the burden of financing specific investments in order to strengthen their bargaining position. The workers' loss risk has to be sufficiently large to prevent blackmailing blockades intended to extract rents from the stockholders.

To the individual employee, the necessity of earning quasi-rents in order to recover his share in sunk costs creates a need for protection by unions and/or codetermination bodies. Unions, for evident reasons, systematically engage in intensifying protective needs by enlarging the worker's share of investment and extending its pay-off period. Interest symbiosis between labor's representatives and "job-owners" explains why bargaining on behalf of workers with high seniority is of utmost importance on the strategic agenda of unions and codetermination bodies, whether the workers' interests are organized on the plant, company, or industry level.

Empirical studies in the United States, where collective bargaining usually takes place at the plant or firm level, show significant correlations between unionization and seniority rights and fringe benefits (Blau, F.D., and Kahn, L.M., 1983; Freeman, R.B. 1981); fringe benefits typically depend on years of seniority or even on the worker's remaining with the firm until retirement. Recently, there has been a growing tendency toward two-tier wage contracts providing for large wage differentials between newly hired and senior workers with the same jobs.[7] Collective bargaining in Germany, usually organized on an industry level, likewise redistributes rents in favor of older workers. Protection against the consequences of technological change and even explicitly guaranteed wages for less productive workers with high seniority are afforded by numerous union contracts.[8]

Quasi-rents of employees with high seniority are consequently very large precisely because workers organize themselves collectively (cf. Black, D.A., and Parker, D.F., 1985). In general, therefore, voluntary exit is associated with substantial financial losses. Thus, the individual is heavily exposed to and needs protection against the exercise of power. As a consequence, many undesired effects are to be expected. Reduced exit options increase the susceptibility of the organization to corruption. Workers' representatives will try to profit from their rights to influence the distribution of quasi-rents among workers, management, and stockholders. The frequency of legal action increases, and stockholders are ready to invest

7) This is especially true for the airlines. Major carriers such as American Airlines have wage differentials of 20 - 50 per cent.

8) For a comprehensive survey of union contracts cf. Weis, P., 1983.

large amounts in the relevant decision makers.[9]

Moreover, the monitoring of management becomes more and more complicated. The higher the workers' quasi-rents, the stronger the argument in favor of relieving managers of their function as stockholders' agents and converting them into mediators between capital and labor or even advocates of the commonweal.[10] How far managers are meeting such a demand can hardly be monitored because such monitoring presupposes not only the availability of financial information but also knowledge of many far less accessible efficiency indicators. Incumbent managers, therefore, can expect reduced monitoring if they are promoted to the status of advocates of the commonweal. This provides a reasonable explanation as to why numerous directors of large German business firms are very open-minded with respect to the abandonment of capitalistic enterprise (Reuter, E., 1981).

Additional problems result from a deterioration in risk allocation. Stockholders, who in general are in a superior position to diversify the risks of specialized investments, are no longer willing to take these risks, if the employees cannot be prevented from appropriating quasi-rents by exercising codetermination rights or threatening with a strike. Consequently, employees have to share such risks; their inability to build up a diversified portfolio of risky quasi-rents from different jobs, however, will result in pressure on management to follow risk-avoiding business strategies. With protective rights of incumbent workers, the net present value of an individual's lifetime income is no longer insured by the capital and labor markets; hence "protected" workers have a vital interest in reducing the risks taken by their employer firm.

To sum up, the consequences of protective rights are among others, risk-avoiding business policies, bureaucratic investment decisions and implementations, payment depending on seniority, proportionate increases in quasi-rents, extreme immobility of labor and reduced adaptability to changing market conditions.

VI. The Question of Institutional Change

The considerations of the preceding section suggest that the workers' position would be improved not by conceiving workable codetermination arrangements or granting other protec-

9) The relevant practices are mostly illegal and therefore kept secret, but sometimes emerge in the courts. Recently, a court invalidated an election of the members of a workers' council, because a large automobile manufacturer had financed and otherwise supported the election campaign of "friendly" candidates (cf. Wenger, E., 1986b). A good example of the high costs involved in the decision process is the requirement of mandatory arbitration in codetermination affairs. Here, judges of labor courts mutually appoint themselves as chairmen of arbitration commissions. The resulting discretionary power forces employers to tolerate high arbitration fees. For a day's work as chairman of an arbitration commission a judge frequently receives more than his monthly earnings as a civil servant (Schlochauer, U., 1983).

10) The related paternalistic attitude on the basis of a collectivist-functional interpretation of the workings of society is codified in the so-called *Davoser Manifest* of leading European managers (European Management Forum, 1973).

tive rights, but by just the opposite. Instead of implementing institutional devices which aggravate imperfections in the labor market, instead of protecting quasi-rents of employees, one should investigate how these imperfections might be reduced.

As a first step it is useful to carry the reduction to the limit where the worker's quasi-rents are always zero. This implies that he can always change his job without affecting the net present value of his lifetime income because all specialized investments are financed by the employer. This can be achieved by choosing a wage path which can be maintained in alternative uses because it does not render the next employer's refraining investment unprofitable. Such a wage path may be called exploitation-free in the sense that an opportunistic employer cannot exploit his workers by expropriation of quasi-rents, because the worker is fully protected by his exit option.

We start with the most simple model, which is based on the assumption that the value of the worker's product is certain and does not depend on his age, but increases linearly during a learning phase each time the worker enters a new firm. The length of the learning phase is L, the productive life of the worker begins at zero and ends with retirement in R. The instantaneous product of a fully trained worker is normalized to unity. Under these assumptions, the path of the worker's value product over time is represented by the dashed line p(t) in figure 2, if the worker remains with the first employer during his worklife.

Figure 2

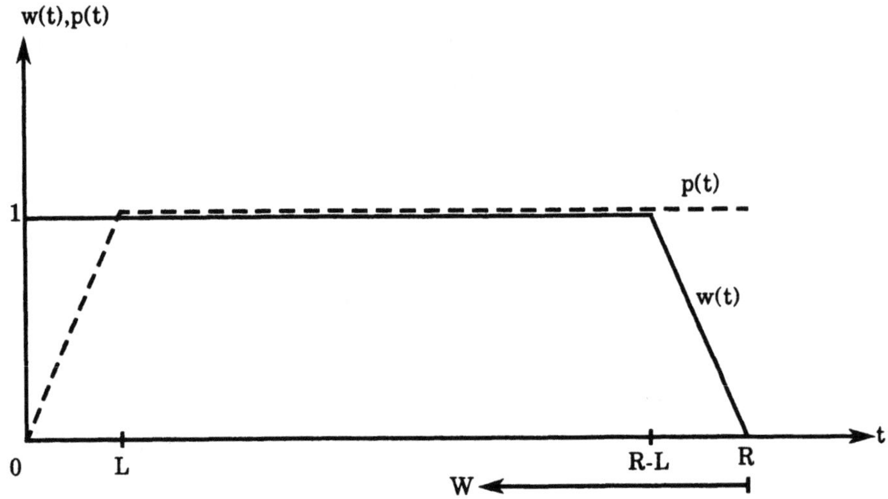

In order to compute the exploitation-free wage path we have to start from its defining property, namely that the wage path can be maintained in a new job. This presupposes that, given the wage path, a retraining investment of a new employer will not be unprofitable. With ex ante perfect labor markets, such a retraining investment will just break even. Hence an employer who hires a worker with a remaining worklife W has to pay the net present value of the product the worker can produce between R-W and retirement in R. For the sake of simplicity, we assume a zero interest rate. Thus, given the length of the learning phase and the path of the worker's value product, the net present value N(W) can be computed as follows:

(1) $$N(W) = \int_{R-W}^{R} \frac{t-(R-W)}{L}\,dt = \frac{W^2}{2L} \qquad \text{if } W \le L$$

(2) $$N(W) = \int_{R-W}^{R-W+L} \frac{t-(R-W)}{L}\,dt + \int_{R-W+L}^{R} dt = \frac{L}{2} + (W-L) \quad \text{if } W \ge L$$

The distribution of wages over time follows from the fact that the instantaneous wage rate w(t) must compensate for the reduction of N (W) in each phase of the worklife. Hence we have

(3) $$w(t) = w(R-W) = -\frac{d}{dt}N(W) = \frac{d}{dW}N(W)$$

The exploitation-free wage path that results from Eq. (1), (2), and (3), is represented by the solid line in figure 2 and is governed by the following equations:

(4) $$w(t) = w(R-W) = \frac{W}{L} \quad \text{if } W \le L$$

(5) $$w(t) = w(R-W) = 1 \quad \text{if } W \ge L$$

By definition, this wage path does not depend on how often the worker is induced to leave his job by employer opportunism, because the employer finances specific investments alone; in this simple model, of course, quits will not happen, because employers refrain from opportunistic behavior in order to avoid a loss of their specialized investments in workers.

Our simple model suggests wage reductions for older workers even if there is no decline in productivity. This conclusion is reinforced if we replace the assumption of a certain and age-independent value product by the most simple stochastic modification. This modification consists in a product price governed by a discrete stochastic process with Markoff and Martingale properties. For the sake of simplicity we assume further that we have a risk-neutral capital market and the learning phase is as long as the steps of the discrete process.[11] If new jobs start with a product price of 1, which will increase or decrease by 20 % in the next period with an equal probability of 0.5, the exploitation-free wage path is deterministic and declines from the beginning:

period	Exploitation free wage
1	1.2759025
2	1.23034
3	1.18575
4	1.1225
5	1.055
6	1
7	1
8	0.5

That wages exceed one until period 5 in the presented eight period example[12], is a consequence of mutually advantageous separations if prices have fallen more than is justified to continue the employment relation; thus, the excess over one is a product of worker mobility.

The wages of older workers must decline even more if we take into account their lower productivity. The decline in productivity starts around the age of forty, and this is true even for professions where most people believe in the importance of the productivity-enhancing effects of experience. Average job performance ratings of managers and engineers have their highs in the early or late thirties, as one can see from figure 3 (Source: Medoff, J.L., and Abraham, K.C., 1980, p. 731).

Of course, there exist several effects which prevent the full realization of an exploitation-free wage path; rising wages at the beginning of the worklife or employment relations can be explained by quality uncertainty of workers or incentive effects or the accumulation of non-specific human capital; but what cannot be explained by such effects is the course of the representative empirical wage path during the second half of the worklife. Even if it is inevitable that workers share some costs of specialized investment, this does not explain why wages of

11) As in the deterministic case, we assume that during the learning phase a worker is on average half as productive as a fully trained worker.

12) As business cycles are flattened out in our model, each step of our stochastic process may be interpreted as a condensed representation for the average of one business cycle. 8 business cycles may be taken as an approximation for the length of a worklife. For further computational details see the Appendix of Wenger, E., 1986a.

older workers in big business firms usually are so high that firms would prefer to get rid of workers if these workers were not protected by union contracts, mandatory codetermination rights or other legal devices or by social customs originating from or supported by the institutional restraints of unionized settings[13] (cf. Edwards, R., 1981, pp. 145, 165, 184-187, 203; Elbaum, B., 1983).

Figure 3

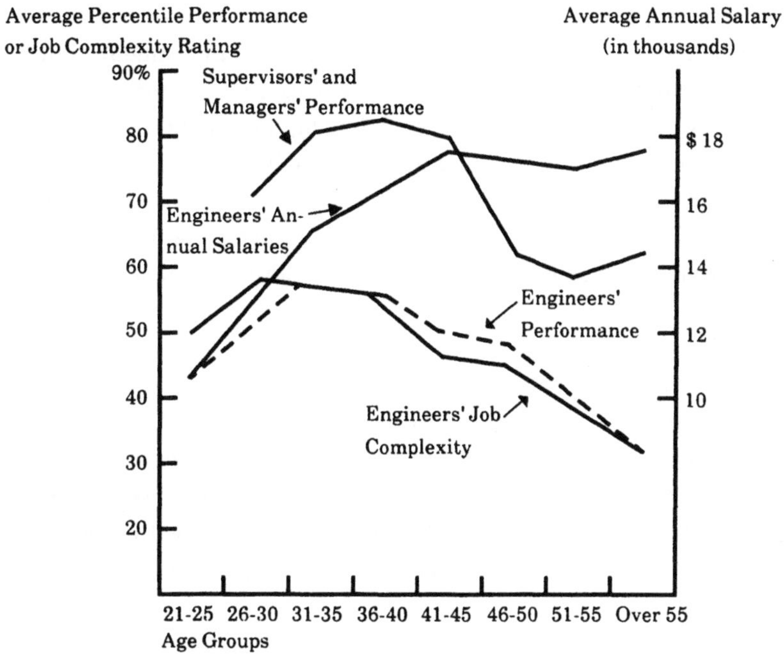

Hence organized labor's collective action lies at the heart of our problem and is the main obstacle against a wage policy trying to approach an exploitation-free wage path. If such a wage path could be realized, at least approximately, the worker's quasi-rents would be negligible, and the sunk costs of labor-financed investment in human capital would be insignificant. Consequently, the risk of labor income related to the worker's life-cycle would be considerably reduced and the need for protection would be met by the worker's option to leave his job. Hence employees' quasi-rents could be ignored in management decision-making and the widespread but dubious claim to include workers' interests in corporate goals would lose both purpose and justification.

13) Considerable spillover from wage and employment policies of unionized firms into the nonunionized sector is stated by Foulkes, F., 1980, p. 145: "Some companies claimed they give very little weight to seniority in their promotion decisions, saying this is one of the advantages of being nonunion. Many other companies will give considerable weight to seniority, thereby ignoring this alleged advantage of being nonunion. The practices of the latter group may help them increase the probability of their remaining nonunion, for they will have no favoritism complaints". For an extensive discussion of the role of social customs in wage and employment policies, see Akerlof, G.A., 1980.

Obviously, this solution implies that the risks of specific investments are shifted to stockholders in a much larger part than today. As they are in a much better position to diversify risks, this will improve allocative efficiency; the willingness of stockholders, however, to accept the higher burden of prefinancing specialized investments, presupposes that workers can be prevented from appropriating the return on such investments.

As to firm-specific investments, it seems to be sufficient to exclude the workers' right to collective action via unionization, strikes or codetermination schemes by contractual arrangements. If stockholders bear the whole risk of specialized investment, they are able to commit themselves credibly to a strategy of not accepting the demands of individual employees for higher wages unless another employer offers higher remuneration. As specialized workers in general do not gain from job-hopping and as isolated shifts are not a major problem for a firm, the quasi-rents of stockholders are relatively well protected against the expropriation efforts of individual employees. Hence, the guideline for the firm's wage policy in a world without collective action should be to pay just enough to dissuade profitable workers from using their exit option.

Industry-specific investments in human capital need not be financed by stockholders if workers are to be protected only by the exit option; such investments do not lose their value if the worker chooses another job within the same industry. Industry-specific investment, however, though not linked to an individual firm, is exposed to nonsystematic risk. Hence it may also be desirable to shift the financing and risk on to stockholders. Their willingness to take such risks depends on measures to prevent uncompensated job changes within the same industry.

If both firm- and industry-specific human capital is financed by the employer, an individual worker essentially bears the risk of a devaluation of his general earning abilities but is relatively well protected against the risks of the division of labor. The result is a considerably reduced risk in terms of lifetime income. Running counter to conventional thinking, this reduction is brought about by transforming the "risk" of declining labor income into a sure prospect.

In comparison with a codetermination arrangement, the labor market reform outlined above seems to be so superior that inevitably one wonders which deficiencies have been overlooked. We offer a preliminary conjecture rather than an answer: the possible deficiencies do not outweigh the advantages. If that is true, why doesn't the labor market produce the suggested solution by itself? The strong tendency of workers to organize indicates that the ideal presented is incompatible with the interests of the parties involved. That, however, is true only from the viewpoint of an already employed "job-owner". An economic perspective is different. Though it has to be conceded that a "job-owner" will not renounce his right to unionize and strike if his employer is already exposed to that right, the economist's question is whether a worker who is not yet employed will be willing to sell his rights to organize and strike in exchange for a higher initial wage.

A similar problem is to prevent workers from going over to competing firms after the employer has financed industry-specific human capital. After the employer's investment the worker will not renounce his right to leave or to enforce a higher wage by threatening to leave; before the investment, however, he may be willing to accept a restraint-of-competition clause.

If one again takes up the question of why labor markets do not produce the suggested reform by themselves, two reasons are obvious. Both are related to restrictions of the freedom of contract imposed by law. Workers cannot sell their right to organize and strike at the time they are hired.[14] A promise not to organize and strike is void, because it cannot be enforced in court. The same holds with respect to clauses restraining competition. In many cases, they are invalidated by judicial decision. If they are to be acknowledged, the employer usually has to pay compensation, which in Germany amounts to one half of the last salary for the time to which the clause applies.[15] Consequently, an employer willing to invest in industry-specific human capital cannot rely on restraint of competition-clauses. In theory, he could instead secure a claim to be refunded by the employee if the latter leaves the firm too early after employer-financed training; in practice, the amounts to be refunded and the periods of commitment acknowledged by German courts are so small that a rational employer is restricted to financing minor investments in workers unless the investment is firm-specific or his employees are locked in by high quasi-rents.

Obviously, the workability of the suggested reorganization of the labor market can be easily tested by observing the consequences of suspending imposed institutional and legal restrictions. Whether contractual structures that have evolved under these restrictions will survive in a world of free labor contracts is doubtful because the current status of unionization and codetermination is mainly the result of far-reaching government intervention.

Whether an institutional reform following the intentions outlined above can be brought

14) In Germany, the right to organize and strike follows directly from the Constitution (Art. 9 Abs. 3 Grundgesetz) and cannot be disposed of by individual contracts. In the United States, it is an unfair labor practice under Section 8 (a)3 of the National Labor Relations Act to discourage membership in any labor organization by discrimination in regard to hire or any condition of employment. Many countries have enacted similar restrictions on freedom of contract. It is interesting to note that the expansion of organized labor in the United States is significantly related to the prohibition of the "yellow dog contract", that is, a contract not to organize. The first major wave of unionization took place during the last decade of the nineteenth century when newly enacted State laws prohibited the yellow dog contract. At the end of the decade, these laws were held unconstitutional. The growth in union membership was considerably reduced or even reversed after 1904, when employers took the offensive against unions. During World War I, a National War Labor Board had to settle labor-management differences and recommended that the rights to organize should not be denied or abridged by employers. Union membership grew rapidly through 1920 and then fell back sharply until 1933. The enactment of the National Industrial Recovery Act in June 1933 was the beginning of the most extensive organization drive in the history of the American Labor Movement. According to the law, no one seeking employment was to be compelled to refrain from joining a labor union. In the following twelve years, union membership rose from 2.9 to 14.8 million (Taft. P., 1964, pp. 162, 164, 212-229, 317, 319, 414, 417-419; Reynolds, L.G. 1978, p. 339).

15) The maximum time is two years and many other restrictions must be observed as laid down in §§ 74-82a of the commercial law code (Handelsgesetzbuch).

about in Germany in the decades to come seems to be very doubtful, considering the current status of the political system. One has to bear in mind, however, that the whole complex of codetermination and union wage policy amounts to a considerable redistribution in favor of the older generation, which aggravates the intergenerational problems inherent in our social security system. Thus, the conservation of union privileges, codetermination and many other institutional devices of modern labor law do not promote social peace, as many people still believe, but increases the risks of its breakdown when coming generations try to get rid of the burden placed on them by the older generation.

References

(1) Akerlof, G.A. (1980),
A Theory of Social Custom, of Which Unemployment May be One Consequence, in: Quarterly Journal of Economics, Vol. 94 (1980), pp. 749-775.

(2) Alchian, A.A. (1984),
Specificity, Specialisation, and Coalitions, in: Zeitschrift für die gesamte Staatswissenschaft, Vol. 140 (1984), pp. 34-39.

(3) Alchian, A.A. and Demsetz, H. (1972),
Production, Information Costs, and Economic Organization, in: American Economic Review, Vol. 62 (1972), pp. 777 - 795.

(4) Alchian A.A. and Woodward, S. (1986),
Reflections on the Theory of the Firm, Paper presented at the Wallerfangen Conference, Wallerfangen, West Germany, June 1986.

(5) Bauer, O. (1931),
Kapitalismus und Sozialismus nach dem Weltkrieg, Band 1: Rationalisierung - Fehlrationalisierung, Berlin 1931.

(6) Beuthien, V. (1982),
Der Sozialauftrag des Sozialplans - Arbeitsplatzabfindung und arbeitsvertragliche Risikoverteilung, in: Zeitschrift für Arbeitsrecht, Vol. 13 (1982), pp. 181-205.

(7) Black. D.A. and Parker, D.F. (1985),
The Division of Union Rents, in: Journal of Labor Research, Vol. 6 (1985), pp. 281-288.

(8) Blau, F.D. and Kahn, L.M. (1983),
Unionism, Seniority, and Turnover, in: Industrial Relations, Vol. 22 (1983), pp. 362-373.

(9) Buchanan, J.M. and Faith, R.L. (1981),
Entrepreneurship and the Internalization of Externalities, in: Journal of Law and Economics, Vol. 24 (1981), pp. 95-111.

(10) Coase, R. (1937),
The Nature of the Firm, in: Economica, Vol. 4 (1937), pp. 386-405.

(11) Coase R. (1960),
The Problem of Social Cost, in: Journal of Law and Economics, Vol. 3 (1960), pp. 1-44.

(12) Downs, A. (1957),
An Economic Theory of Democracy, New York 1957.

(13) Edwards, R. (1981),
Herrschaft im modernen Produktionsprozeß, Frankfurt/New York 1981.

(14) Eich, R.A. (1983),
Einstweilige Verfügung auf Unterlassung der Betriebsänderung in: Der Betrieb, Vol. 36 (1983), pp. 657-662.

(15) Elbaum, B. (1983),
The Internalization of Labor Markets: Causes and Consequences, in: American Economic Review, Vol. 73 (1983), pp. 260-264.

(16) European Management Forum (Ed.) (1973),
Third European Management Symposium, Summary of the Plenary Sessions, A final Report, Davos 1973.

(17) Foulkes, F. (1980),
Personnel Policies in Large Nonunion Companies, Englewood Cliffs 1980.

(18) Freeman, R.B. (1981),
The Effect of Unionism on Fringe Benefits, in: Industrial and Labor Relations Review, Vol. 34 (1981), pp. 489-509.

(19) Furubotn, E.G. (1987),
A General Model of Codetermination, in: Backhaus, J. and Nutzinger, H.G. (Eds.), Codetermination, Berlin, Heidelberg, New York 1987.

(20) Furubotn, E.G. and Wiggins, S.N. (1984),
Plant Closing, Worker Reallocation Costs and Efficiency Gains to Labor Representation on Boards of Directors, in: Zeitschrift für die gesamte Staatswissenschaft, Vol. 140 (1984), pp. 176-192.

(21) Gessner, V. and Plett, K. (1982),
Der Sozialplan im Konkursunternehmen: Die Praxis eines autonomen Regelungsmodells im Schnittpunkt von Arbeits- und Konkursrecht, Köln 1982.

(22) Grub, V. (1983),
Sozialplanwillkür? Thesen aus der Sicht des Praktikers, in: Zeitschrift für Insolvenzpraxis, Vol. 4 (1983), pp. 873-875.

(23) Hart, O.D. (1983),
Optimal Labour Contracts under Asymmetric Information: An Introduction, in: Review of Economic Studies, Vol. 50 (1983), pp. 3-35.

(24) Klein, B., Crawford, R. and Alchian, A.A. (1978),
Vertical Integration, Appropriable Rents, and the Competitive Contracting Process, in: Journal of Law and Economics, Vol. 21 (1978), pp. 297-326.

(25) Medoff, J.L. and Abraham, K.G. (1980),
Experience, Performance and Earnings, in: Quarterly Journal of Economics, Vol. 95 (1980), pp. 703-736.

(26) Monissen, H.G. (1976),
Haftungsregeln und Allokation: Einige einfache analytische Zusammenhänge, in: Jahrbuch für Sozialwissenschaft, Vol. 27 (1976), pp. 391-412.

(27) Monissen, H.G. (1978),
The current status of labor participation in the management of business firms in Germany, in: Pejovich, S. (Ed.), The Codetermination Movement in the West, Lexington 1978, pp. 57-84.

(28) Monissen H.G. (1983),
Externalitäten und Wirtschaftspolitik: Anmerkungen zu einigen Neuinterpretationen, in: Woll, A. (Ed.), Aktuelle Wege der Wirtschaftspolitik (Schriften des Vereins für Socialpolitik, Neue Folge, Band 130) Berlin 1983, pp. 51-78.

(29) Monissen, H.G. and Wenger, E. (1987),
Organizational Problems with Specific Human Capital: Reflections on Furubotn's General Model of Codetermination, in: Backhaus, J. and Nutzinger, H.G. (Eds.), Codetermination, Berlin, Heidelberg, New York 1987.

(30) Reuter, D. (1980),
Gemeinsame Anmerkung zu den Entscheidungen des Bundesarbeitsgerichts vom 22.5.1979, 1 AZR 848/76 und 1 ABR 17/77, in: Sammlung arbeitsrechtlicher Entscheidungen, Heft 3, 1980 pp. 96-98.

(31) Reuter, E. (1981),
Wir verschenken kostbarste Zeit, in: Manager-Magazin, Vol. 11 (1981), pp. 88-91.

(32) Reynolds, L.G. (1978),
Labor Economics and Labor Relations, Englewood Cliffs 1978.

(33) Schlochauer, U. (1983),
Die betriebliche Einigungsstelle: Ein zunehmendes Ärgernis, in: Rüthers, E. und Hacker, W. (Eds.), Das Betriebsverfassungsgesetz auf dem Prüfstand, Stuttgart 1983, pp. 99-103.

(34) Schneider, H. (1983),
Mitbestimmung, unvollständige Information und Leistungsanreize: Überlegungen zu einer funktionsfähigen Unternehmensverfassung, in: Schweizerische Zeitschrift für Volkswirtschaft und Statistik, Vol. 119 (1983), pp. 337-354.

(35) Taft, P. (1964),
Organized Labor in American History, New York 1964.

(36) Vogt, A. (1981),
Sozialpläne in der betrieblichen Praxis, 2nd. ed., Köln 1981.

(37) Weis, P. (1983),
Zur arbeitsmarktpolitischen Problematik von Kündigungs- und Besitzstandsregelungen für ältere Arbeitnehmer, in: Zeitschrift für Wirtschafts- und Sozialwissenschaften, Vol. 103 (1983), pp. 255-281.

(38) Wenger, E. (1984),
Die Verteilung von Entscheidungskompetenzen im Rahmen von Arbeitsverträgen, in: Neumann, M. (Ed.), Ansprüche, Eigentums- und Verfügungsrechte (Schriften des Vereins für Socialpolitik, Neue Folge, Band 140), Berlin 1984, S. 199-217.

(39) Wenger, E. (1986a),
Freiwillig vereinbarte und erzwungene Organisationsregeln - Eine Analyse ihrer Wirkungen, dargestellt am Beispiel von Beschäftigungsverhältnissen, Habilitationsschrift, München 1986.

(40) Wenger, E. (1986b),
Unternehmensverfassung und Arbeitsmarkt: Die Berücksichtigung von Arbeitnehmerinteressen im Entscheidungsprozeß der Unternehmung, in: Leipold, H. und Schüller, A. (Eds.), Zur Interdependenz von Unternehmens- und Wirtschaftsordnung, Stuttgart 1986, pp. 153-185.

Comment on H. G. Monissen and E. Wenger: "Specific Human Capital and Collective Codetermination Rights"

by

Louis De Alessi

If employees undertake firm-specific investments, whether in their own human capital or in other assets, then they have a stake in the performance of the firm. This possiblity has been interpreted by some observers, including a number of economists, politicians, and labor leaders, as providing an explanation as well as a theoretical justification for the German system of codetermination.

Professors Monissen and Wenger offer a detailed criticism of this conclusion. Their general argument is well taken, and their analysis seems sound. Accordingly, the present comment takes the form of an addendum, noting some points that Monissen and Wenger might have discussed in more detail and raising some additional considerations in support of their position.

The reasons why codetermination evolved presumably are complex. For present purposes, it is useful to focus upon the alternative hypotheses that it evolved to (1) protect firm-specific investments by employees, or (2) redistribute wealth from shareholders to some employees through unanticipated changes in the employment contract. Which hypothesis dominates is an empirical question that, unfortunately, awaits rigorous testing.

In the absence of such tests, several empirical considerations suggest a tentative conclusion. Perhaps most important, in the real world codetermination does not appear to rise through voluntary contracts in open markets. Rather, it rises through imposition by the state or by labor unions with state-sanctioned power to strike. This observation suggests that codetermination is obtained by groups with a comparative advantage in the use of political power and is sought as a means for redistributing wealth from shareholders to some employees.

Additionally, the factors determining whether a firm is subject to codetermination do not appear to be good proxies for an employee's investment in firm-specific capital. For example, firms initially covered were in industries (e.g., mining, iron and steel) with large specific investment by shareholders, and the pattern seems to have been followed in subsequent extensions of the act; there is no indication that shareholders' specific investment is positively correlated with such investments by employees, although it is certainly suggestive of the expropriable quasi-rents available. Similarly, firms with few employees (e.g., less than 100 in the iron and steel industry) are exempt; size of labor force seems a better proxy for political power than for a worker's investment in firm-specific capital.

Theoretical arguments of the sort raised by Monissen and Wenger support the redistribution hypothesis. Within this context, the following points deserve note.

First, the existence of positive transaction costs implies that some events are simply too costly to take into account. Thus, there is no indication that the amount of firm-specific investment by individual employees covered by codetermination is significant. To the extent that such investments are small and/or amortized over a relatively short period of time, they may not be worth protecting with arrangements as costly as codetermination.

Second, firm-specific investment in an employee typically is undertaken by both the employee *and* the employer. Accordingly, the employee's investment is protected not only by the employment contract, but also by the employer's investment and by the constraints associated with continuous dealings. Thus, if an employer were to act opportunistically and seek to reduce an employee's wage to what he or she could earn elsewhere, the employee would leave, thereby destroying the employer's share of the specific investment. Moreover, if the employer acted opportunistically, it would have to pay higher wages to actual and prospective employees to compensate them for the increased risk.

Third, firm-specific investment by the employee -- just like employee-specific investment by the firm -- may be viewed as a performance bond. Current theory suggest that firms arise to solve the shirking-monitoring problem of joint production. Although the firm may arise to control shirking, it does not eliminate it. Accordingly, firm-specific investment by employees may be used as a bond to inhibit shirking. Employees who are detected shirking and lose their jobs will lose the present value of the quasi-rents generated by the infirm specific investment.

Indeed, even in the absence of any firm-specific investment, under open market conditions employers may choose to pay employees a wage above the amount they could earn elsewhere. The present value of this premium, which would be lost on dismissal, then acts to inhibit shirking by employees.

Fourth, codetermination weakens the effectiveness of the corporation as an institution for organizing productive activity, thereby encouraging the evolution and adoption of higher-cost alternatives. One effect of codetermination is to reduce the gains to shareholders from monitoring managers. As a result, less monitoring takes place and managers have increased opportunity for discretionary behavior.

More importantly, codetermination shifts the focus of the firm's behavior from the dominating objective of maximizing shareholders' wealth. Rather than seeking to maximize the expected present value of the firm's net income stream, decision makers within a firm subject to codetermination must resolve conflict regarding both the sharing and the timing of the income. Whereas shareholders can capitalize future returns into current transfer prices, employees typically can only capture them through higher wages during their emplyoment period. Thus, among other things, employees have a stronger preference for present relative to future returns. Resources are allocated less effectively within the firm and wealth is smaller.

Moreover, to the extent that employees are successful in using codetermination to expropriate some of the shareholders' quasi-rents, future firm-specific investments by shareholders will be inhibited.

In concluding, a few words about efficiency may be appropriate. Various statements made at this conference seem to suggest that generally acceptable criteria of efficiency are readily available.

Even Pareto efficiency, however, is not value-free. Viewing economics as a scientific system for predicting choices under constraints, it seems useful to regard the outcome of a constrained maximization problem -- whether the constraints are institutional or not -- as efficient. The relative merits of the (efficient) outcomes associated with alternative constraints may then be assessed according to an explicit set of value criteria.

Free Riders and Voluntary Contributions Reconsidered

by

Rüdiger Pethig[1)]

1. The Problem

The Cournot-Nash model of "independent adjustment" or "voluntary contributions" is still the prototype description of market provision for non-exclusive public goods.[2)] But this approach is quite inappropriate for explaining the allocation of all those (group-specific) public goods which are provided by organizations raising their funds through membership dues. This paper develops a membership-dues procedure and compares it with the standard voluntary contribution approach as well as with exclusive market provision. It is shown that uniform membership dues reduce free rider incentives thus mitigating the exploitation of the great by the small (Olson 1965).

We suggest to approach the free rider problem in allocating non-exclusive public goods by looking at the allocation displacement effects of non-exclusive provision as compared to the market allocation with complete and costless price exclusion. Roughly speaking, a free rider is considered a person who does not purchase the public good in the absence of exclusion but would have done so if price exclusion were implemented.[3)] Such a definition is not meaningful unless we provide an unambiguous reference allocation resulting from an exclusive market procedure. Unfortunately, in its present state the "price theory of public goods" is rather fragmentary. But for expository purposes assume that the (excludable) public good under consideration is supplied by a single firm under the zero-profit constraint, at uniform prices, and on an all-or-nothing basis (Pethig 1983). For simplicity, we refer to this market model as "the" *exclusive procedure*. In general, the public good will be sold to many consumers under these conditions.[4)]

1) This paper is part of the author's research program in the Sonderforschungsbereich 5: Staatliche Allokationspolitik im marktwirtschaftlichen System, financed by the Deutsche Forschungsgemeinschaft. Helpful comments from Wolfgang Blümel and Oskar von dem Hagen are gratefully acknowledged.

2) This model has received various refinements in recent contributions which will be entirely disregarded in the present paper. For details see Blümel, Pethig, and von dem Hagen (1986).

3) This concept of free riding focusses on the exclusion principle. Primarily, it is meant to be descriptive rather than normative and efficiency-oriented. Quite a different approach relies on Hurwicz's concept of individual incentive compatibility. See Pethig (1977).

4) It is well-known that the mere fact of excluding agents who have positive willingness-to-pay renders an allocation Pareto inefficient. However, we are not preoccupied with normative efficiency comparisons in the present paper.

Pethig Schlieper (Eds.)
Efficiency, Institutions, and Economic Policy

On the other hand, if price exclusion is not applied - or impossible, for that matter - everybody enjoys what somebody else has bought. Each consumer has an incentive to take a free ride hoping that somebody else will buy the public good in his place. The "classical" approach to explain the resulting allocation is to assume non-cooperative Cournot-type behavior for all consumers and to apply the Cournot-Nash equilibrium as the appropriate solution concept. It is easy to see (and restated below) that in such models no self-interested consumer is willing to buy if the maximum marginal willingness-to-pay of the highest-demand consumer is less than marginal production cost. But even if the opposite inequality holds the number of buyers may be very small. This approach to the "market provision" of non-exclusive public goods has already been employed by Olson (1965, p. 22-33) and further elaborated and discussed by Buchanan (1968) and Malinvaud (1972). For convenience we take up Malinvaud's notion and call it the *subscription procedure*. In the context of Olson's (1965) *Logic of Collective Action* the subscription procedure was used to demonstrate the obstacles to the formation of those organizations which seek to promote the provision of group-specific public goods.[5)]

In a broader perspective this procedure is only one out of several possible sales strategies being at an entrepreneur's disposal in the market for non-exclusive public goods. Another sales strategy is to give everybody the opportunity to buy a piece of the public good where both the sales price and the amount to be acquired are fixed by the entrepreneur with price and quantity sold being uniform across the agents. We call this strategy the *(uniform-)dues procedure* because one particularly interesting interpretation of it is that a (political) entrepreneur aims at forming an association or a lobbying organization. In this framework accepting the all-or-nothing offer is tantamount to paying the uniform membership dues as fixed by the entrepreneur. Hence an individual is a member of the association, if and only if he or she is a public-good buyer.

It is the principle purpose of this paper to elaborate the allocative implications of this dues procedure and to compare it both to the exclusive and to the subscription procedure. An individual is called a free rider under the subscription procedure [the dues procedure, respectively] if for some given public good supplied he or she accepts the entrepreneur's offer under the exclusive procedure but not under the subscription procedure [the dues procedure]. We will demonstrate that the incentives to free ride are stronger in the subscription procedure than in case of uniform membership dues.

It would be desirable to reach such a conclusion within a theoretic framework being as general as possible. But unfortunately there is a severe trade-off between generality of assumptions and specificy of results. We chose to compromise on generality in favour of clear-cut

5) Olson's distinction between small and large groups is irrelevant in our model. He seems to use the implicit assumption that in large groups even the highest-demand consumers' marginal willingness-to-pay is insufficiently low.

conclusions and comparisons. More specifically, the subsequent analysis is carried out under the assumptions

- that marginal production costs are below the highest-demand consumer's marginal willingness-to-pay and
- that the demand side of the market can be described by a linear demand distribution (Burns and Walsh 1981, Pethig 1983).

These conditions imply that one and only one, namely the highest-demand consumer, purchases some positive amount of public good under the subscription procedure. Even though this result seems to be quite implausible on empirical grounds, it gives us a convenient point of reference for applying different institutional rules to the same demand environment and for comparing their impact on the number of buyers and on quantities provided.

In the next section the subscription procedure with the one-buyer-only equilibrium allocation is algebraically restated. Then it is shown that in the exclusive procedure the number of purchasers is generally much greater than under subscription. Section 3 introduces and discusses the uniform-dues procedure under the same demand conditions. The comparative analysis reveals that under this scheme the number of free riders is positive but smaller than with subscription.

As a basis for all comparisons it is presupposed that under each scheme the same amount of public good is provided. This strategy is viable because the unique equilibrium provision under subscription is contained in the set of equilibrium quantities under both the exclusive and the dues procedure. While this indeterminacy of the equilibrium allocations helps to "isolate" the free-rider behavior, it clearly disqualifies the dues procedures as a descriptive approach. The last section of the present paper offers an analysis as to which outcome might be predicted for the dues procedure if the purchasers are assumed to exert influence on the determination of membership dues. Our basic hypothesis is that an organization is stable in the medium term, if it is impossible to find a majority of its membership voting either for a reduction or a rise of membership dues. Using our theoretical framework it turns out that there exists a stable organization with at least two members. The question whether high-demand members have an incentive to offer gifts in addition to their dues is also addressed, and it is found that uniform membership dues determined by majority vote tend to discourage those gifts. We believe that the dues procedure as specified in Section 4 has explanatory power for the allocation of all those non-congestible and non-exclusive public goods that are provided in clubs[6)], lobbying organizations, associations etc. raising their funds through membership dues.

6) It should be emphasized that the present investigation is not a contribution to the economic theory of clubs. Club goods are congestible and non-members are excluded from their consumption. In contrast, our public good is both non-congestible and nonexclusive. For details of these distinctions see Blümel, Pethig, and von dem Hagen (1986).

2. Free Riding under the Subscription Procedure

Consider an economy with m consumers who have quadratic and quasi-linear utility functions

$$(1) \quad u^i = h^i z^i - b z^{i2} + x^i \text{ with } h^i := h - (m+1-i)e \qquad (i = 1, ..., m).$$

In (1) we have h, e, b > 0, and z^i and x^i is agent i's consumption of some public good (good Z) and some private good (good X), respectively. In order to assure that the lowest-demand consumer (i=1) has a positive marginal utility for the first unit of good Z, we assume[7] h > em. Good X is the numéraire, and we write p for the public-good price and w^i for the consumer's fixed real income. Under the subscription procedure an agent i buys (or subscribes to) the amount s^i of good Z at the supplier's price p = c where the marginal production cost, c, is assumed to be positive and constant.[8]

We define $s^{-i} := \Sigma_{j \neq i} s^j$, $z^i := s^i + s^{-i}$ and obtain i's utility as

$$(2) \quad U^i(s^i, s^{-i}) := h^i(s^i + s^{-i} I) - b(s^i + s^{-i})^2 + w^i - cs^i .$$

A strategy m-tuple $(s^{1*}, ..., s^{m*})$ constitutes a Cournot-Nash equilibrium, if for all i and for all s^i in some suitably defined strategy set the following condition holds:

$$(3) \quad U^i(s^{i*}, s^{-i*}) \geq U^i(s^i, s^{-i*}) .$$

It is easy to see from (2) that agent i's best response to alternatively given s^{-i} (i.e. his reaction function) is

$$(4) \quad s^i \begin{cases} = \dfrac{h^i - c}{2b} - s^{-i}, \text{ if } \dfrac{h^i - c}{2b} \geq s^{-i} \geq 0, \\[2ex] = 0 \text{ otherwise.} \end{cases}$$

7) This assumption is not restrictive. m > h/e would mean that we include agents into our analysis, who rather belong to the group opposing the provision of good Z.

8) Under the subscription procedure (as well as under the dues procedure) marginal-cost pricing (p=c) is equivalent to satisfying the zero-profit constraint. This constraint will be used throughout the paper. Right now, its introduction is quite ad hoc, but we will argue in Section 4 why this assumption appears to be empirically plausible for an important class of problems.

Since all reaction functions are parallel lines with 45-degree slopes, the unique Cournot-Nash equilibrium is characterized by $s^{j*} = 0$ for all $j \neq m$ and

(5) $$s^{m*} = \frac{h^m - c}{2b} = \frac{h - e - c}{2b} =: z^* .$$

In order to assess the allocative impact of the absence of exclusion, we now presuppose costless price exclusion and compare the resulting allocation with that of the subscription procedure. Associated to the individual preferences from (1) are the demand function

(6) $$p = h^i - 2bz$$

and the all-or-nothing demand function[9)]

(7) $$p = h^i - bz.$$

Assume, furthermore, that the firm determines an offer (p,z) and leaves each consumer with the option either to accept it or to refreign from public-good consumption altogether. This sales strategy constitutes the *exclusive procedure.*
For predetermined $p_0 > 0$ individual i's utility-maximizing public good consumption is $z_0 = (h^i - p_0)/2b$, and the associated consumer's surplus is bz_0^2. Clearly, consumer i will accept the offer (p_0, z) if and only if z is in $[0,2z_0)$ and reject it for $z > 2z_0$. For $z = 2z_0$ he or she is indifferent, i.e. in case of accepting, his or her surplus is completely absorbed by the firm. This consideration demonstrates that if (p_0, z_0) satisfies (6) then consumer i is the marginal buyer under the exclusive procedure provided that the firm's offer is $(p_0, 2z_0)$.

In what follows it is convenient to apply the real-number approximation for consumers (as in Pethig (1983)), that is, to substitute i in {1, ..., m} by i in [1,m]. If i in [1,m] is not an integer it is understood to approximate the individual who is associated with the next lower integer. Substituting $n = m + 1 - i$ in (7) we thus obtain the *all-or-nothing demand distribution*

(7') $$p = h - en - bz.$$

For every (p,z) in some feasible domain, $n = (h - bz - p)/b$ from (7') determines the number of consumers who accept the offer (p,z). Equation (7') and the zero-profit constraint $npz - cz = 0$

9) Equation (6) represents what Samuelson (1969) calls a pseudo-demand function in case of non-exclusion. The all-or-nothing demand function associates to each z that unit price p which is equal to consumer i's maximum average willingness-to-pay. If (p,z) satisfies (7) then accepting to buy z for pz dollars yields the same utility for consumer i as rejecting the offer and being excluded from public-good consumption altogether.

imply that a sales strategy is feasible if and only if $p = c/n$ and $z = Z^e(n) \geq 0$, where (Pethig (1983, p. 393))

(8) $$Z^e(n) := \frac{hn - en^2 - c}{bn}.$$

For our purpose to identify free riders under the subscription procedure it is advantageous that the exclusive market allocation is not unique. We are now interested in knowing whether z^* from (5) can be provided under the exclusive procedure, that is, whether z^* belongs to the range of the function Z^e as defined in (8). To answer this question observe that $n_A := \sqrt{c/e}$ is the unique maximizer of Z^e. Define $z_A := Z^e(n_A) = (h - 2\sqrt{ec})/b$. For all z in $[0, z_A]$ we denote by $N^e(z)$ the maximum value[10] of n which satisfies $Z^e[N^e(z)] = z$. Simple calculation yields

(9) $$N^e(z) := \frac{h - bz + \sqrt{(h - bz)^2 - 4ec}}{2e}$$

We are now in the position to conclude that $[p = c / N^e(z^*), z^*]$ is a feasible sales strategy under the exclusive procedure, because

$$\begin{aligned} z_A - z^* &= (h + e + c - 4\sqrt{ec})/2b \\ &= [h - 2ec + (\sqrt{e} - \sqrt{c})^2]/2b \\ &= [z_A + (\sqrt{e} - \sqrt{c})^2]/2b > 0. \end{aligned}$$

Using (5), (8) and (9) yields

(9') $$n_e^* := N^e(z^*) = \frac{h + e + c + R(c)}{4e},$$

$$\text{where } R(c) := \sqrt{(h + e + c)^2 - 16ec}.$$

It would be desirable to have some information about the order of magnitude of n_e^*. For that purpose consider

(9'') $$N_c^e(z^*) := \frac{\partial N^e(z^*)}{\partial c} = [R(c) + c + h - 7e]/4eR(c).$$

10) For more details see the "régime A" in Pethig (1983, p. 393 n.).

Inspection of (9") and R (c) as defined in (9') reveals that $h \geq 7e$ is sufficient for $R(c) > 0$ and also for $N_c^e(z^*) > 0$. For $c = 0$, (9') yields $N^e(z^*; c = 0) =: n_{eo} = (h+e) / 2e$. These observations imply that if $h \geq 7e$, then $n_e^* > n_{eo}$ for all positive c. Since $h > em$ by assumption $h \geq 7e$ implies $m \geq 7$ and $n_{eo} > (m + 1) / 2$. Consequently, except for small groups ($m \leq 6$) we established that $n_e^* > m/2$. Defining free riders under the subscription procedure as those agents who are purchasers (of z^*) in the market but not under subscription, we therefore conclude that at least every second consumer takes a free ride in the case of voluntary contributions (subscription).

Figure 1: Subscription and exclusion in comparison

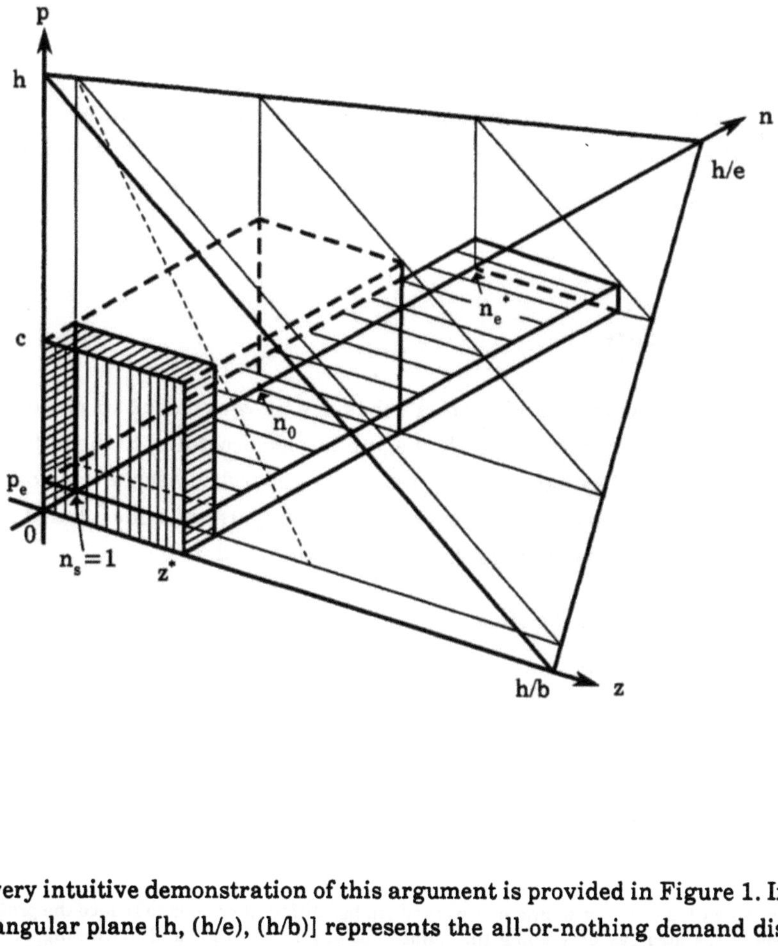

A very intuitive demonstration of this argument is provided in Figure 1. In that diagram the triangular plane [h, (h/e), (h/b)] represents the all-or-nothing demand distribution (7'), and the shaded box with length z^*, height c, and with depth 1 is the equilibrium allocation under subscription. By construction, this shaded area is the money value of the public good, pz^*, sold to the hightest-demand consumer. pz^* is equal to cz^*, the production cost of z^*, because $p = c$. Suppose now, the exclusion procedure applies and the entrepreneur extends the all-or-nothing offer (c,z^*) to everybody. It follows from Figure 1 that n_0 will accept this offer so that the firm's revenue is given by the medium-sized box in Figure 1, whose front is the shaded area c times z^* and whose depth is n_o. Since, by assumption, the cost of producing z^* is already covered when z^* is sold only once the profit associated with the strategy ($p = c, z^*$) is equal to $(n_o - 1)cz^*$ which is positive for $n_o > 1$.

A meaningful comparison between subscription and exclusion not only requires to stick with the same quantity supplied (here z^*) but also to run the exclusion procedure under the zero-profit constraint. Suppose that initially the positive-profit allocation $p = c, z^*$ and n_o is given. We now ask the firm to maintain the amount supplied, z^*, but to lower p until total revenue shrinked to become equal to total cost. Clearly, price reductions raise the number of buyers until some $p = p_e$ and $n = n_e > n_o$ is reached satisfying $p_e = h - en_e - bz^*$ and $p_e z^* n_e = cz^*$. In Figure 1 this allocation corresponds to the flat and long box with height p_e', length z^* and depth n_e.[11]

By definition, $i = m$ is the highest-demand consumer, and the $n_e^* - 1$ individuals also buying the public good under the exclusive procedure are those with the next highest demand, that is the consumers $i = m - 1, m - 2, \ldots, m + 1 - n_e^*$. All these consumers are free riders under subscription.[12]

3. The Uniform Dues Procedure

In order to define and characterize this allocation scheme it is convenient to proceed in several steps. Suppose first, the entrepreneur sells the public good according to the following rules: He announces a price-quantity pair ($p = c, y$) and gives everybody the all-or-nothing option to buy y units of the public good at the price $p = c$. Non-buyers are not excluded from consuming the public good bought by other agents. It is convenient to define

$$(10) \qquad s^i \begin{cases} = 0, \text{ if i rejects the offer,} \\ = y \text{ otherwise,} \end{cases}$$

and we use $s^{-i} := \Sigma_{j \neq i} s^j$ as above. Then the consumer i's utility is described in equation (2) and his decision problem is to maximize $U^i(s^i, s^{-i})$ over s^i in $\{0,y\}$ for predetermined $s^{-i} \geq 0$. For any $s^{-i} \geq 0$ consumer i obviously chooses $s^i = y$ if and only if[13]

11) Observe that starting with $p = c$, $z = z^*$ and $n = n_o$ the firm has different options to reduce the profit to zero. One of these is the strategy of keeping the number of buyers constant and expanding output; another one is to maximize output (Pethig 1983).

12) If $n_e < m$ there is still another group of agents who consume (part of) the public good in the absence of exclusion but who would not buy the good under the exclusive procedure. In a broader sense these agents are also free riders but they exhibit consistent behaviour insofar as they are not public-good buyers - neither under subscription nor under the exclusive procedure.

13) The "if and only" formulation is not quite correct because in case of the equality sign consumer i is indifferent between choosing $s^i = y$ or $s^i = 0$.

(11) $U^i(y, s^i) \geq U^i(0, s^{-i})$.

Recalling (1), (2), and (10), the inequality (11) is equivalent to

(12) $h^i - by - 2bs^{-i} - p \geq 0$.

Figure 2: The consumer's choice in the uniform-dues procedure

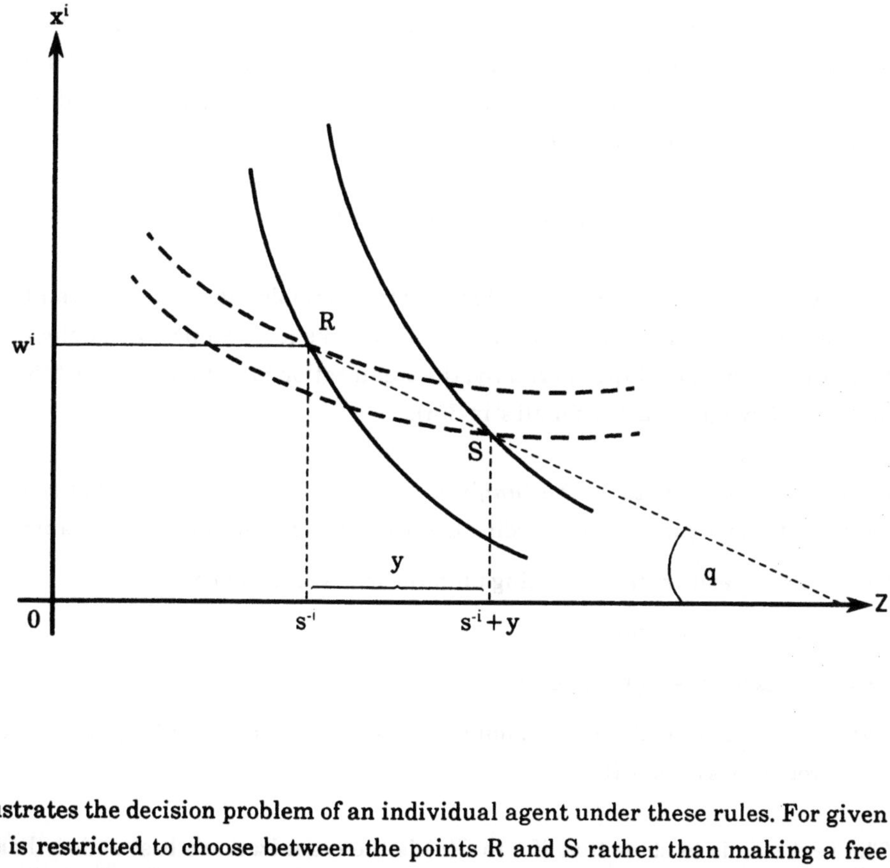

Figure 2 illustrates the decision problem of an individual agent under these rules. For given s^{-i} he or she is restricted to choose between the points R and S rather than making a free selection from the budget line segments RT. If his or her utility at point S [R, respectively] is greater than at R [S] then the individual chooses $s^i = y$ [$s^i = 0$]. The solid indifference curves through R and S trigger the decision $s^i = y$ whereas $s^i = 0$ is chosen when the dashed indifference curves apply.

As in Section 2, (s^{1*},...,s^{m*}), is a Cournot-Nash equilibrium if condition (3) holds for every i and all admissible s^i. It is interesting to observe that the only difference between this allocation rule and the subscription procedure is that, in the former, the consumer's strategy sets are restricted to a binary choice (where, in addition, the non-zero option is determined by the entrepreneur) whereas, in the latter, consumers can choose arbitrary amounts within some feasibility bounds. From the theoretical viewpoint we now deal with a "constrained" subscription scheme.

Denote by S the set of all Cournot-Nash equilibria. That is, $s^* := (s^{1*}, \ldots, s^{m*})$ is an element in S,
(i) if s^{i*} is in $\{0, y\}$ for all i and for some given y
(ii) and if (3) is satisfied for all i.
Consequently, every s in S determines implicitly the membership dues cy, the number of members $n = \Sigma_i s^i / y$, and the total public-good supply $z = ny$. It is easy to see that under certain parameter constellations there exist s, s' in S such that $\Sigma_i s^i = \Sigma s'^i$ but $n \neq n'$ and $y \neq y'$ or there may exist s, s' in S such that $n = n'$, but $y \neq y'$. The latter possibility can also be expressed by saying that the set

$$S(n) := \{ s \in S / \text{there is } y > 0 \text{ such that } \Sigma_i s^i = ny \}$$

may have more than one element. However this possible indeterminacy can be resolved by the plausible assumption that the organization seeks to maximize the public-good provision for any given membership n. Formally, the organization is assumed to select that particular s in S (n) satisfying $\Sigma_i s^i \geq \Sigma_i s'^i$ for all s' in S(n).

In summary, we denote as the *(uniform-) dues procedure* the non-exclusive public-good provision by an organization according to the following set of rules: The organization

(i) raises membership dues being uniform across all members;

(ii) operates at zero profit;

(iii) wants to have a given number of members;

(iv) wishes to provide the maximum possible amount of public good given the above conditions (i) to (iii).

The next step is to show that if s in S(n) is the organization's best action then its lowest-demand member must be the marginal member to join the oganization. Suppose not. Then (12) implies $h^j - by - 2b(n-1)y - c > 0$ or

$$y < y^j := \frac{h^j - c}{(2n-1)b} \tag{13}$$

if j is the lowest-demand member associated to the Cournot-Nash equilibrium s. Define s^+ by $\Sigma_i s^{+i} = ny^j$ where $s^{+i} = y^j$ and $s^{+k} = 0$ whenever $s^i = y$ and $s^k = 0$, respectively. We clearly have s^+ in S (n) and $\Sigma_i s^{+i} > \Sigma_i s^i$ which proves the claim.

To illustrate the marginal member j suppose that for i = j, (12) is satisfied as an equality. Substituting $s^{-j} = z - y$ this equality reads

(12') $$p = h^j + by - 2bz.$$

In Figure 3 the equation (12') is represented by the line FE whereas AD is consumer j's demand curve $p = h^j - 2bz$ (from 6).

Figure 3: The marginal member in the dues procedure

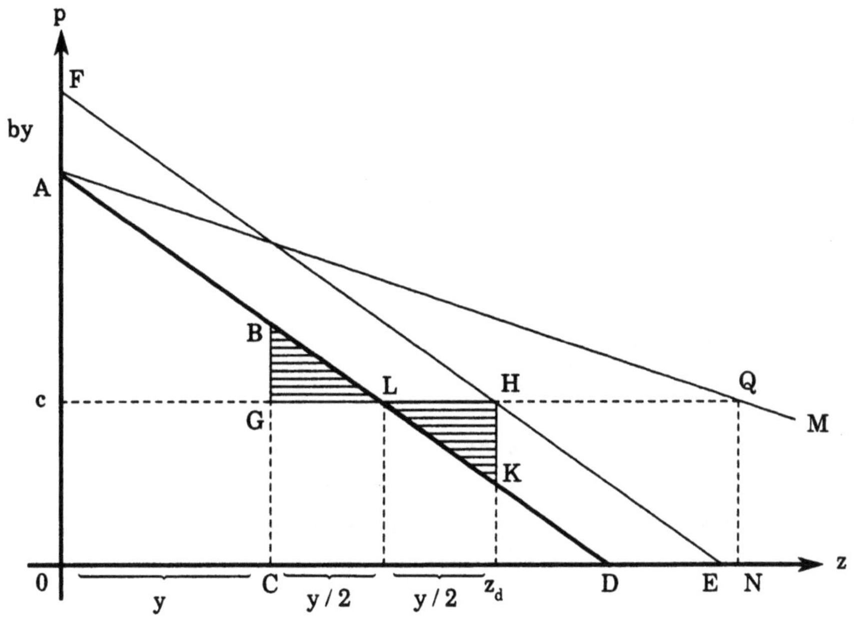

The horizontal distance of these two lines is y/2. Since p = c and $z_d = (h^j + by - c) / 2b$ (because j is the marginal member, by assumption), Figure 3 is drawn in such a way that j = n = 2. Consumer j's dues is $CGHz_d$ and his surplus is

$$OABC + GBL - LHK = OABC > 0 .$$

The equality in size of the shaded triangles GBL and LHK means that consumer j is indifferent between joining and not joining the organization (which makes him or her the marginal member). In other words, his or her surplus of buying the *increment* is zero.

We are now in the position to show that for each n there is one and only one s in S(n) maximizing the public-good provision (hence implying the organization's best action). This Cournot-Nash equilibrium is characterized by $s^i = y$ for all $i \geq m + 1 - n$ and $s^i = 0$ otherwise. To prove this, suppose the contrary holds true. Then the best action is some s' in S(n) such that $s'^j > 0$ for $j < m + 1 - n$, and from (12) we have $h^j - by' - 2b(n-1)y' - c = 0$ or $y' := (h^j - c)/(2n-1)b$. But $j < m + 1 - n$ implies that there is some $k > j$ for which $s'^k = 0$ since otherwise s' is not in S(n). Denote by s" that m-tuple of strategies being equal to s' except that $s''^j = 0$ and $s''^k = y'$. We clearly have s" in S(n) and there is $l > j$ such that $s''^l = y'$ and $s''^i = 0$ for all $i < l$. $l > j$ implies $h^l > h^j$ and $y'' := (h^l - c)/(2n-1)b > y'$. Due to this inequality agent l is an intramarginal member. Define s"' by $\Sigma_i s'''^i = ny''$ where $s'''^i = y''$ ($s'''^i = 0$) if and only if $s''^i = y'$ ($s''^i = 0$). Clearly, $\Sigma_i s'''^i > \Sigma_i s''^i$. This contradiction proves that if s in S(n) is compatible with the organization's best action then $s^i = y$ for all $i \geq m + 1 - n$ and $s^i = 0$ otherwise.

Our preceding findings have an important implication: if the organization's membership is to be n, then $i(n) := m + 1 - n$ must be its marginal member and $s^j > 0$ for all $j > i(n)$. In other words, we have $h^{i(n)} = h - en$, $s^{-i(n)} = (n-1)y$, and $h^{i(n)} - by - 2bs^{-i(n)} - p = 0$ from (12). Using this information we readily obtain

(14) $$p = h - en - \frac{(2n-1)b}{n} z ,$$

which we denote the *membership demand distribution*. The interpretation of (14) is straightforward: If the organization wants to maximize the public-good provision subject to the zero-profit constraint (p=c) and subject to n members then it must produce z such that (p = c, n, z) satisfies (14). More specifically, the organization selects

(15) $$z_d = Z^d(n) := \frac{n(h - en - c)}{(2n-1)b} .$$

Equation (14) is illustrated in Figure 4 by the shaded convex-shaped plane being located between the demand distribution ABD and the all-or-nothing demand distribution AED. The line FG in Figure 4 is the locus of all points (p = c, n, Z^d (n)), i.e. the projection of the line FG to the ground plane is the graph of the function Z^d as defined in (15). The associated "piece" of good Z to be offered to each agent is

(16) $$y = z_d/n = Y^d(n) := \frac{h - en - c}{(2n-1)b} .$$

Figure 5 depicts the Cournot-Nash equilibrium allocation for an example with n = 3 in

Figure 4: The membership demand distribution

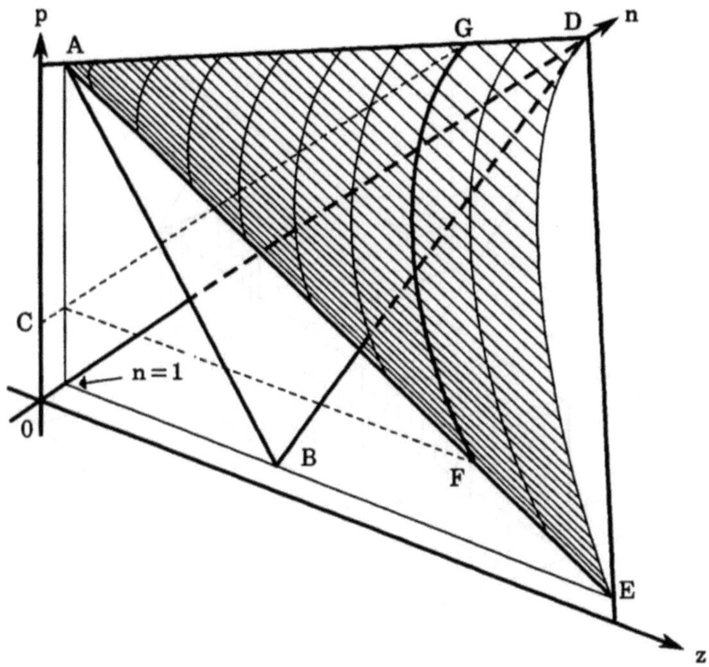

which y and $z_d = 3y$ satisfy the equations (16) and (15), respectively. The shaded box represents the firm's revenue, i.e. three times cy. Observe that at point Q in Figure 5 one corner of this box touches the membership demand distribution (14) from below, because consumer 3 is clearly the marginal public-good buyer.

It is easy to see from (15) that the organization's total public-good provision decreases strictly with increasing membership ($Z_n^d < 0, Z_{nn}^d > 0$). In other words, the larger the membership is the less successful is the organization in providing the public good. The reason for this rather unexpected result ist that each unit of the public good is sold at the (constant) marginal-cost price and that increasing memberhsip implies decreasing willingness to pay of the marginal member, who determines to overall-supply.

Now we have sufficiently characterized the dues procedure so that we can turn to investigating its free-riding incentives. Particularly helpful for answering this question is the form of the function Z^d. Since this function is strictly monotone, there exists an inverse function reading

Figure 5: A Cournot-Nash equilibrium for the dues procedure

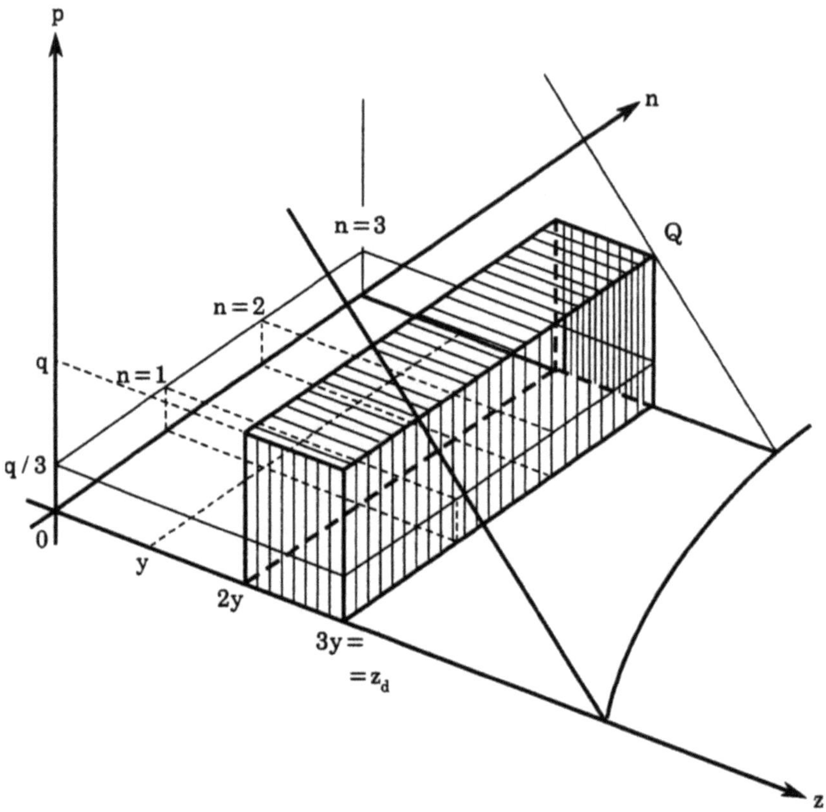

(17)
$$n_d = N^d(z) := [h - 2bz - c + \sqrt{(h - 2bz - c)^2 + 4ebz}] / 2e \; .$$

We choose z = z* to obtain

(17')
$$n_d{}^* = N^d(z^*) = 1/2 + \sqrt{1/4 + \frac{h - c - e}{2e}} \; ,$$

so that the number of free riders under the dues procedure is $n_e{}^*$ - $n_d{}^*$ (with $n_e{}^*$ as defined in (9')). Since $n_e{}^*$ and $n_d{}^*$ depend on the parameters of the model in a complex way (16') and (9') don't provide clear-cut information about the order of magnitude of $n_e{}^*$ - $n_d{}^*$. Therefore we take the route of comparing the graphs of the functions Z^e and Z^d from (8) and (14), respectively.

Figure 6: The number of free riders in the dues procedure

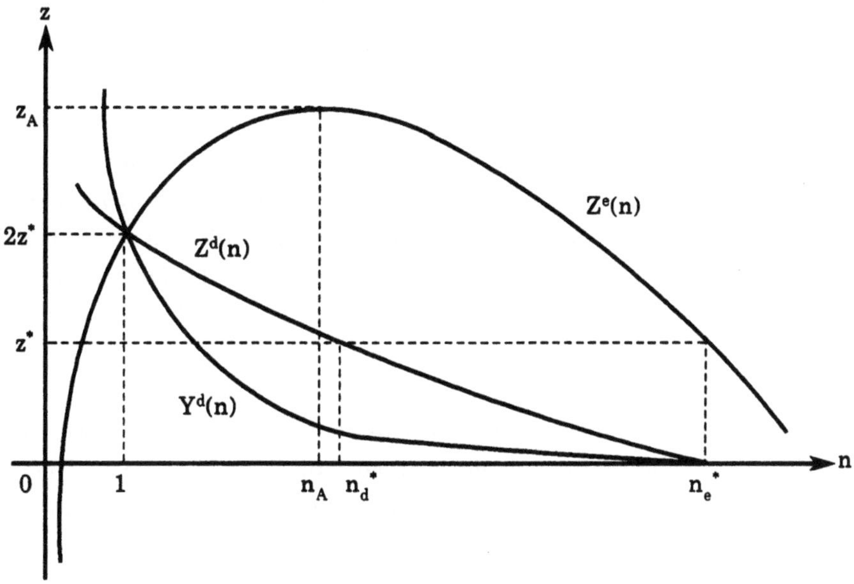

The function Z^e is drawn in Figure 6 so that $z_A < 2z^*$ which presupposes $c>e$. Observe also that $Z^e(n) = Z^d(n)$ for $n = 1$ and that $n_{eo} > n_{do}$ where n_{eo} and n_{do} are defined by the conditions $Z^e(n_{eo}) = 0$ and $Z^d(n_{do}) = 0$, respectively. In addition, z_e is strictly concave while Z^d is strictly convex. Therefore $N^e(z^*) - N^d(z) > 0$ for all z in $[0,2z^*]$. Figure 6 also shows that $N^d(z^*)$ is strictly greater than one. Hence there are free riders in the dues procedure but less than in the subscription procedure. (17') reveals that the comparative advantage of dues over subscription in mitigating the free rider problem (as measured by $n_d^* - 1$) is the greater, the greater is h and the smaller is c or e.[14]

4. The Dues Procedure as a Descriptive Approach to Group Formation

In the preceding section we confined our attention to the number of buyers as compared with that under exclusive market provision. The dues procedure as discussed so far turned out to be indeterminate in its equilibrium allocation which renders it highly inappropriate as an explanatory device. We now wish to investigate the causes of this indeterminacy and how it could be mitigated or resolved.

14) See also Table 1 and its interpretation in the section 4.2 below.

4.1. Behavioral Assumptions and Incentives

First we reconsider our assumption about entrepreneurial behavior. To see its allocative impact suppose an entrepreneur applies the uniform-dues strategy but seeks to maximize profit. If he or she determines some sales price p ($p \geq c$) and some z, then the arguments in the context of inequality (12) imply that the marginal buyer $i(n) = m + 1 - n$ is uniquely determined by the equation (12') whenever y is assigned any value less than z. Observe that equation (12') enables us then to select the correct value of y, namely $y = z/n$ (for predetermined p and z). Given this information the entrepreneur's problem is to maximize his or her profit $\pi = pz - cz = (h - en - bz)\, z - cz$ subject to $n \geq 1$. Since $\pi_n < 0$ for $z > 0$ a necessary condition for maximum profit is clearly to choose $n = 1$. Moreover, for $n = 1$ the first-order condition $\pi_z = h - en - 2bz - c = 0$ yields $z = z^*$ (with z^* from (5)) as the profit-maximizing public-good supply.

This result has several interesting implications: First of all, it is shown that profit-maximizing behavior yields a uniquely determined equilibrium allocation. The associated values of n and z are exactly those being obtained under subscription when the zero-profit constraint holds. In fact, $i = m$ is the only buyer in both cases. But in the zero-profit subscription procedure m's surplus attains its maximum whereas his or her surplus is zero under the profit-maximizing dues strategy. In this case the only member of the association is completely exploited by the organization's manager. This observation raises serious doubts as to whether profit-maximizing behavior is empirically relevant: Whenever "buying the public good" means that the buyer becomes a member in some special-interest organization with $cY^d(n)$ interpreted as the membership dues it is very ofter the case that the zero-profit constraint is part of the association's statutory rules. This constraint could also be imposed and enforced by government regulation.[15)]

Given zero-profit supply let us now ask the question whether the demand-side behavior was adequately modeled in Section 3. It was assumed that the firm fixes $p = c$ and y while the consumers react by adopting that offer or not. Recall that the firm has at its disposal a large set of different values of y, consistent with an equilibrium, and that the firm is indifferent between these offers due to the zero-profit condition. But the consumers are not indifferent between these offers, as can easily be seen by considering the all-or-nothing offer ($p = c$, $y = 2z^*$). In that limiting case the highest-demand consumer is the only buyer, so that we are basically confronted with a bilateral monopoly and hence a bargaining situation. But the rules of the game disregard completely this particular or similarly special market structures. In case of one buyer only the rules determine to exploit the consumer's entire surplus. It is

15) In some cases government regulation even encompasses compulsory membership of all the organization's potential beneficiary. But such an institutional arrangement leaves no room for voluntary contributions any more, and it will therefore be disregarded. See also Pethig (1986).

obvious that the highest-demand agent would not accept these rules but would rather ask a different entrepreneur to offer him or her utility-maximizing amount of the public good ($z^* < 2z^*$). These considerations suggest that high-demand buyers have an incentive to induce the firm to lower the uniform dues thus increasing both the number of buyers and their own utility. On the other hand, those not accepting some given offer might oppose any decrease in y because that could reduce their surplus.

To be more specific, suppose all consumers know the functions Z^d and Y^d from (15) and (16), respectively, and the firm offers ($p = c$, $Y^d(n)$) for some n in [1,(h – c) / e)].Then for all i in [m+1–n, m] consumer i's utlity is

(18) $$V(i, n) := h^i Z^d(n) - b[Z^d(n)]^2 + w^i - c\,Y^d(n),$$

where $h^i := h - (m + 1 - i)\,e$. The first derivative of function V is

(19) $$V_n(i, n) = Z_n{}^d(n)\,(h^i - 2bZ^d(n)) - cY_n{}^d(n).$$

It is easy to see that $V_n(i = m, n = 1) > 0$ implying that the highest-demand consumer doesn't want to be the only member. Note also that $\partial V_n(i, n) / \partial i > 0$. Hence if i is one out of some organization's given membership n and is asked whether he or she prefers the membership dues, then with decreasing i the consumer's net advantage of increasing membership diminishes and may eventually become negative.

4.2. Stability by Voting on Dues

In many associations members have considerable influence on the organization's policy, in particular on the determination of membership dues. Moreover, the arguments presented in the preceding paragraphs suggest that members are not at all indifferent as to the size of the organization, or equivalently, as to the dues. In what follows we assume, therefore, that the membership dues is determined by majority vote of all members. More precisely, the procedure may be interpreted to be a vote on an incremenal reduction or rise of dues. Define $N^+(n)$ and $N^-(n)$ to be the cardinality of the set $\{i \text{ in } [m + 1 - n, m] / V_n(i, n) > 0\}$ and $\{i \text{ in } [m + 1 - n, m] / V_n(i, n) \le 0\}$, respectively. Since $\partial V_n(i, n) / \partial i > 0$, we clearly have $N^+(n) + N^-(n) = n$. It follows that the organization with present membership n decides to reduce [increase] its dues (and hence to increase [reduce] its membership) if and only if $N^+(n) > N^-(n)$ [$N^+(n) < N^-(n)$]. These considerations suggest to define a stable membership by that number n_b which satisfies $N^+(n_b) = N^-(n_b)$. If the membership is n_b the organization itself may be called stable in the sense that no majority of members can be found to support a change in membership dues and hence a change in membership. The equality $N^+(n) = N^-(n)$ is equivalent to the condition that the median voter $i_n := m + 1 - n / 2$ cannot improve upon his or her utility by either increasing or reducing the membership. Algebraically this conditions reads $V_n(i_n, n) = 0$. Unfortunately, the function V has no straightforward properties for $i = i_n$. But its special structure suggests to proceed as follows. We define

$$(20) \qquad V^b(n) := b[V(i_n, n) - w^{i_n}] = F(n) Z^d(n) - [Z^d(n)]^2$$

where $F(n) := (2hn - en^2 - 2c) / 2bn$ and where w^{i_n} is the wealth of the median voter $i_n = m + 1 - n/2$. The first and second derivative of V^b are

$$(21) \qquad V_n^b = F_n Z^d + F(-z^d) Z_n^d$$

$$(22) \qquad V_{nn}^b = F_{nn} Z^d + 2F_n Z_n^d + (F - Z^d) Z_{nn}^d - (Z_n^d)^2 .$$

The sign of V_n^b depends on that of the difference $F - Z^d$. Define n_a by the condition

$$(23) \qquad Z^d(n_a) = F(n_a) > 0.$$

We now show that n_a exists and is unique if and only if $h^2 > 2ec$. Observe that F is strictly concave in n and that $F(n) = 0$ for $n_{\alpha/\beta} = (h \pm \sqrt{h^2 - 2ec})/e$. Therefore $F(n) = 0$ presupposes $h^2 > 2ec$. Consider $n_\gamma := (h - c)/e$ defined by $Z^d(n_\gamma) = 0$ and note that n_β satisfies both $F(n_\beta) = 0$ and $F(n) < 0$ for all $n > n_\beta$. Under $h^2 > 2ec$ this implies $n_\beta > n_\gamma$. Moreover Z^d is strictly decreasing in n. Therefore (21) is satisfied for one and only one value of n, which we denote n_a.

The point of intersection n_a is illustrated in Figures 7 and 8. It may turn out that $n_a < n_F$ or $n_a > n_F$, where $n_F := 2c/e$ is the unique maximizer of F. The Figures 7 and 8 illustrate these two cases. When the information from the upper panels of these figures is combined with the equations (21) and (22) we are able to determine several basic properties of the function V^b There is some interval $[1, \min(n_a, n_F)]$ in which V^b is strictly increasing and strictly concave, and there is another interval $[\max(n_a, n_F), n]$ in which V^b is strictly decreasing (but not possibly nonconcave). Consequently

(24) $\qquad n_b$ is in the (open) interval $(\min(n_a, n_F), \max(n_a, n_F))$.

In Figure 7 we illustrate the case that n_b is in (n_a, n_F), and Figure 8 shows n_b in (n_F, n_a). Since (23) cannot be explicitly solved for n_a one may wish to determine some range for n_b without using n_a. For that purpose define $Z^f(k, n) := (h - en - c)/kb$ and observe that $Z^f(k, n) = Z^d(n)$ for $k = (2n - 1)/n$. Moreover, for every $n \geq 1$ there is k in $[1,2]$, such that $Z^f(k, n) = Z^d(n)$. Let

$$n_u := (-c + \sqrt{c^2 + 2ce})/e \text{ and}$$
$$n_o := (h - 2c + \sqrt{(h - 2c)^2 + 6ce})/3.$$

Figure 7 and 8: The stable membership

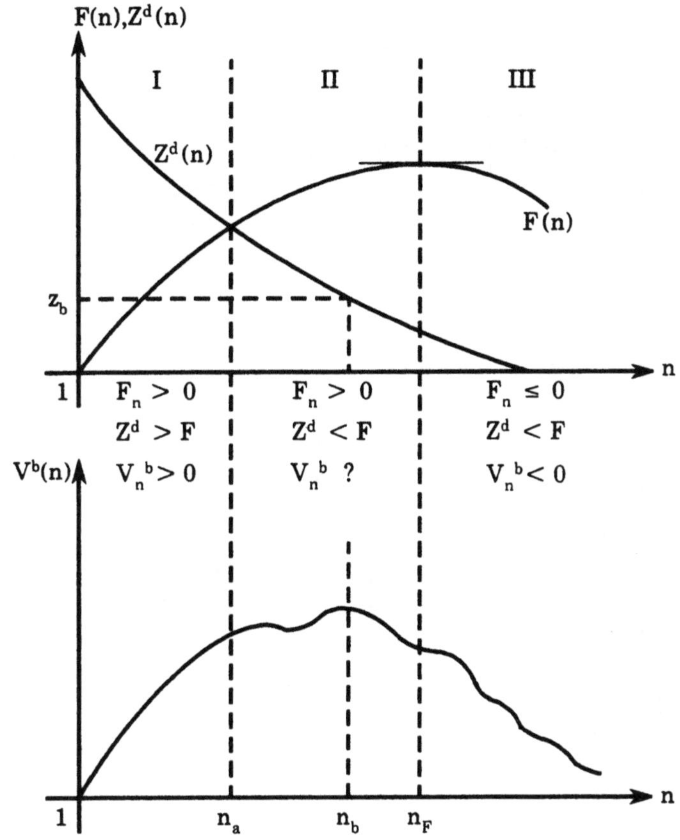

Figure 7

By definition, n_u solves $Z^f(k = 2, n) = F(n)$ and hence underestimates n_a. Conversely, n_o solves $Z^f(k = 1, n) = F(n)$ and hence overestimates n_a. We conclude, therefore, that

$$n_b \text{ is in } \begin{cases} (n_u, n_F), \text{ if } n_a < n_F, \\ (n_F, n_o), \text{ if } n_a > n_F\,. \end{cases}$$

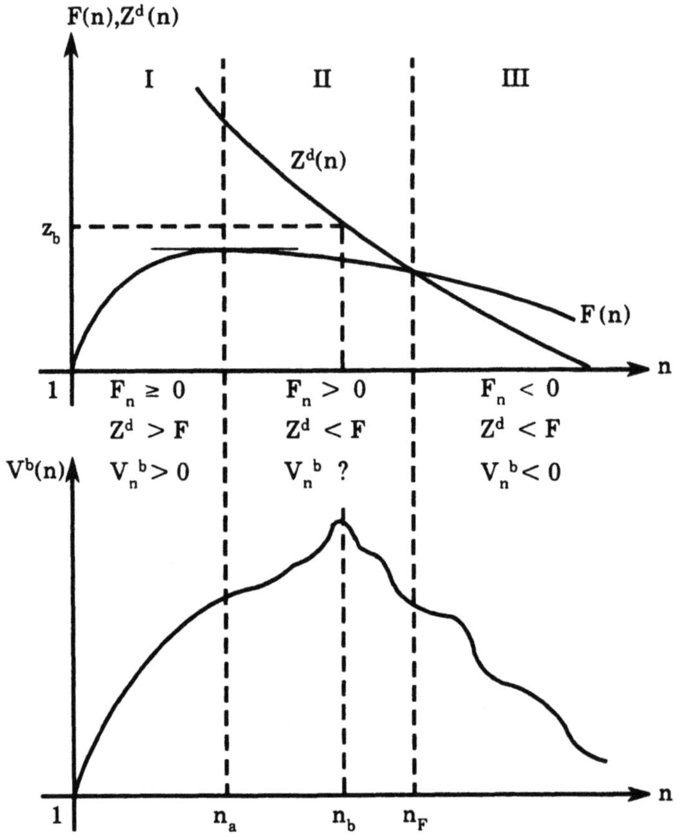

Figure 8

What can be said about the relationship between $[n_b, z_b = Z^d(n_b)]$ and $[n_d^* z^* = Z^d(n_d^*)]$ (with n_d^* and z^* defined in (16')and (5), respectively)? Since $F(n_F) > z^*$ it turns out that the sign of the differences $n_b - n_d^*$ and $z^* - z_b$ cannot be determined by graphical means. To see this, consider Figure 9, assuming $n_a < n_d^* < n_F$. We know that n_b is in (n_a, n_F). Figure 9 is drawn in such a way that $z_b > z^*$ if n_b is in $(n_a, n_d^*)$and $z_b < z^*$ if n_b is in (n_d^*, n_F). A similar argument applies if $n_a > n_F$ if presupposed.

Unfortunately the function V^b as defined in (20) is so complex that n_b cannot be determined algebraically. (We do not even know whether its maximum is unique). We therefore rewrite (20) as

Figure 9: Properties of the voting equilibrium allocation

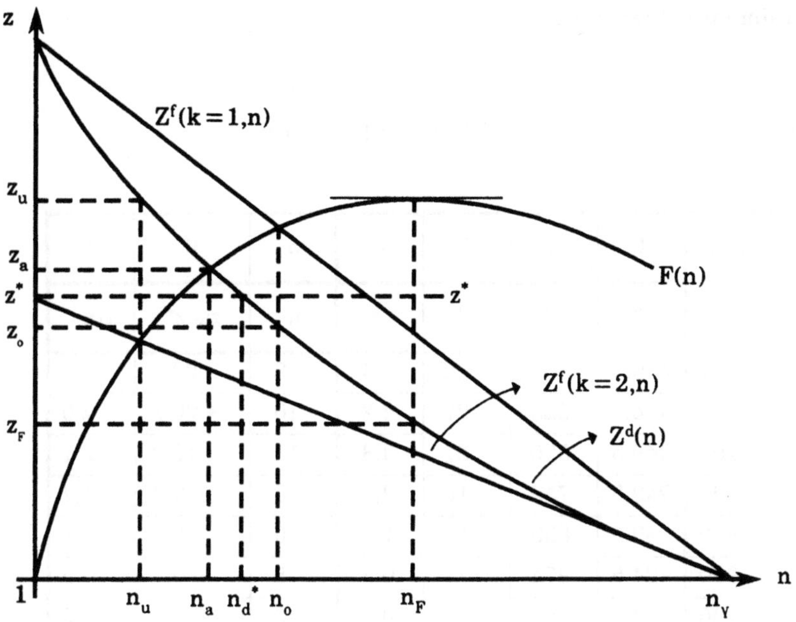

(20')
$$V^b(n) = \frac{-a_1 n^3 + a_2 n^2 - a_3 n + 2(h-c)c}{4b^2(4n^2 - 4n - 1)}$$

with $a_1 := e(2h + 2c + e)$,

$a_2 := (h - c)(2h + 2c + e) + 2e(2c + h)$,

$a_3 := 2(h - c)(2c + h) + 2ce$,

and calculate its maximizer, n_b, for some numerical values of b, c, e and h. The upper eight rows of Table 1 presuppose $b = c = 1$, $h = 1000$ and various values of c. The lower six rows assume[16] $b = 1$, $c = 100$, $h - e = 999$ and various values of e. Observe that the choice of parameters implies that the third row from above is the same as the fifth row from below. Column 4 is defined by $\Delta n^* := 100 n_d^* / n_e^*$, i.e. Δn^* denotes the organization's member-ship as a percentage rate of all those agents who would have bought the public good in case of exclusion. By definition, $100\Delta n^*$ is the percentage of free riders in the dues procedure.

16) We chose to keep the difference h-e constant because that leaves the highest-demand agent's utility function unchanged.

Column 6 contains the difference of public-good provision between the stable organization ($z_b = Z^d(n_b)$) and subscription (z^*), and in column 7 we have $\Delta n_b : 100 n_b / N^e(z_b)$ with an interpretation similar to that of Δn^*.

Table 1: Numerical outcomes of the dues procedure

h = 1000 b = e = 1	1	2	3	4	5	6	7
c	z^*	n_e^*	n_d^*	Δn^*	n_b	$z_b - z^*$	Δn_b
1	499,0	501	22	4,4	8	+29,5	1,7
50	474,5	525	22	4,2	10	+20,2	2,0
100	449,5	550	21	3,8	11	+16,2	2,1
500	249,5	749	16	2,1	13	+ 3,7	1,7
800	99,5	899	10	1,1	10	+ 0	1,1
950	24,5	974	5	0,5	5	+ 0	0,5
990	4,5	994	2	0,2	2	+ 0	0,2
998	0,5	998	1	0,1	1	+ 0	0,1
e							
0,1	449,5	5495	67	1,2	31	+ 5,8	0,6
1	449,5	550	21	3,8	11	+16,2	2,1
10	449,5	55	7	12,7	4	+47,1	7,8
50	449,5	11	3	27,3	2	+116,5	22,2
100	449,5	6	2	33,3	2	+83,2	40,0
200	449,5	3	1	33,3	1	-	-

The main results of Table 1 are summarized as follows:

(i) The maximizer n_b of the function V^b is unique.

(ii) The stable organization provides at least as much of the public good as under subscription. It is a corrollary, that n_b never exceeds n_d^*.

(iii) The membership of the stable organization is largest, ceteris paribus, when production costs are intermediate, and it increases with decreasing e. While constant-output organizations react qualitatively in the same way as stable organizations with respect to variations in e they differ in that their membership increases monotonely with decreasing c.

(iv) For both stable and constant-output organizations it is true that their propensity to discourage free rides (as measured by Δn_b and Δn^*, respectively) does not vary significantly with c (and is very low for h = 1000, b = e = 1). But it grows substantially with increasing values of e - even though all organizations' absolute membership is strictly increasing in e.

These observations can be taken as conjectures, at best, because there seems to be no easy way to generalize them beyond the parameter values used in Table 1.

4.3 Membership dues and gifts

By definition, stable organization satisfying $N^+(n) = N^-(n)$ contain all those high-demand agents (and members) who prefer to increase the organization's public-good output by decreasing its membership along with raising the dues. This observation suggests that high-demand members may find it in their self-interest to offer voluntary contributions (gifts, donations) in excess of their dues. It is beyond the scope of the present paper to offer a model in which donations are systematically incorporated as an additional option to the payment of dues. It is however possible to reveal the nature of the problem by simply assuming that nobody but the highest-demand agent (i = m) considers to make a gift in addition to the membership dues.

To fix our ideas let us assume that consumer i = m anounces to make a contribution g in addition to the membership dues. Indidvidual i ≠ m will then decide to become a member if and only if

(11') $$U^i(y, s^{-i} + g) \geq U^i(0, s^{-i} + g).$$

Using $s^{-i} = (n\text{-}1)y$ and $z = ny + g$, (14) and (15), respectively, turn into

(14') $$p = h - en - \frac{(2n-1)b}{n} z - \frac{bg}{n},$$

(15') $$z = Z^g(n, g) := Z^d(n) - \frac{g}{2n-1}.$$

Equation (15') implies that the supply of good Z diminishes with increasing gift if the organization keeps its membership constant (by reducing the dues). Gifts clearly discourage low-demand agents to join the organization. The decisive point is, however, how the equilibrium membership reacts to a change in gifts. The median voter's "utility" now reads

(19')
$$V^g(n,g) := F(n)Z^g(n,g) - [Z^g(n,g)]^2 + \frac{cg}{n}.$$

(19') shows that the algebra of this problem has become even less tractable than for g = 0. But a few general observations can be made. Assume that V^g has a unique maximum with respect to n and define

$$N(g) := \underset{n}{\text{Max}}\, V^g(n,g) \quad \text{and} \quad Z(g) := Z^g[N(g), g].$$

Consider

$$Z_g = Z_n^d N_g - 1/(2n-1) + 2gN_g/(2n-1)^2$$

$$= \frac{2[z^* + en(2n-1)/2b - g]}{(2n-1)^2} - \frac{1}{2n-1}.$$

If $g \geq z^*$ is ruled out, the conditions $Z_g \leq 0$ is equivalent to

$$N_g \geq N_g^0 := \frac{2n-1}{2[z^* + en(2n-1)/2b - g]} < 0.$$

In that case making a gift is pleinly self-defeating for the highest-demand consumer: He or she pays a larger part of the public good which is smaller than or the same as before. In contrast, if $Z_g \geq 1$ or, equivalently, $N_g \leq 2nN_g^0 < 0$, then the gift would be clearly advantageous for the donator. It is now obvious from these arguments that there is a threshold value, say N_g^1, in the open interval $(2nN_g^0, N_g^0)$ such that an extra dollar of gifts pays for the highest-demand agent if an only if $N_g < N_g^1$, or

$$\int_{N(g+1)}^{N(g)} [h - e - 2bZ^g(n,g)]dn > c.$$

Suppose, n_b is the equilibrium membership for g = 0, that is, $V_n^g(n_b, 0) = 0$. An increase in g has the effect

$$V_{ng}^g(n_b, 0) = (F_n - Z_g^g)Z_n^g + (F - Z^d)Z_{ng}^g - c/n^2.$$

Assume first, n_b satisfies the conditions of Figure 6. Then $(F_n - Z_g^g) Z_n^g < 0$ but $(F - Z^g) Z_{ng}^g > 0$ and hence the sign of $V_{ng}^g(n_b, 0)$ is indeterminate. A similar ambiguity applies if n_b is as drawn in Figure 8. These arguments suggest that $N_g < 0$ cannot be algebraically secured. A fortiori, it is therefore questionable under which conditions $N_g < N_g^1$ is fulfilled. In summary, the highest-demand consumer's incentives to make a donation in addition to the membership dues (if $z_b < z^*$) could not be determined unambiguously. But even if one considers it plausible that the equilibrium membership shrinks with increasing gifts ($N_g < 0$)it is not clear whether the shrinkage is sufficiently great ($N_g < N_g^1 < 0$) to make the gift advantageous for the donator. We conjecture, therefore, that the uniform membership procedure tends to discourage gifts.

5. Concluding Remarks

This paper aims at making a descriptrive contribution to the market theory of allocating non-exclusive public goods. The analysis is carried out in a theoretical framework in which the standard Cournot-Nash model of voluntary contributions (subscription procedure) generates "one-person-only organizations". It is shown how uniform membership dues induce rational individuals to join the organization thus explaining a membership greater than one in an environment for which the subscription procedure predicts only one member. The obvious interpretation of this observation is that the institutional rule of raising uniform membership dues, per se, is an approriate means to reduce free rider incentives.

The formation of a "one-person-only organization" means that *the* highest-demand consumer is exploited by all other agents. With uniform dues the highest-demand consumer is no longer the only buyer, in general, and no buyer is completely exploited. In fact, the highest-demand consumer is considerably relieved in the dues procedure in which the lowest-demand buyer carries the heaviest relative burden. Low-demand agents still take a free ride so that it remains correct to say that this subgroup "exploits" the (higher-demand) buyers.

It is a common feature of the subscription and the dues procedure that group formation may fail completely if individual marginal willingness-to-pay is too low relative to marginal production cost. If in situations of that type positive public good provision would be Pareto efficient we face a classical total "market failure". In both procedures the marginal unit is always sold at marginal production cost so that there is a threshold value of marginal cost beyond which nothing at all is sold. Observe that in the exclusive procedure the sales price (being uniform across both units and agents)is $p = c/n$ which is well below marginal cost (c) when the number of buyers (n) is large.

Olson (1965) considers situations described in the preceding paragraph as empirically relevant for large (latent) groups. According to his so-called by-product theory of group formation, successful organization presupposes the creation of selective incentives to the effect that "...those who do not join the organization ... can be treated differently from those who do" (Olson 1965, p. 51). In our uniform-dues procedure, positive selective incentives can be interpreted to shift consumer i's all-or-nothing demand function upward (that is, h^i

increases in (7)) if i is a member of the organization. As a consequence, the organization will gain a few additional members. But the "production" of selective incentives is not costless so that this activitity pays if and only if the dues revenue gained from the additional members exceed the incentive production costs (Pethig 1985). These few remarks demonstrate that the issue of selective incentives can be fruitfully integrated in our analysis.

References

(1) Blümel, Wolfgang, Pethig, Rüdiger, and von dem Hagen, Oskar (1986), "The theory of public goods: A survey of recent issues", *Journal of Institutional and Theoretical Economics* 142, 241-309.

(2) Buchanan, James M. (1968), *Demand Supply of Public Goods*, Rand McNally, Chicago.

(3) Burns, Michael, E., and Walsh, Cliff (1981), "Market provision of price-excludable public goods: A general analysis", *Journal of Political Economy* 89, 166-191.

(4) Malinvaud, Edmond (1972), *Lectures on Microeconomic Theory*, North-Holland, Amsterdam.

(5) Olson, Mancur (1965), *The Logic of Collective Action*, Harvard University Press, Cambridge (Mass.).

(6) Pethig, Rüdiger (1978), "Das Freifahrerproblem in der Theorie der öffentlichen Güter", in: Helmstädter, Ernst (ed.), *Neuere Entwicklungen in den Wirtschaftswissenschaften*, Duncker & Humblot, Berlin, 75-100.

(7) Pethig, Rüdiger (1983), "On the production and distribution of information", *Zeitschrift für Nationalökonomie* 43, 383-403.

(8) Pethig, Rüdiger (1985), "Competitive lobbying for group-specific public goods", in: Pethig, Rüdiger (ed.), *Public Goods and Public Allocation Policy*, Peter Lang, Frankfurt a.M., Bern, New York, 63-92.

(9) Pethig, Rüdiger (1986), "Verbände als Produzenten öffentlicher Güter", Wirtschaftspolitische Blätter, 30, 145-154.

(10) Samuelson, Paul A. (1969), "Pure theory of public expenditure and taxation", in: Margolis, Julius, and Guitton, Henri (eds.), *Public Economics*, New York, 98-123.

Comment on R. Pethig: "Free Riders and Voluntary Contributions Reconsidered"

by

Charles B. Blankart

Rüdiger Pethig presents an illuminating new procedure for revealing the demand for public goods. His contribution is a very valuable one in an important and growing field of research. His proposal can be evaluated from a normative and a positive point of view, normative in the sense of what rule should be applied for eliciting undistorted demands for public goods, and positive in the sense of explaining why institutions supplying public goods can survive. Let me first address the normative problem and then turn to the positive one. What should a lobby manager do to reduce free riding for the services he produces? Pethig proposes that he should levy uniform dues upon the members of the organization. Uniform membership-dues imply (according to Pethig) an all-or-nothing choice and therefore give more of an incentive to the individuals to participate in the financing of a public good than e.g. voluntary provision. All-or-nothing choice increases the detrimental effects of free riding for an individual and therefore makes such a behavior less attractive.

Pethig's uniform membership-dues procedure may be devided in two steps for expository purposes: First, a mutually beneficial bargain is struck between the supplying entrepreneur and one single buyer. This result, however, is supposed to be stable only in the limiting case. For the single buyer could benefit from attracting more demanders who are willing to share his costs. In the second step therefore the demander will negotiate with the supplier for proposing other all-or-nothing choices implying larger numbers of buyers. To understand the influence of group size, one has to consider that Pethig's all-or-nothing choice takes place only at the margin, i.e. for one additional member of the lobby. This "marginal" effect is likely to be very small when group size is large, e.g. 1 million or so, though Pethig is right that an individual's incentives to reveal his true preferences are still larger in his procedure than under voluntary provision.

The second step is, however, not without difficulties. For here we are moving from a small group problem to a large group problem involving an increase of the incentive to behave stragegically. In my view this negative effect comes about quite apart of the positive effects implied in the all-or-nothing choice. It occurs always when group size grows.

But how could an alternative theory of a lobbying organization be designed? Or, more specifically, why do lobbying organizations exist? Here, the design of a conceptual history of lobbying organizations could help to understand the problem. With "conceptual history" I mean the methodological tool often used in economic textbooks to explain the existence e.g. of banks which are said to originate from goldsmith shops. How could such a conceptual history of the emergence of a lobbying organization look like? Three stages of development could be invisaged.

First, in the early stage of the development of an industry, lobbying is made independently by each firm on a voluntary basis. There is no coordination of activities. On a second level of development, some of these firms will see the potential economies of scale in coordinating their activities. They will form a lobbying organization under some statutory rules of collective decision making, while other firms remain outside the organization.

At the third stage, the lobbying organization will attempt to increase its membership and to eliminate free riding. If government support for establishing compulsory membership is unavailable, the lobbying organization has to search for other means to attract more members. As an information producing firm the lobbying organization may exploit its economies of scope to produce other sorts of information, particularly private good information, e.g. information on market trends and data, on changes in laws and regulations, consulting etc. So the lobbying organization will become a multiservice firm producing public goods in connection with private goods as it has been suggested by Olson more than 20 years ago. The multiproduct enterprise considered here will be stable in the market though it supplies some services unpriced. This is so because it exploits economies of scope. So, an old argument that Olsons's byproduct theory is not viable, is weakened.

Let me now contrast this positive view of a lobbying organization with Pethig's view that a lobbying organization sells its services under all-or-nothing contracts. One cannot resist that this latter explanation looks a little strange as compared with the former. But why? Strange is particularly Pethig's assumption on exclusion costs. Clearly assumptions cannot be criticized per se. But they shape the view of a problem and affect the relevance of an approach. Pethig assumes that the amount of exclusion costs a firm faces is given exogeneously. They are either zero as in the exclusive market provision procedure or infinite as in the voluntary contribution procedure and in the uniform membership-dues procedure. These assumptions are very unrealistic. For exclusion costs are instruments rather than data in an enterpreneur's supply policy. They are means for attracting more paying consumers. It is very unlikely that an entrepreneur will not use them for the goods he supplies as it is suggested in Pethig's uniform membership-dues procedure. But as soon as we allow some goods in his production bundle to be priced and some not, we end up again at Olson's byproduct theory. I wonder whether such an alternative explanation would not contribute as much to our understanding of why lobbying organizations exist as Pethig's uniform membership dues procedure.

Nevertheless, Pethig's paper is stimulating and interesting enough to think about. I also like Pethig's goal not to strive for an optimal, but only for a satisficing solution of the free rider problem.

Competition versus Monopoly in the Supply of Public Goods

by

Werner Güth and Martin Hellwig

I. Introduction

In an earlier paper (Güth and Hellwig (1986)), we studied the supply of a public good by a profit-maximizing monopolistic producer. A major finding of our analysis was that the private monopoly supply of a public good is inefficient because, as in the case of a private good, the monopolist makes his supply artificially scarce. In this paper we study the question whether the inefficiency would disappear if there was a sufficient amount of competition among actual or potential providers of the public good.

As in our earlier paper we consider a public good *without individual exclusion*. It is technically infeasible to provide this good selectively to some agents without providing it to everybody else as well. If the good is provided at all, then *all* potential users benefit from it. As examples of such a good, we may consider a water treatment plant which benefits all downstream users of water or Samuelson's (1954,1955) outdoor circus performance which anybody can watch if he likes. In contrast, an indoor circus performance would correspond to a public good *with* individual exclusion where anybody who does not pay for admission will not see the show.

Given the lack of exclusion on an individual basis, the supplier(s) of the public good must negotiate with the potential beneficiaries collectively. In this collective negotiation, a supplier will threaten not to supply the public good at all unless the users are willing to pay him a sufficient amount of money. The question then is how the presence or absence of another potential supplier affects his negotiating strength and negotiating strategy.

Relations between potential suppliers and users of the public good are characterized by the usual information and incentive problems. On the one hand, a profit-maximizing seller wants to know the public's willingness to pay for the public good so that he can extract as large a share of the surplus as possible. On the other hand, depending on how the payment for the public good is shared among the beneficiaries, each beneficiary may have an incentive to underreport his willingness to pay in order to reduce his payment to the supplier, or he may

Financial support by the Deutsche Forschungsgemeinschaft through the Sonderforschungsbereich 303 is gratefully acknowledged.

Pethig Schlieper (Eds.)
Efficiency, Institutions, and Economic Policy

have an incentive to overreport his willingness to pay in order to increase the chances of having the public good supplied at the other beneficiaries' expense.

Following the approach taken in our earlier paper, we study these issues by means of a *sequential game* with incomplete information. At the first stage of the game, each supplier proposes a *mechanism* for the provision of the public good, i.e. a system of rules which specify the conditions under which he will provide the public good and the amounts that the beneficiaries have to pay. At the second stage of the game, the potential beneficiaries vote on whether to accept one of the mechanisms that have been proposed. Approval of a mechanism must be unanimous so that no mechanism can be implemented which makes an agent worse off than he would be without the public good. If at this voting stage, a mechanism is accepted at all, then at the final stage of the game, the users of the public good implement this mechanism, i.e. they choose whatever actions serve as inputs for the mechanism and thereby determine a final outcome. At any one stage of the game, the different players moving at that stage do so independently and simultaneously. In making his decisions, each user of the public good is assumed to know his willingness to pay, but not that of any other user. Suppliers of the public good do not know any user's willingness to pay.

In our earlier paper we showed that from a welfare point of view it would be most desirable to implement a mechanism which entails the supply of the public good if and only if the aggregate surplus generated by the public good is positive, i.e. if the aggregate willingness to pay for the public good exceeds the cost of providing it. However, we also found that under the individual rationality constraints that are imposed by the voting stage of the game, such a first-best mechanism can only be implemented if it involves a set of payment schemes for the "buyers" of the public good that impose an expected loss on the supplier. Hence, in the absence of a subsidy from the "general" government budget, the first-best mechanism cannot be taken as a suitable welfare standard in an incomplete-information setting.

As an alternative, we therefore looked at second-best mechanisms, i.e. those mechanisms which maximize the expected aggregate surplus from the provision of the public good and which can still be implemented in an incentive-compatible way without imposing a loss on the supplier. Upon comparing such second-best mechanisms to the mechanisms that a profit-maximizing monopolistic supplier of the public good would propose, we found that any profit-maximizing mechanism is inefficient and involves an undersupply of the public good even though second-best mechanisms already involve a smaller supply than first-best mechanisms.

Taking this observation as the starting point for the present paper, we consider the question whether this inefficiency of the private supply of a public good will disappear if there is more than one potential supplier. With more than one supplier the first stage of our game may be interpreted as a *Bertrand model* in which the different suppliers bid for the franchise to supply the public good. As usual in Bertrand models, one might expect that in equilibrium the suppliers have to propose the second-best mechanism because otherwise a supplier who fails to get the franchise can improve his position by proposing another mechanism which the public prefers to whatever is currently available (see, e.g., Demsetz (1968)). In particular, such Bertrand competition should eliminate the inefficient monopoly solution.

This intuition is partly borne out by our results. We do indeed find equilibria of the sequential game in which each supplier proposes the second-best mechanism (which provides him with zero expected profits), at the second stage one of these suppliers is chosen, and finally the second-best mechanism is implemented.

However, we also find equilibria in which each supplier proposes the monopoly mechanism, one of the suppliers gets the franchise, and finally the monopoly mechanism is implemented. This result is due to the unanimity requirement at the second stage of the game. For suppose that at the first stage of the game one of the suppliers who do not get the franchise deviates to proposing a mechanism which the public unanimously prefers to the monopoly mechanism. Given the choice between the monopoly mechanism and the preferred mechanism, there may still be a unanimous vote for the monopoly mechanism. The point is that given the other buyers' votes for the monopoly mechanism, a single voter expects a vote for the alternative mchanism to lead to a split vote and hence to the non-supply of the public good rather than acceptance of the alternative mechanism.

Our analysis thus points to an important difference between competition in the supply of private goods and competition in the supply of public goods. Competition in the supply of private goods involves an attempt to find favour with individuals. Each individual knows what he wants and can award the prize to the supplier whose offer comes closest to the optimum. In contrast, competition in the supply of public goods involves an attempt to find favour with a social body. Even if each member of the community knows what he or she wants, the aggregation of these indiviudal preferences still involves a problem of social choice. The actual outcome here will of course depend upon the rules of the voting game among the buyers of the public good. However, there is no presumption that the collective will pick the "best" supplier with the same rigour as the individual. As we mentioned above, simultaneous unanimity voting may be stuck at an inefficient solution. Of course, this difficulty would not arise under majority voting. However, under majority voting, the game in which the suppliers bid for the franchise to supply the public good does not have an equilibrium in pure strategies at all because a firm that is left out in the cold can always upset a given solution by proposing a mechanism that appeals to a majority of underdogs.

Beyond the special model that we analyse, our results have important implications for the general theory of natural monopoly. Beginning with Demsetz (1968), a number of authors (e.g. Goldberg (1976), v. Weizsäcker (1980)) have proposed not to regulate natural monopolies, but to organize auctions at which various potential suppliers bid for the right to run the natural monopoly by proposing a price structure (e.g. a single price, or a two-part tariff), a quality level, etc. In theory, the franchise should be awarded to the "best" bid. However, except for the case of unidimensional bids involving only a price, it is not clear how the "best" bid is to be determined. Presumably, this is a problem of social choice which involves the same difficulties as the award of the franchise to supply a public good in the present paper.

The paper is organized as follows. Section 2 develops the basic conceptual framework. Section 3 surveys some results of our earlier paper, including in particular the characterization of monopoly, first-best and second-best mechnisms. Section 4 contains our analysis of voting to choose the supplier of the public good.

II. The Model

As in our earlier paper, we study the provision of a public good which comes as a single indivisible unit. There are m potential suppliers and n potential users of the public good. There is no exclusion on an individual basis, i.e. once the public good has been provided, nobody can be denied its use. One can only exclude *all* potential users jointly by not providing the public good at all.

The basic allocation problem is to determine in what circumstances the public good is to be provided, which of the m suppliers is to provide it, and what payments are to be made from users to suppliers. Two distinct issues arise. First, given that the provision of the public good is a natural monopoly, how is the monopoly franchise to be awarded? Second, given that individual exclusion is not feasible, how are the beneficiaries of the public good made to pay for its use?

As in our earlier paper, we look at the second issue as a problem of mechanism design. By a *mechanism*, we understand a set of rules which specify the conditions under which the public good is made available as well as the payments that the beneficiaries have to make to the supplier. We allow for stochastic rules so that e.g. in any situation the supplier may randomize over whether he makes the public good available. Formally, a mechanism then is a vector $\mu = (A, q, p)$ such that:

(2.1) $A = (A_1, ..., A_n)$, and A_i is a set of feasible actions for beneficiary i;

(2.2) $q: A \rightarrow [0,1]$ is a function that indicates for each $(a_1, ..., a_n) \in A$ the probability $q(a_1,...,a_n)$ that the public good is provided if the potential users take actions $a_1, ..., a_n$;

(2.3) $p = (p_1,..., p_n): A \rightarrow \mathbf{R}_+{}^n$ is a vector-valued function that indicates for each $(a_1,...,a_n) \in A$ the expected payment $p_i(a_1,...,a_n)$ of any user i to the supplier if the users 1,...,n take actions $a_1, ..., a_n$.

A concrete example of such a mechanism is provided by a bidding scheme under which each potential user of the public good submits a bid $a_i \in \mathbb{R}_+$ knowing that the public good will be provided and the bids will be paid up if and only if the sum of the bids exceeds a critical revenue level $\rho \geq 0$. For a given value of ρ, such a bidding scheme corresponds to the mechanism

$\mu^\rho = (\mathbb{R}_+{}^n, q^\rho, p^\rho)$ such that $q^\rho(a_1, ..., a_n) = 1$ and for $i = 1, ..., n$, $p^\rho{}_i(a_1, ..., a_n) = a_i$ if and only if

$$\sum_{i=1}^{n} a_i > \rho,$$

whereas $q^\rho(a_1, ..., a_n) = 0$ and for $i = 1, ..., n$, $p^\rho{}_i(a_1, ..., a_n) = 0$ if

$$\sum_{i=1}^{n} a_i \leq \rho.$$

We assume that the potential suppliers compete with each other to obtain the monopoly franchise for providing the public good. For this purpose, each supplier k proposes a mechanism μ^k which is to be implemented if he receives the franchise. Given the proposed mechanisms $\mu^1, ..., \mu^m$, the potential users vote on which proposal, if any, is to be accepted. A supplier receives the franchise if *all* potential users vote for his proposal. If there is a split vote, then *no* supplier receives the franchise and the public good is not provided.

We require voting to be unanimous because we want to ensure that a mechanism is not implemented unless it is individually rational. In contrast, under majority voting, a conspiracy between a supplier and a majority of the voters might impose a mechanism that exploits the minority. We realize that in practice this type of redistribution among voters plays an important role. Nevertheless, we want to abstract from it in order to concentrate on the competition among suppliers. Therefore, we impose the unanimity condition, which gives each potential user of the public good a veto against any supplier and any proposed mechanism. We prefer this method of deriving individual rationality from the underlying strategic interactions over a formulation with majority voting and an exogenous constraint that only individually rational mechanisms can be proposed.

Altogether, the strategic interactions between potential suppliers and potential users of the public good have the following sequential structure.

Stage 1: Each potential supplier $k = 1, ..., m$ independently proposes a mechanism $\mu^k = (A^k, q^k, p^k)$.

Stage 2: Each potential user $i = 1, ..., n$ independently chooses a vote $V_i = k$ for one of the proposed mechanisms μ^k or a vote $V_i = 0$ to reject all proposed mechanisms. If none of the mechanisms $\mu^1, ..., \mu^m$ is accepted unanimously, the game ends.

Stage 3: If a mechanism μ^k has been unanimously accepted, then each potential user i = 1, ..., n of the public good independently chooses an action a_i from his action set A_i^k.

We assume that all potential suppliers and all potential beneficiaries of the public good are risk neutral. All suppliers have the same cost $c \geq 0$ of providing the public good. Beneficiary i assigns a money value $v_i \in [0,1]$ to the use of the public good. If the mechanism $\mu^k = (A^k, q^k, p^k)$ of supplier k is accepted and if the actions $a_1, ..., a_n$ are taken at stage 3 then the payoffs are:

(2.4) $$v_i q^k(a_1, ..., a_n) - p_i^k(a_1, ..., a_n)$$

for beneficiaries i = 1, ..., n ,

(2.5) $$\sum_{i=1}^{n} p_i^k(a_1, ..., a_n) - cq^k(a_1, ..., a_n)$$

for supplier k, and zero for the other suppliers. If no mechansim is accepted at stage 2, then all potential beneficiaries and suppliers receive zero payoffs.

For i = 1, ..., n, the valuation v_i of beneficiary i is taken to be known by himself, but not by any of the other beneficiaries of the public good or by any of the suppliers. In contrast, the production cost c is taken to be common knowledge among all agents.

We have thus specified a strategic game with incomplete information among the m potential suppliers and n potential users of the public good. Following Harsanyi (1967/68), we transform this game into a game with complete, but imperfect information. We introduce a prior stage 0 at which nature as an additional player chooses the vector $v = (v_1, ..., v_n)$ of valuations for the public good according to the joint probability distribution F, which is known to all players. We assume that the valuations $v_1, ..., v_n$ are mutually independent so that F may be written as $F = F_1 \times .... \times F_n$. At stage 1, the suppliers of the public good do not know nature's choice and must rely on their knowledge of the distribution F. At stages 2 and 3, each user i of the public good knows his component v_i of the vector v, but *not* the vector v_{-i} of the other components of v. Therefore, he must rely on his knowledge of the probability distribution $F_{-i} = F_1 \times .... \times F_{i-1} \times F_{i+1} \times ... \times F_n$ of the vector v_{-i}.

In the game with imperfect information, a pure strategy for supplier k is simply the choice of a mechanism μ^k. A pure strategy for user i is an (m+1)-tuple of functions $(V_i, f_i^1, ..., f_i^m)$ such that for any valuation $v_i \in [0,1]$ and any possible constellation $\underline{\mu} = (\mu^1, ..., \mu^m)$ of proposed mechanisms, $V_i(v_i, \underline{\mu}) \in \{0, 1, 2, ..., m\}$ is his vote at stage 2, and for k = 1, ..., m, the choice $f^k_i(v_i, \underline{\mu}) \in A_i^k$ is his action at stage 3 if supplier k with the mechanism μ^k has been awarded the franchise. A mixed (behavioural) strategy for user i is an (m+1)–tuple of functions $(V_i^*, \phi^*{}_i^1, ..., \phi^*{}_i^m)$ that associate with $(v_i, \underline{\mu})$ a probability measure $V_i^*(\,.\,; v_i, \underline{\mu})$ over the set $\{0,1, \ldots, m\}$ of possible votes at stage 2 and for $k = 1, \ldots, m$, a probability measure $\phi^{*k}_i(\,.\,; v_i, \underline{\mu})$ over the set A_i^k of feasible actions under the mechanism μ^k at stage 3. For simplicity, we denote the probability of a vote for supplier k as $V^{*k}_i(v_i, \underline{\mu})$ rather than $V^*_i(\{k\}; v_i, \underline{\mu})$ and the probability of a vote against all proposals as $V^{*0}_i(v_i, \underline{\mu})$ rather than $V^*_i(\{0\}; v_i, \underline{\mu})$.

Given an n-tuple $(V^*_i, \phi^{*1}_i, \ldots, \phi^{*m}_i)^n_{i=1}$ of mixed strategies for users $1, \ldots, n$, we write Ψ for the n-tuple (V_i^*) of voting strategies for stage 2 and Φ for the n-tuple $(\phi^*_i)^n_{i=1}$ of action strategies $\phi^*_i = (\phi^{*1}_i, \ldots, \phi^{*m}_i)$ for stage 3. Given nature's choice v, the constellation $\underline{\mu} = (\mu^1, \ldots, \mu^m)$ of proposed mechanisms, and the constellation $\Psi = (V_i^*)$ of voting strategies, the probability that supplier k receives the franchise at stage 2 is

$$\text{(2.6)} \qquad \Pi^k(v, \underline{\mu}, \psi) = V^{*k}_1(v_1, \underline{\mu}) \times \ldots \times V^{*k}_n(v_n, \underline{\mu}).$$

If supplier k receives the franchise at stage 2, then the payoffs at stage 3 are

$$\text{(2.7)} \qquad u_i^k(v, \underline{\mu}, \Phi) = \int_{A^k} \left[v_i q^k(.) - p_i^k(.) \right] d\phi_1^{*k}(.\,; v_1, \underline{\mu}) \ldots d\phi_n^{*k}(.\,; v_n, \underline{\mu})$$

for users $i = 1, \ldots, n$ and

$$\text{(2.8)} \qquad u_S^k(v, \underline{\mu}, \Phi) = \int_{A^k} \left[\sum_{i=1}^{n} p_i^k(.) - c q^k(.) \right] d\phi_1^{*k}(.\,; v_1, \underline{\mu}) \ldots d\phi_n^{*k}(.\,; v_n, \underline{\mu})$$

for supplier k. Hence the overall ex ante expected payoffs under the strategies $\underline{\mu}$, ψ, Φ are

$$\text{(2.9)} \qquad U_i(\underline{\mu}, \psi, \Phi) = \sum_{k=1}^{m} \int \Pi^k(v, \underline{\mu}, \psi)\, u_i^k(v, \underline{\mu}, \phi)\, dF(v)$$

for users $i = 1, \ldots, n$ and

$$\text{(2.10)} \qquad U_S^k(\underline{\mu}, \psi, \Phi) = \int \Pi^k(v, \underline{\mu}, \psi)\, u_S^k(v, \underline{\mu}, \phi)\, dF(v)$$

for suppliers $k = 1, \ldots, m$.

A strategy constellation $(\underline{\mu}, \psi, \Phi)$ is a *Nash equilibrium* if the following conditions hold:

(2.11) For $k = 1, \ldots, m$ and any alternative proposal $\hat{\mu}^k$ for supplier k,

$$U_S^k(\mu^1, \ldots, \mu^{k-1}, \hat{\mu}^k, \mu^{k+1}, \ldots, \mu^m, \psi, \Phi) \leq U_i^k(\underline{\mu}, \psi, \Phi).$$

(2.12) For $i = 1, \ldots, n$ and any alternative strategy

$$(\hat{V}_i, \hat{\phi}_i^1, \ldots, \hat{\phi}_i^m)$$

for user i,

$$U_i(\underline{\mu}, (V_1^*, \phi_1^{*1}, \ldots, \phi_1^{*m}), \ldots, (\hat{V}_i, \hat{\phi}_i^1, \ldots, \hat{\phi}_i^m), \ldots, (V_n^*, \phi_n^{*1}, \ldots, \phi_n^{*m})) \leq U_i(\underline{\mu}, \psi, \Phi).$$

In addition to the Nash equilibrium conditions (2.11) and (2.12), we want to impose some *sequential rationality conditions*. Without such additional conditions, there are trivial no-trade equilibria of the following type: Every supplier proposes a mechanism in which the supply probability for the public good as well as the payments from the users to the supplier are identically equal to zero; the proposal of an alternative mechanism is not profitable because any such proposal would be vetoed; the strategy of vetoing any alternative proposal is acceptable because in equilibrium no such proposal is made, so that the vetoes are never actually implemented.

We find it implausible that votes on alternative proposals should be justified solely by the consideration that these votes do not matter because in equilibrium, the proposal in question will never actually be made. Voting on any set $\underline{\mu}$ of mechanisms should rather be based on outcomes that these mechanisms may yield. Similarly, an action that one plans to take at stage 3 under a mechanism μ should be chosen not because one expects that μ will never be implemented anyway, but because the action is the best one can take in the situation in which one is called upon to take it.

Formally, we say that $(V^*_i(\,.\,, \hat{\underline{\mu}}), \phi^*_i(\,.\,, \hat{\underline{\mu}}))^n_{i=1}$, is an *equilibrium continuation for the offer constellation* $\hat{\underline{\mu}}$ if the following conditions are satisfied:

(2.13) For any supplier k, any buyer i, any valuation $v_i \in [0,1]$ and any alternative $\hat{\phi}_i$ of buyer i for stage 3,

$$\int u_i^k(v, \hat{\underline{\mu}}, \phi_1^*, \ldots, \hat{\phi}_i, \ldots, \phi_n^*)\, dF_{-i}(v_{-i} \mid k, \hat{\underline{\mu}}) \leq \int u_i^k(v, \hat{\underline{\mu}}, (\phi_j^*))\, dF_{-i}(v_{-i} \mid k, \hat{\underline{\mu}}),$$

where $F_{-i}(\,.\, \mid k, \hat{\underline{\mu}}) \in \mathcal{M}([0,1]^{n-1})$ is a regular conditional distribution of v_{-i} given the event

$$\left\{ \bigtimes_{j \neq i} V_j^k(v_j', \hat{\underline{\mu}}) = 1 \right\}$$

that at the offer constellation $\underline{\mu}$, all agents $j \neq i$ vote for supplier k.

(2.14) For any supplier k, any buyer i and any valuation $v_i \in [0,1]$,

$$V^{*k}_i(v_i, \hat{\underline{\mu}}) = 0 \text{ if} \int u_i^k(v, \hat{\underline{\mu}}, (\phi_j^*))\, dF_{-i}(v_{-i} \mid k, \hat{\underline{\mu}}) < 0.$$

(2.15) For any buyer i and any valuation $v_i \in [0,1]$,

$$V^{*0}_i(v_i, \hat{\underline{\mu}}) = 0 \text{ if} \int u_i^k(v, \hat{\underline{\mu}}, (\phi_j^*))\, dF_{-i}(v_{-i} \mid k, \hat{\underline{\mu}}) > 0$$

for some k.

Let $\underline{M}$ be the set of offer constellations $\underline{\mu}$ for which an equilibrium continuation exists. In the spirit of Kreps and Wilson (1982), we say that a Nash equilibrium $(\underline{\mu}, \psi, \Phi) = (\underline{\mu}, (V^*_i), (\phi^*_i))$ is a *sequential equilibrium* if for every $\hat{\underline{\mu}} \in \underline{M}$, $(V^*_i(\,.\,, \hat{\underline{\mu}}), \phi^*_i(\,.\,, \hat{\underline{\mu}}))^n_{i=1}$ is an equilibrium continuation for $\hat{\underline{\mu}}$.

Without loss of generality, we restrict our analysis to sequential equilibria with offer constellations $\underline{\mu} \in \underline{M}$. If an offer constellation $\underline{\mu}$ does not belong to $\underline{M}$, then for one or more suppliers k, the mechanism μ^k must involve a discontinuity or noncompactness which causes difficulties for the equilibrium condition (2.13) at stage 3. If $\underline{\mu}$ nevertheless arises in a Nash equilibrium of the overall game, then the voting strategies at stage 2 must ensure that these mechanisms μ^k are rejected whenever (2.13) cannot be satisfied at the third stage. But then the equilibrium involves the same allocation as another equilibrium with offer constellation $\tilde{\underline{\mu}} \in \underline{M}$ where for each k, $\tilde{\mu}^k$ is a mechanism which yields the same results as μ^k in those circumstances in which μ^k is accepted and which involves a zero supply probability and zero payments in those circumstances in which μ^k is not accepted at stage 2. Hence we do not lose anything by considering only equilibria with mechanisms in $\underline{M}$.

III. Profit-Maximizing versus Welfare-Maximizing Revelation Mechanisms

In this section we discuss some mechanisms that play a central role in our analysis. First we need some terminology. A mechnism $\mu = (A, q, p)$ is called *direct* if $A_i = [0,1]$ for $i = 1, \dots, n$, with the interpretation that each buyer i just announces a money value $\hat{v}_i \in A_i$ that he assigns to the public good. We are interested in direct mechanisms that induce buyers to tell the truth, i.e. to always announce a money value $\hat{v}_i$ equal to the true value v_i. However, each agent i's behaviour at the third stage of the game depends on his probabilistic beliefs $\hat{F}_{-i}(\,.\,)$ about the vector v_{-i} of the other buyers' valuations for the public good. A direct mechanism $\mu = ([0,1]^n, q, p)$ will be called *incentive compatible under the beliefs* $(\hat{F}_{-i})^n_{i=1}$ if for every buyer i, any valuation $v_i \in [0,1]$ and any measure ϕ^*_i on [0,1],

(3.1)
$$\int_{[0,1]^n} [v_i q(v_1, \dots, \hat{v}_i, \dots, v_n) - p_i(v_1, \dots, \hat{v}_i, \dots, v_n)]\, d\hat{F}_{-i}(v_{-i})\, d\phi^*_i(\hat{v}_i)$$

$$\leq \int_{[0,1]^{n-1}} [v_i q(v_1, \dots, v_i, \dots, v_n) - p_i(v_1, \dots, v_i, \dots, v_n)]\, d\hat{F}_{-i}(v_{-i}),$$

i.e. if truthtelling is a Bayesian-Nash equilibrium under the beliefs $(\hat{F}_{-i})$ at the third stage. A constellation of direct mechanisms $\underline{\mu} = (\mu^1, \dots, \mu^m)$ will be called *incentive compatible* if there exists an equilibrium continuation $(V^*_i(\,.\,, \underline{\mu}), \phi^*_i(\,.\,, \underline{\mu}))^n_{i=1}$ for $\underline{\mu}$ such that for each k, the mechanism μ^k is incentive compatible under the (regular conditional) beliefs $(F_{-i}(\,.\,|k, \underline{\mu}))^n_{i=1}$ that are determined (up to null sets, which we disregard) by the voting strategies (V^*_j) according to (2.13). Such an incentive compatible constellation of direct mechanisms will be referred to as a *revelation offer constellation*. The corresponding equilibrium continuation $(V^*_i(.,\underline{\mu}), \phi^*_i(.,\underline{\mu}))^n_{i=1}$ is called the *revelation continuation* for $\underline{\mu}$.

By the well-known *revelation principle* (see, e.g., Dasgupta, Hammond, and Maskin (1979), Myerson (1979), and also Section 3 of Güth and Hellwig (1986)) we can restrict our analysis to revelation offer constellations and continuations. We say that two offer constellations $\underline{\mu}$ and $\hat{\underline{\mu}}$ with equilibrium continuations $(V^*_i(.,\underline{\mu}), \phi^*_i(.,\underline{\mu}))$ and $V^*_i(.,\hat{\underline{\mu}}), \phi^*_i(.,\hat{\underline{\mu}}))$ are *equivalent* if they satisfay the conditions:

(3.1) $$V_i^{*k}(v_i,\underline{\mu}) = V_i^{*k}(v_i,\hat{\underline{\mu}})$$
for $i = 1, \ldots, n$, all $v_i \in [0,1]$, and all k;

(3.2) $$\int_{A^k} q^k(.)\,d\phi_1^{*k}(.;v_1,\underline{\mu}) \ldots d\phi_n^{*k}(.;v_n,\underline{\mu}) = \int_{\hat{A}^k} \hat{q}^k(.)\,d\phi_1^{*k}(.;v_1,\hat{\underline{\mu}}) \ldots d\phi_n^{*k}(.;v_n,\hat{\underline{\mu}})$$
for all k and $v = (v_1, \ldots, v_n) \in [0,1]^n$;

(3.3) $$\int_{A^k} p_i^k(.)\,d\phi_1^{*k}(.;v_1,\underline{\mu}) \ldots d\phi_n^{*k}(.;v_n,\underline{\mu}) = \int_{\hat{A}^k} \hat{p}_i^k(.)\,d\phi_1^{*k}(.;v_1,\hat{\underline{\mu}}) \ldots d\phi_n^{*k}(.;v_n,\hat{\underline{\mu}})$$
for all k, $i = 1, \ldots, n$, and $v = (v_1, \ldots, v_n) \in [0,1]$.

Any two equivalent offer constellations and continuations give rise to the same allocation, i.e., the same voting behaviours, the same supply probabilities and individual expected payments from buyers to sellers.

A sequential equilibrium $(\underline{\mu}, \psi, \Phi) = (\underline{\mu}, (V^*_i), (\phi^*_i))$ is called a *revelation equilibrium* if $\underline{\mu}$ is a revelation offer constellation and $(V^*_i(.,\underline{\mu}), \phi^*_i(.,\underline{\mu}))$ a revelation continuation for $\underline{\mu}$. The main implication of the revelation principle may now be stated as

Proposition 3.1: For any sequential equilibrium $(\underline{\mu}, (V^*_i), (\phi^*_i))$ there exists a revelation equilibrium $(\hat{\underline{\mu}}, (\hat{V}_i), (\hat{\phi}_i))$ such that $\underline{\mu}, (V^*_i(.,\underline{\mu}), \phi^*_i(.,\underline{\mu}))$ and $\hat{\underline{\mu}}, (\hat{V}_i(.,\hat{\underline{\mu}}), \hat{\phi}_i(.,\hat{\underline{\mu}}))$ are equivalent.

Apart from some obvious modifications, the proof of Proposition 3.1 is the same as that of Proposition 3.2 in Güth and Hellwig (1986) and is left to the reader. Proposition 3.1 shows that we can restrict our attention to revelation equilibria without changing the equilibrium allocations in the game. This is convenient because revelation equilibria are much easier to analyse.

The condition of incentive compatibility imposes strong conditions on revelation equilibria. Consider a strategy constellation $(\underline{\mu}, \psi, \Phi)$ such that for any k and j, ϕ^{*k}_j is a truthtelling strategy, i.e. $\phi^{*k}_j(v_j, \underline{\mu}) = \delta_{v_j}$ for all $v_j \in [0,1]$, where δ_{v_j} is the probability measure with unit mass at v_j. Given this strategy constellation, the question is what incentive a given buyer i has to implement ϕ^*_i at the third stage of the game. If the franchise has been awarded to seller k and if buyer i with a true value v_i announces the value $\hat{v}_i$, then his (conditionally) expected payoff is:

(3.4) $$v_i \int q^k(v_1, \ldots, \hat{v}_i, \ldots, v_n)\, dF_{-i}(v_{-i}|k,\underline{\mu}) - \int p_i^k(v_1, \ldots, \hat{v}_i, \ldots, v_n)\, dF_{-i}(v_{-i}|k,\underline{\mu}),$$

or more compactly,

(3.4') $$v_i Q_i^k(\hat{v}_i, \underline{\mu}, F_{-i}(.|k,\underline{\mu})) - P_i^k(\hat{v}_i, \underline{\mu}, F_{-i}(.|k,\underline{\mu})),$$

where we define

(3.5a) $$Q_i^k(\hat{v}_i, \underline{\mu}, F_{-i}(.|k,\underline{\mu})) := \int q^k(v_1, \ldots, \hat{v}_i, \ldots, v_n)\, dF_{-i}(v_{-i}|k,\underline{\mu})$$

and

(3.5b) $$P_i^k(\hat{v}_i, \underline{\mu}, F_{-i}(.|k,\underline{\mu})) := \int p_i^k(v_1, \ldots, \hat{v}_i, \ldots, v_n)\, dF_{-i}(v_{-i}|k,\underline{\mu}).$$

If truthtelling actually is optimal for buyer i, then for any $v_i \in [0,1]$, the payoff expectation (3.4') must be maximized by setting $\hat{v}_i = v_i$. A well known argument (see, e.g., van Damme (1985) or Güth and Hellwig (1986)) then yields the following characterization result:

Proposition 3.2: An offer constellation $\underline{\mu} = (\mu^1, \ldots, \mu^m)$ of direct mechanisms is a revelation offer constellation if and only if there exists a constellation (V^*_i) of voting strategies such for $k = 1, \ldots, m$ and $i = 1, \ldots, n$, the following are true:

i: The expression

$$Q_i^k(\hat{v}_i, \underline{\mu}, F_{-i}(.|k,\underline{\mu}))$$

in (3.5a) is nondecreasing in $\hat{v}_i$.

ii: The expression

$$P_i^k(\hat{v}_i, \underline{\mu}, F_{-i}(.|k,\underline{\mu}))$$

in (3.5b) satisfies

(3.6) $$P_i^k(\hat{v}_i, \underline{\mu}, F_{-i}(.|k,\underline{\mu})) = P_i^k(0, \underline{\mu}, F_{-i}(.|k,\underline{\mu})) + \int_0^{\hat{v}_i} x\, dQ_i^k(x, \underline{\mu}, F_{-i}(.|k,\underline{\mu}))$$

for all $\hat{v}_i \in [0,1]$.

iii: For

(3.7a) $$\underline{v}_i^k := \sup\left\{ v_i \in [0,1] \,\Big|\, \int_0^{v_i} Q_i^k(x, \underline{\mu}, F_{-i}(.|k,\underline{\mu}))\, dx - P_i^k(0, \underline{\mu}, F_{-i}(.|k,\underline{\mu})) \le 0 \right\},$$

the voting strategy $V^{*k}_{i}(\,.\,,\underline{\mu})$ satisfies:

(3.7b) either

$$Q^k_i(\underline{v}^k_i, \underline{\mu}, F_{-i}(.\,|k, \underline{\mu})) = P^k_i(0, \underline{\mu}, F_{-i}(.\,|k, \underline{\mu})) = 0,$$

or

$$V^{*k}_i(v_i, \underline{\mu}) = 0 \text{ if } v_i < \underline{v}^k_i .$$

Moreover

(3.7c) $$V^{*0}_i(v_i, \underline{\mu}) = 0 \text{ if } v_i > \min_k \underline{v}^k_i$$

With some obvious modifications, the proof of Proposition 3.2 is again the same as the proof of Proposition 3.3 in Güth and Hellwig (1986) and is left to the reader. Conditions (ii) and (i) are roughly the same as the requirement that for all $v_i \in [0,1]$, the announcement $\hat{v}_i = v_i$ satisfy the first and second order conditions for maximizing the payoff expectation (3.4'). Given the structure provided by (i) and (ii), condition (iii) is simply a reformulation of (2.14) and 2.15).

Proposition 3.2 can be used to evaluate the different agents' expected payoffs from a revelation offer constellation and continuation. Conditions (i) - (iii) imply that the expected payment from buyer i to seller k is entirely determined by the seller's supply probability function q^k and the different buyers' voting strategies. Formally we have:

Lemma 3.3: Let $\underline{\mu}$ be a revelation offer constellation and let $(V^*_j(\,.\,,\underline{\mu}), \phi^*_j(\,.\,,\underline{\mu}))$ be a revelation continuation for $\underline{\mu}$. Then the expected payment from buyer i to seller k is:

(3.8) $$\int \Pi^k(v, \underline{\mu}, (V^*_j))\, p^k_i(v)\, dF(v)$$

$$= \int \Pi^k(v, \underline{\mu}, (V^*_j))\, q^k(v)\, v_i\, dF(v)$$

$$- \int \Pi^k(v, \underline{\mu}, (V^*_j)) \int_{\underline{v}^k_i}^{v_i} q^k(x, v_{-i})\, dx\, dF(v) .$$

The proof of this lemma replicates the proof of formula (4.4) in Güth and Hellwig (1986) and is left to the reader. The interpretation of formula (3.8) is fairly straightforward. Consider a given valuation vector v. At this valuation vector, $\Pi^k(v, \underline{\mu}, (V^*_j))\, q^k(v)$ is the effective probability that supplier k provides the public good, and v_i is the benefit that buyer i obtains in this case. Hence the first term is simply the expectation of the benefit to buyer i of the provision of the public good by supplier k.

The second term in (3.8) corresponds to the fact that the incentive compatibility constraints prevent the supplier from appropriating *all* the benefits that he generates. A buyer with a valuation $v_i > 0$ can always ensure himself a strictly positive payoff by pretending to have a valuation $\hat{v}_i = v_i / 2$. Given the report $\hat{v}_i = v_i / 2$, the seller can at most appropriate benefit that corresponds to the valuation $v_i / 2$, leaving the buyer with the expectation of the difference $v_i - \hat{v}_i = v_i - v_i / 2 = v_i / 2$, which is strictly positive unless the report $\hat{v}_i$ entails the nonsupply of the public good with probability one. Formally, these considerations appear in the incentive-compatibility constraint (3.6) because the integral on the right hand side is less than $v_i\, Q_i^k(\hat{v}_i, \underline{\mu}, F_{-i}(\,.\,|k, \underline{\mu}))$. Upon using integration by parts and the definition (3.7a) of $\underline{v}_i^k$ we can in fact rewrite (3.6) as

$$(3.6') \qquad P_i^k(\hat{v}_i, \underline{\mu}, F_{-i}(.|k, \underline{\mu})) = \hat{v}_i Q_i^k(\hat{v}_i, \underline{\mu}, F_{-i}(.|k, \underline{\mu})) - \int_{\underline{v}_i^k}^{\hat{v}_i} Q_i^k(x, \underline{\mu}, F_{-i}(.|k, \underline{\mu}))\,dx$$

for all $\hat{v}_i \in [0,1]$.

Now $P_i^k(v_i, \underline{\mu}, F_{-i}(\,.\,|\, k, \underline{\mu}))$ is strictly less than $v_i\, Q_i^k(v_i, \underline{\mu}, F_{-i}(\,.\,|\, k, \underline{\mu}))$ whenever $v_i > \underline{v}_i^k$. The second term in expression (3.8) reflects the same difference between consumer i's expected benefits and his expected payments.

If we use expression (3.8) to substitute for the consumers' expected payments in (2.7) – (2.10), we obtain:

Proposition 3.4: Let $\underline{\mu}$ be a revelation offer constellation and let $(V^*_j(\,.\,, \underline{\mu}), \phi^*_j(\,.\,, \underline{\mu}))$ be a revelation continuation for $\underline{\mu}$. Then supplier k's expected profit is:

$$(3.9) \qquad U_S^k(\underline{\mu}, (V_j^*), (\phi_j^*)) = \int \Pi^k(v, \underline{\mu}, (V_j^*))\, q^k(v) \left[\sum_{i=1}^n v_i - c\right] dF(v)$$

$$- \int \Pi^k(v, \underline{\mu}, (V_j^*)) \sum_{i=1}^n \int_{\underline{v}_i^k}^{v_i} q^k(x, v_{-i})\,dx\,dF(v).$$

Buyer i's expected payoff is

$$(3.10) \qquad U_i(\underline{\mu}, (V_j^*), (\phi_j^*))$$

$$= \sum_{k=1}^m \int \Pi^k(v, \underline{\mu}, (V_j^*)) \int_{\underline{v}_i^k}^{v_i} q^k(x, v_{-i})\,dx\,dF(v).$$

For any valuation vector v, $\Pi^k(v, \underline{\mu}, (V^*_j))\, q^k(v)$ is again the effective probability that supplier k provides the public good, and

$$\sum_{i=1}^n v_i - c$$

is the aggregate surplus that is generated by the provision of the public good. Thus the first term in (3.9) is just the expectation of the aggregate surplus from the provision of the public good by supplier k. From this aggregate surplus we again have to subtract that portion of the buyers' benefits that the supplier cannot appropriate because of the incentive-compatibility constraints. For any buyer i, the expected payoff (3.10) then is simply the sum over all suppliers of the differences between his individual expected benefits from the provision of the public good and his expected payments for the provision of the public good.

In the monopoly case (m=1), expressions (3.9) and (3.10) are particularly simple. In this case, condition (3.7c) implies $V^*_i{}^1(v_i, \underline{\mu}) = 1$ if $v_i > \underline{v}_i{}^1$ and hence $\Pi^1(v, \underline{\mu}, (V^*_j)) = 1$ if

$$v \in \mathop{\times}_{j=1}^{n} (\underline{v}_j^1, 1].$$

It is then easy to evaluate the double integrals in (3.9) and (3.10) through integration by parts. Specificially, if the distributions $F_1, \dots, F_n$ have strictly positive densities $f_1, \dots, f_n$, then for m = 1, expressions (3.9) and (3.10) may be rewritten as:

$$(3.11)\qquad U_S^1(\underline{\mu}, (V_j^*), (\phi_j^*)) = \int_Y q^1(v) \left\{ \sum_{i=1}^{n} \left[v_i - \frac{1-F_i(v_i)}{f_i(v_i)} \right] - c \right\} dF(v)$$

and

$$(3.12)\qquad U_i(\underline{\mu}, (V_j^*), (\phi_j^*)) = \int_Y q^1(v) \frac{1-F_i(v_i)}{f_i(v_i)} dF(v),$$

where $Y = (\underline{v}_1{}^1, 1] \times \dots \times (\underline{v}_n{}^1, 1]$.

A direct mechanism μ^* is called a *profit-maximizing revelation mechanism* if there exists a revelation continuation $(V^*_i(\,.\,, (\mu^*)), \phi^*_i(\,.\,, (\mu^*)))$ for the monopoly offer (μ^*) such that for m=1, $U_S{}^1((\mu^*), (V^*_i), (\phi^*_i))$ is maximal over all revelation offer constellations and continuations. If μ^* is a profit-maximizing revelation mechanism, one easily shows that for m=1, there exists a constellation $(V^*_i, \phi^*_i)_{i=1}{}^n$ of buyers' strategies such that $(V^*_i(\,.\,, (\mu^*))$, $\phi^*_i(\,.\,, (\mu^*))$ is a revelation continuation for (μ^*), $((\mu^*), (V^*_i), (\phi^*_i))$ is a sequential equilibrium, and moreover there exists no other sequential equilibrium that the monopolist prefers to $((\mu^*), (V^*_i), (\phi^*_i))$ (Güth and Hellwig (1986), Proposition 4.1).

Equation (3.11) suggests that the monopolist's profits are maximized by the mechanism $\mu^* = ([0,1]^n, q^*, p^*)$ such that

$$(3.13)\qquad q^*(v) = \begin{cases} 0 & \text{if } \sum_{i=1}^{n} \left[v_i - \frac{1-F_i(v_i)}{f_i(v_i)} \right] \le c \\ 1 & \text{if } \sum_{i=1}^{n} \left[v_i - \frac{1-F_i(v_i)}{f_i(v_i)} \right] > c \end{cases}$$

for any $v \in [0,1]^n$, and for $i = 1, \ldots, n$,

$$(3.14)\qquad p_i^*(v) = \int_0^{v_i} x \, dQ_i^*(x)$$

for any $v \in [0,1]^n$, regardless of v_{-i}, where for $v_i \in [0,1]$,

$$(3.15)\qquad Q_i^*(v_i) = \int q^*(v) \, dF_{-i}(v_{-i})$$

is the conditional expectation of $q^*(\,.\,)$ given v_i. To ensure that μ^* actually is a revelation mechanism, we impose the assumption

A.1: For $i = 1, \ldots, n$, the distribution F_i has strictly positive density f_i; the hazard rate $f(v_i)/(1-F_i(v_i))$ is a nondecreasing function of v_i.

Under Assumption A.1, $q^*(v)$ and hence $Q^*_i(v_i)$ are nondecreasing in v_i. Given the voting strategies V^*_i such that $V^{*1}_i(v_i, (\mu^*)) = 1$ for all $v_i \in [0,1]$ and $i = 1, \ldots, n$, we have $Q_i^1(v_i, (\mu^*), F_{-i}(\,.\,, |1, (\mu^*))) = Q^*_i(v_i)$ for all $v_i \in [0,1]$ and $i = 1, \ldots, n$ so that under A.1,the incentive compatibility condition (i) of Proposition 3.2 is automatically fulfilled. Since (3.14) implies that conditions (ii) and (iii) of Proposition 3.2 are also satisfied, it follows that unanimous approval and truthtelling are indeed a revelation continuation for the monopoly offer (μ^*). Using (3.11) one can therefore show easily that μ^* is indeed a profit-maximizing revelation mechanism (Güth and Hellwig (1986), Proposition 4.3).

We contrast the results of profit maximization by a monopolist with the results of welfare maximization. As our welfare criterion, we take the expectation of the aggregate surplus

$$\sum_{i=1}^{n} v_i - c$$

from the provision of the public good. A direct mechanism μ^F is called a *first-best welfare-maximizing mechanism* if there exists a revelation continuation $(V^*_i(\,.\,, (\mu^F)), \phi^*_i(\,.\,, (\mu^F)))$ for the monopolist's offer (μ^F) such that for $m = 1$, the expectation

$$W((\mu^F), (V_j^*), (\phi_j^*)) = \int \Pi^1(v, (\mu^F), (V_j^*)) \, q^F(v) \left[\sum_{i=1}^{n} v_i - c \right] dF(v)$$

is maximal over all revelation offer constellations and continuations. Under Assumption A.1, one easily finds that a first-best welfare-maximizing mechanism is given by $\mu^F = ([0,1]^n, q^F, p^F)$ where

$$(3.16) \qquad q^F(v) = \begin{cases} 0 & \text{if } \sum_{i=1}^{n} v_i \leq c \\ 1 & \text{if } \sum_{i=1}^{n} v_i > c \end{cases}$$

for any $v \in [0,1]^n$ and for $i = 1, \ldots, n$,

$$(3.17) \qquad p_i^F(v) = \int_0^{v_i} x \, dQ_i^F(x)$$

for any $v \in [0,1]^n$, regardless of v_{-i}, where for $v_i \in [0,1]$,

$$(3.18) \qquad Q_i^F(v_i) := \int q^F(v) \, dF_{-i}(v_{-i})$$

is the conditional expectation of q^F given v_i. Unfortunately though, the mechanism μ^F - and indeed any other first-best mechanism - imposes a loss on the supplier whenever $n \geq 2$ and $0 < c < n$ so that the public good is provided with positive probability (see Güth and Hellwig (1986), Propositions 5.1 - 5.4).

We are therefore lead to a second-best welfare analysis. A direct mechanism μ^S is called a *second-best welfare-maximizing mechanism* if there exists a revelation continuation $(V^*_i(\,.\,,(\mu^S)), \phi^*_i(\,.\,,(\mu^S)))$ for the monopolist's offer (μ^S) such that for $m = 1$

$$U_S^1((\mu^S), (V^*_j), (\phi^*_j)) \geq 0$$

and moreover the expectation

$$W((\mu^S), (V_j^*), (\phi_j^*)) = \int \Pi^1(v, (\mu^S), (V_j^*)) \, q^S(v) \left[\sum_{i=1}^{n} v_i - c \right] dF(v)$$

is maximal over all revelation offer constellations and continuations that yield nonnegative profits to the seller.

To find a second-best mechanism, we use a Lagrange multiplier approach. For $\lambda \geq 0$, let $\mu_\lambda = ([0,1]^n, q_\lambda, p_\lambda)$ be such that

(3.19)
$$q_\lambda(v) = \begin{cases} 0 & \text{if } (1+\lambda)\left[\sum_{i=1}^{n} v_i - c\right] - \lambda \sum_{i=1}^{n} \frac{1-F_i(v_i)}{f_i(v_i)} \leq 0 \\ 1 & \text{if } (1+\lambda)\left[\sum_{i=1}^{n} v_i - c\right] - \lambda \sum_{i=1}^{n} \frac{1-F_i(v_i)}{f_i(v_i)} > 0 \end{cases}$$

for any $v \in [0,1]^n$ and for $i = 1, \ldots, n$,

(3.20)
$$p_{i\lambda}(v) = \int_0^{v_i} x \, dQ_{i\lambda}(x)$$

for any $v \in [0,1]^n$, regardless of v_{-i}, where for $v_i \in [0,1]$,

(3.21)
$$Q_{i\lambda}(v_i) := \int q_\lambda(v) \, dF_{-i}(v_{-i})$$

is the conditional expectation of q_λ given v_i. For any λ, one easily verifies that unanimous approval and truthtelling are an equilibrium continuation for the single seller's offer of μ_λ. Moreover (3.11) shows that the resulting profits $U_S^1((\mu_\lambda), (V^*_j), (\phi^*_j))$ of the seller are continuous and strictly increasing in λ with

$$\lim_{\lambda \to 0} U_S^1((\mu_\lambda), (V^*_j), (\phi^*_j)) = U_S^1((\mu^F), (V^*_j), (\phi^*_j)) \leq 0$$

$$\lim_{\lambda \to \infty} U_S^1((\mu_\lambda), (V^*_j), (\phi^*_j)) = U_S^1((\mu^*), (V^*_j), (\phi^*_j)) \geq 0$$

where at least one of the inequalities is strict if the public good is provided at all with positive probability. Therefore there exists a unique λ^* such that $U_S((\mu_{\lambda^*}), (V^*_j), (\phi^*_j)) = 0$ so that the seller makes exactly zero profits. One can show that the mechanism $\mu^S = \mu_{\lambda^*}$ is indeed a second-best revelation mechanism (Güth and Hellwig (1986), Proposition 5.6).

Figure 1 illustrates the mechanisms μ^*, μ^F, μ^S for a particular example. In this example, $n = 2$, $c = 2/3$, and for $i = 1,2$, the distribution F_i has the uniform density $f_i(v_i) = 1$ for all $v_i \in [0,1]$. Then $(1-F_i(v_i))/f_i(v_i) = 1-v_i$ and (3.11) becomes

$$U_S^1((\mu), \Psi, \Phi) = \int_Y q(v)[2(v_1 + v_2) - 2 - c] \, dF(v).$$

Figure 1

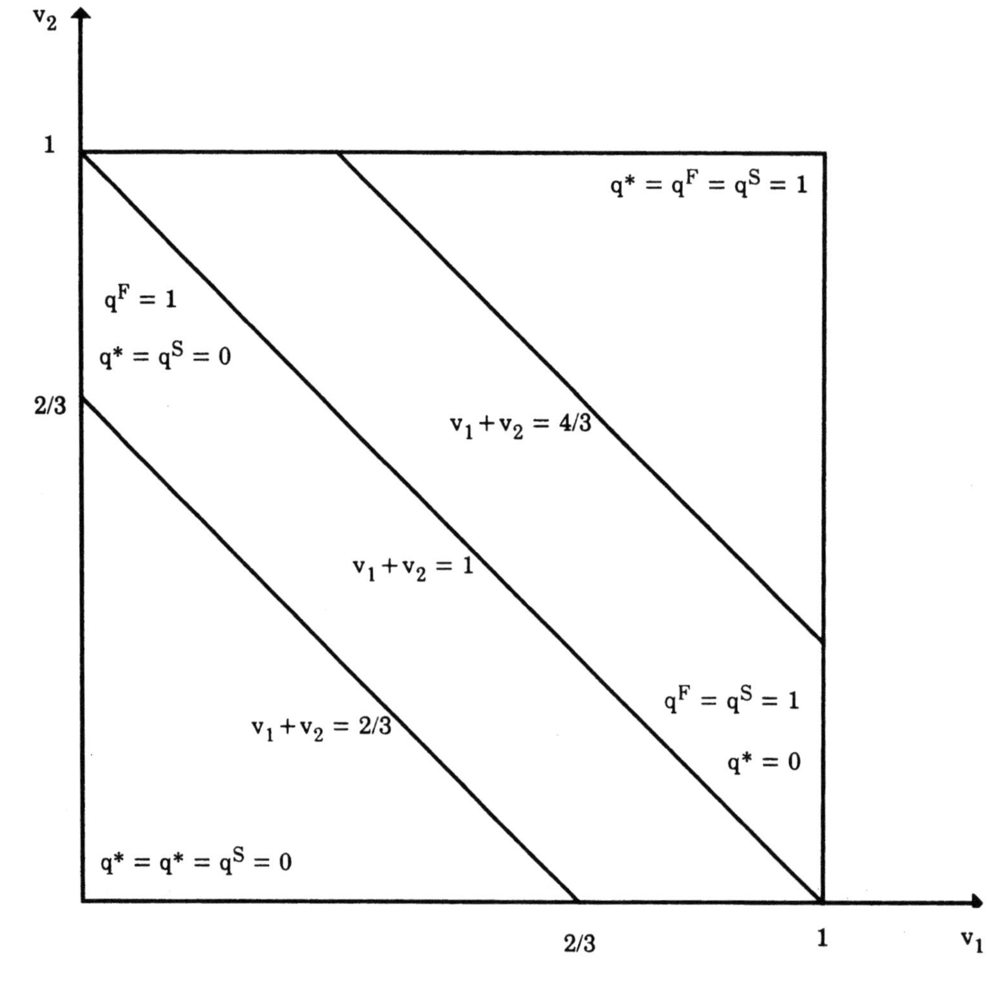

The profit-maximizing mechanism μ^* entails $q^*(v) = 1$ if and only if $2(v_1 + v_2) - 2 > c$ or, for $c = 2/3$, $v_1 + v_2 > 4/3$. The first-best mechanism μ^F entails $q^F(v) = 1$ if and only if $v_1 + v_2 > 2/3$. The mechanisms μ_λ involve $q_\lambda(v) = 1$ if and only if $v_1 + v_2 > k(\lambda)$, where

$$k(\lambda) := \frac{2}{3}\,\frac{1+4\lambda}{1+2\lambda}.$$

The corresponding profit levels can be evaluated as $-2/3\,(1-k(\lambda))\,(k(\lambda)^2 - 2k(\lambda) - 1) < 0$ if $\lambda < 1/2$, $k(\lambda) < 1$ and $2/3\,(k(\lambda) - 1)\,(2 - k(\lambda))^2$ if $\lambda \geq 1/2$, $k(\lambda) \geq 1$. As λ varies over the positive real numbers and $k(\lambda)$ varies from 2/3 to 4/3, the seller's expected profits rise from the level -22/81 at the first-best mechanism ($\lambda = 0$) to the maximal level 8/81 at the monopoly mechanism. Profits are zero for $k(\lambda^*) = 1$, or $\lambda^* = 1/2$, so that the second-best welfare-maximizing mechanism μ^S is equal to $\mu_{1/2}$. Therefore $q^S = 1$ if and only if $v_1 + v_2 > 1$. The corresponding levels of the expected aggregate surpluis are $W^F = 31/81$ under the first-best mechanism μ^F, $W^S = 1/3$ under the second-best mechanism μ^S, and $W^* = 16/81$ under the profit-maximizing mechanism μ^*.[1)]

If we compare the mechanisms μ^*, μ^F, and μ^S, we observe the same conflict between welfare maximization and monopolistic profit maximization as in the market for a private good. The expected supply probability for the public good is strictly lower under the profit-maximizing mechanism μ^* than under the second-best mechanism μ^S (and again strictly lower under μ^S than under the first-best mechanism μ^F). As in the market for a private good, the monopolist keeps his supply artificially scarce in order to raise the price. He thereby raises his expected profits from the level zero under the second-best mechanism to a positive level. However, the increase in his expected profits is not sufficient to compensate for the consumers' loss.

In the market for a private good, these undesirable effects of profit maximization by the suppliers disappear once the suppliers are exposed to the pressures of competition. The question is whether a similar result is available for public goods. In other words, how do the sequential equilibria of our model with $m > 1$ relate to (a) the profit-maximizing mechanism μ^* and (b) the welfare-maximizing mechanisms μ^F and μ^S? A partial answer to this question is given by

Proposition 3.5: Any sequential equilibrium $(\underline{\mu}, (V^*_j), (\phi^*_j))$ satisfies the following:

a: The sum of the suppliers' expected profits,

$$\sum_{k=1}^{m} U_S^k(\underline{\mu}, (V_j^*), (\phi_j^*))$$

does not exceed the expected profit $U_S^1(\mu^*), (V^*_j), (\phi^*_j))$ that a monopolist obtains through the profit-maximizing mechanism μ^*.

b: The aggregate expected surplus

$$W(\underline{\mu}, (V_j^*), (\phi_j^*)) = \sum_{k=1}^{m} U_S^k(\underline{\mu}, (V_j^*), (\phi_j^*)) + \sum_{i=1}^{n} U_i(\underline{\mu}, (V_j^*), (\phi_j^*))$$

does not exceed the expected surplus that can be obtained from a single supplier through the second-best welfare-maximizing mechanism μ^S.

Proof: By Proposition 3.1, we may assume without loss of generality that $(\underline{\mu}, (V^*_j), (\phi^*_j))$ is a revelation equilibrium. Given the revelation offer constellation $\underline{\mu} = (\mu^k) = (A^k, q^k, p^k)$, we define a new mechanism $\hat{\mu} = (\hat{A}, \hat{q}, \hat{p})$ as follows:

For $i = 1, ..., n$, $\hat{A}_i := \{0, 1, ..., m\} \times [0,1]^m$.

1) More generally, the surplus level under the mechanism μ_λ can be evaluated as $W_\lambda = 1/3\ (1 + k(\lambda)^2 (1 - k(\lambda)))$ if $k(\lambda) < 1$ and $W_\lambda = 1/3\ k(\lambda)\ (2 - k(\lambda))^2$ if $k(\lambda) \geq 1$.

For $a = \{(k_i, \hat{v}_i^1, \ldots, \hat{v}_i^m)\}^n_{i=1} \in \hat{A}$ set $\hat{q}(a) = \hat{p}_1(a) = \ldots \hat{p}_n(a) = 0$
unless $k_1 = \ldots = k_n \neq 0$. If $k_1 = \ldots = k_n = k \neq 0$, then:

$$\hat{q}(a) = q^k(\hat{v}_1{}^k, \ldots, \hat{v}_n{}^k)$$

and for $i = 1, \ldots, n$,

$$\hat{p}_i(a) = p_i^k(\hat{v}_1{}^k, \ldots, \hat{v}_n{}^k).$$

Heuristically, $\hat{\mu}$ is a single mechanism which encompasses both the voting stage, at which either nothing or one of the mechanisms μ^k in the offer constellation $\underline{\mu}$ is selected, and the implementation stage, at which the mechanism μ^k that has been selected is put to work. Given this analogy between the offer constellation $\underline{\mu}$ and the single mechanism $\hat{\mu}$, we can find a continuation $(\hat{V}_j(\,.\,, \hat{\mu}))$, $\hat{\phi}_j(\,.\,, (\hat{\mu})))^n_{j=1}$ for $\hat{\mu}$ that replicates the equilibrium continuation $(V^*_j(\,.\,, \underline{\mu}), \phi^*_j(\,.\,, \underline{\mu}))^n_{j=1}$ for $\underline{\mu}$. For this purpose we set:

$$\hat{V}_j^1(v_j, (\hat{\mu})) = 1$$

and

$$\hat{\phi}_j^1(\,.\,; v_j, (\hat{\mu})) = V_j^*(\,.\,; v_j, \underline{\mu}) \times \phi^{*1}_j(\,.\,; v_j, \underline{\mu}) \times \ldots \times \phi^{*m}_j(\,.\,; v_j, \underline{\mu})$$

for $j=1, \ldots, n$ and all $v_j \in [0,1]$, so that (i) the mechanism $\hat{\mu}$ is always accepted and (ii) for any j and $v_j \in [0,1]$, the mixed strategy $\hat{\phi}_j^1(\,.\,; v_j, (\hat{\mu}))$ on the product $\{0,1, \ldots, m\} \times [0,1]^m$ is simply the product of the original strategies $V^*_j(\,.\,; v_j, \underline{\mu})$ on $\{0,1, \ldots, m\}$ and $\phi^*{}_j^k(\,.\,; v_j, \underline{\mu})$ on $[0,1]$, $k=1, \ldots, m$. One easily verifies that the mechanism $\hat{\mu}$ with the continuation $(\hat{V}_j(\,.\,, (\hat{\mu}))$, $\hat{\phi}_j(.,(\hat{\mu})))$ is equivalent (in the sense of Proposition 3.1) to the offer constellation $\underline{\mu}$ with the continuation $(V^*_j(\,.\,, \underline{\mu}), \phi^*_j(\,.\,, \underline{\mu}))$. In particular, $((\hat{\mu}), (\hat{V}^*_j), (\hat{\phi}^*_j))$ and $(\underline{\mu}, (V^*_j), (\phi^*_j))$yield the same payoffs to the buyers and the same aggregate profits, i.e.

$U_j(\underline{\mu}, (V^*_j), (\phi^*_j)) = U_j((\hat{\mu}), (\hat{V}_j), (\hat{\phi}_j))$.
for $j = 1, \ldots, n$, and

$$\sum_{k=1}^{m} U_S^k(\underline{\mu}, (V_j^*), (\phi_j^*)) = U_S^1((\hat{\mu}), (\hat{V}_j), (\hat{\phi}_j)).$$

It is therefore sufficient to prove that $U_S{}^1((\hat{\mu}), (\hat{V}_j), (\hat{\phi}_j))$ does not exceed $U_S{}^1((\mu^*), (V^*_j), (\phi^*_j))$ and that $W((\hat{\mu}), (\hat{V}_j), (\hat{\phi}_j))$ does not exceed $W((\mu^S), (V^*_j), (\phi^*_j))$.

For this purpose we claim that $(\hat{V}_j(\,.\,, (\hat{\mu})), \hat{\phi}_j(\,.\,, (\hat{\mu})))$ is in fact an *equilibrium* continuation for the offer of $\hat{\mu}$ by a single supplier. For suppose that this claim were false. Then there would exist a buyer j and a valuation $v_j \in [0,1]$ such that $\hat{V}_j(\,.\,; v_j, (\hat{\mu}))$ violates (2.14) or (2.15) or $\hat{\phi}_j(\,.\,; v_j, (\hat{\mu}))$ violates (2.13). However, by construction $\hat{V}_j^\circ(v_j; (\hat{\mu})) = 0$ for all v_j, so that (2.15) cannot be violated. Moreover the validity of (2.14) at $(\underline{\mu}, (V^*_i), (\phi^*_i))$ implies

$$\int \Pi^k(v, \underline{\mu}, (V_i^*))\, u_j^k(v, \underline{\mu}, (\phi_i^*))\, dF_{-j}(v_{-j}) \geq 0, k=1, \ldots, m$$

for all v_j, and hence

$$\int u_j^1(v,(\hat{\mu}),(\hat{\phi}_i))dF_{-j}(v_{-j}) = \sum_{k=1}^{m} \int \Pi^k(v,\underline{\mu},(V_i^*))\, u_j^k(v,\underline{\mu},(\phi_i^*))\, dF_{-j}(v_{-j}) \geq 0$$

for all $v_j \in [0,1]$. Hence it cannot be the case that $\hat{V}_j(\,.\,,(\hat{\mu}))$ violates (2.14) for some $v_j \in [0,1]$.

There remains the possibility that $\hat{\phi}_j(\,.\,,(\hat{\mu}))$ violates (2.13). Then there exists an alternative strategy $\tilde{\phi}_j$ such that for some $v_j \in [0,1]$

$$\int u_j^1(v,(\hat{\mu}),\hat{\phi}_1,\ldots,\tilde{\phi}_j,\ldots,\tilde{\phi}_n)dF_{-j}(v_{-j}) > \int u_j^1(v,(\hat{\mu}),\hat{\phi}_1,\ldots,\hat{\phi}_n)dF_{-j}(v_{-j})$$

But then we can use $\tilde{\phi}_j$ to construct an alternative strategy $(\tilde{V}^*_j(\,.\,,\underline{\mu}),\tilde{\phi}^*_j(\,.\,,\underline{\mu}))$ that dominates the presumed equilibrium strategy $(V^*_j(\,.\,,\underline{\mu}),\phi^*_j(\,.\,,\underline{\mu}))$. Specifically, let $(\tilde{V}^*_j(\,.\,;v_j\,,\underline{\mu})$ be the *marginal* probability distribution of the vote of buyer j with valuation v_j under the strategy $\tilde{\phi}_j(\,.\,;v_j\,,(\hat{\mu}))$; moreover for k = 1, ... ,m, let $\tilde{\phi}^{*k}_j(\,.\,;v_j,\underline{\mu})$ be the probability distribution of the k-th message $\hat{v}_j^k$ of buyer j with valuation v_j under the strategy $\tilde{\phi}_j(\,.\,;v_j;(\hat{\mu}))$ conditional on the event $\{V_j^k(v_j,(\hat{\mu})) = 1\}$ that agent j has cast his vote for k. It is easy to see that if $\tilde{\phi}_j$ dominates $\hat{\phi}_j$ in the implementation of the mechanism $\hat{\mu}$, then $(\tilde{V}^*_j,(\,.\,,\underline{\mu}),\tilde{\phi}^*_j(\,.\,,\underline{\mu}))$ dominates $(V^*_j(\,.\,,\underline{\mu}),\phi^*_j(\,.\,,\underline{\mu}))$ in the game following the offer constellation $\underline{\mu}$. Hence, the assumption that $(\hat{V}_i(\,.\,,(\hat{\mu})),\hat{\phi}_i(\,.\,,(\hat{\mu})))$ fails to be an equilibrium continuation for the offer of μ by a single seller leads to a contradiction and must be false.

Given that $(\hat{V}_j(\,.\,,(\hat{\mu})),\hat{\phi}_j(\,.\,,(\hat{\mu})))$ is an equilibrium continuation for $(\hat{\mu})$, the revelation principle implies the existence of a revelation mechanism μ^R and a revelation continuation $(V^*_j(\,.\,,(\mu^R)),\phi^*_j(\,.\,,(\mu^R)))$ for the offer of μ^R by a single firm such that $((\mu^R),(V^*_j),(\phi^*_j))$ and $((\hat{\mu}),(\hat{V}_j),(\hat{\phi}_j))$ are equivalent (in the sense of Proposition 3.1; see also Proposition 3.1 of Güth and Hellwig (1986)). Then

$$U_S^1((\hat{\mu}),(\hat{V}_j),(\hat{\phi}_j)) = U_S^1((\mu^R),(V_j^*),(\phi_j^*)).$$

and

$$W((\hat{\mu}),(\hat{V}_j),(\hat{\phi}_j)) = W((\mu^R),(V_j^*),(\phi_j^*))$$

By the definition of a profit-maximizing revelation mechanism, we have

$$U_S^1((\mu^R),(V_j^*),(\phi_j^*)) \leq U_S^1((\mu^*),(V_j^*),(\phi_j^*)),$$

which proves statement (a). By the definition of a second-best welfare-maximizing mechanism, we have either

$$W((\mu^R),(V_j^*),(\phi_j^*)) \leq W((\mu^S),(V_j^*),(\phi_j^*))$$

or

$$U_S^1((\mu^R),(V_j^*),(\phi_j^*) < 0.$$

However, since $(\underline{\mu},(v^*_j),(\phi^*_j))$ is a sequential equilibrium, we must have

$$U_S^k(\underline{\mu}, (V_j^*), (\phi_j^*)) \geq 0$$

for all k and hence

$$\sum_{k=1}^{m} U_S^k(\underline{\mu}, (V_j^*), (\phi_j^*)) \geq 0 .$$

To see this, observe that regardless of the other agents' strategies, each supplier can always guarantee himself a profit of zero by offering a trivial mechanism, (A, q_o, p_o) with $q_o(a) \equiv 0$, $p_o(a) \equiv 0$. Now

$$\sum_{k=1}^{m} U_S^k(\underline{\mu}, (V_j^*), (\phi_j^*)) = U_S^1((\mu^R), (V_j^*), (\phi_j^*))$$

implies

$$U_S^1((\mu^R), (V_j^*), (\phi_j^*)) \geq 0$$

and hence

$$W((\mu^R), (V_j^*), (\phi_j^*)) \leq W((\mu^S), (V_j^*), (\phi_j^*)) ,$$

which proves statement (b). This completes the proof of Proposition 3.5. Q.E.D.

Proposition 3.5 shows that the mechanisms μ^* und μ^S can serve as benchmarks in the analysis of competition as well as monopoly. There is no sequential equilibrium in which suppliers earn more than the monopolist earns from the profit-maximizing mechanism μ^*. Moreover, there is no sequential equilibrium in which the expected aggregate surplus exceeds the level that is reached under the second-best welfare-maximizing mechanism μ^S. In particular, the first-best welfare level cannot be achieved if suppliers are able to avoid losses by offering a mechanism with a zero supply probability for the public good. The question then is to what extent the pressures of competition enforce the implementation of the second-best solution.

IV. Competition in the Supply of the Public Good

We begin with the rather reassuring result that the second-best solution is at least one possible outcome of competition for the franchise to supply the public good.

Proposition 4.1: If $m \geq 2$, there is a sequential equilibrium $(\underline{\mu}, (V^*_j), (\phi^*_j))$ which implements the second-best welfare-maximizing revelation mechanism μ^S and yields the expected aggregate surplus $W((\mu^S), (V^*_j), (\phi^*_j))$.

Proof: Let $\underline{\mu} = (\mu^S, \dots, \mu^S)$. For $j = 1, \dots, n$ and any $v_j \in [0,1]$, let $V^*{}_j^1(v_j, \underline{\mu}) = 1$ and for $k = 1, \dots, m$, $\phi^*{}_j^k(v_j, \underline{\mu}) = \delta v_j$, the degenerate probability measure with unit mass at v_j. Then trivially, by the definition of μ^S, $(V^*_j(\,.\,, \underline{\mu}), \phi^*_j(\,.\,, \underline{\mu}))$ is a revelation continuation for $\underline{\mu}$.

Next we specify the strategies (V^*_j), (ϕ^*_j) off the equilibrium path. Let $\underline{\hat{\mu}} \neq \underline{\mu}$ be any alternative offer constellation. If no equilibrium continuation for $\underline{\hat{\mu}}$ exists, i.e. if $\underline{\hat{\mu}} \notin \underline{M}$, then for $k = 1, \ldots, m$, $j = 1, \ldots, n$ and all $v_j \in [0,1]$, let $V^{*k}_j(v_j, \underline{\hat{\mu}}) = 0$ and let $\phi^{*k}_j(v_j, \underline{\hat{\mu}})$ be arbitrary.

If $\underline{\hat{\mu}} \in \underline{M}$, consider first an arbitrary equilibrium continuation $(\hat{V}_j(\,.\,, \underline{\hat{\mu}}), \hat{\phi}_j(\,.\,, \underline{\hat{\mu}}))$ for $\underline{\hat{\mu}}$. If $\hat{\mu}^k \neq \mu^S$ for all k, set $(V^*_j(\,.\,, \underline{\hat{\mu}}), \phi_j(\,.\,, \underline{\hat{\mu}})) = (\hat{V}_j(\,.\,, \underline{\hat{\mu}}), \hat{\phi}_j(\,.\,, \underline{\hat{\mu}}))$. If $\hat{\mu}^k = \mu^S$ for some k, let k* be the smallest index k for which $\hat{\mu}^k = \mu^S$, and set $V^{*k^*}_j(v_j, \underline{\hat{\mu}}) = 1$, $\phi^{*k^*}_j(v_j, \underline{\hat{\mu}}) = \delta_{v_j}$ for $j = 1, \ldots, n$ and all $v_j \in [0,1]$. Moreover, for $k \neq k^*$, set $V^{*k}_j(v_j, \underline{\hat{\mu}}) = 0$ and $\phi^{*k}_j(v_j, \underline{\hat{\mu}}) = \hat{\phi}^k_j(v^k_j(v_j, \underline{\hat{\mu}})$ for $j = 1, \ldots, n$ and all $v_j \in [0,1]$. One easily checks that the continuation $(V^*_j(\,.\,, \underline{\hat{\mu}}), \phi^*_j(\,.\,, \underline{\hat{\mu}}))$ is again an equilibrium continuation for $\underline{\hat{\mu}}$.[2)]

Given the specified strategies (V^*_j), (ϕ^*_j) of the potential users of the public good, it is now easy to see that none of the suppliers can gain by deviating from the offer constellation $\underline{\mu} = (\mu^S, \ldots, \mu^S)$. If supplier 1 deviates to an offer $\hat{\mu}^1 \neq \mu^S$, then nobody votes for him because all potential users of the public good turn to supplier 2 as the one with the lowest index k among all suppliers who offer μ^S. Therefore $U^1_S(\mu^1, (\mu^S, \ldots, \mu^S), (V^*_j), (\phi^*_j))$, $= 0 = U^1_S(\underline{\mu}, (V^*_j), (\phi^*_j))$, for all alternative offers $\hat{\mu}^1$ of supplier 1: Similarly, if any supplier $k > 1$ deviates to an alternative offer $\hat{\mu}^k \neq \mu^S$, nobody votes for him because under the specified strategies, all potential users of the public good continue to vote for supplier 1: Therefore $U^k_S((\mu^S, \ldots, \hat{\mu}^k, \ldots, \mu^S), (V^*_j), (\phi^*_j)) = 0 = U^k_S(\underline{\mu}, (V^*_j), (\phi^*_j))$ for all alternative offers $\hat{\mu}^k$ of supplier k. The proposition follows immediately.

Q.E.D.

However, the second-best solution is *not* the only possible outcome of competition. We also have:

Proposition 4.2: If $m \geq 2$, there is a sequential equilibrium $(\underline{\mu}, (V^*_j), (\phi^*_j))$ which implements the profit-maximizing revelation mechanism μ^* and yields the aggregate surplus $W((\mu^*), (V^*_j), (\phi^*_j))$.

The proof of Proposition 4.2 is word for word the same as the proof of Proposition 4.1 with μ^S everywhere replaced by μ^*. The main point is the following: If supplier 1 offers the profit-maximizing mechanism μ^* and suppliers $2, \ldots, m$ offer mechanisms $\mu^2, \ldots, \mu^m$ that consumers should find strictly more attractive than μ^*, then there still is an equilibrium continuation under which all potential users of the public good vote for supplier 1. Given that everybody else votes for supplier 1, any one individual strictly prefers to also vote for supplier 1 because a vote say for supplier 2 would merely entail the non-supply of the public good rather than the implementation of the mechanism μ^2.

2) Note that under the voting strategies V^*_j, the acceptance of any seller other than k* is a null event. Thus for $k \neq k^*$, the conditional distribution $F_{-j}(\,.\mid k, \underline{\hat{\mu}})$ of v_{-j} in (2.13) is arbitrary and may be identified with the conditional distribution of v_{-j} under the original voting strategies $\hat{V}_j$. Then the strategies $\phi^*_j(\,.\,, \underline{\hat{\mu}})$ satisfy (2.13) for $k \neq k^*$ because by assumption the original strategies $\hat{\phi}_j(\,.\,, \underline{\hat{\mu}})$ satisfy (2.13) for any k.

More generally, the preceding argument can be used to show that *any* revelation mechanism μ which provides a positive expected payoff to consumers and which yields nonnegative expected profits to the supplier can be implemented by a sequential equilibrium when there are two or more competing suppliers. In any such equilibrium the prevailing offer cannot be displaced because all potential users of the public good vote for it even if a better offer becomes available.

Our model of competition in the supply of public goods thus involves a significant indeterminacy of equilibrium allocations. Indeed the bounds given in Proposition 3.5 provide the sharpest available general characterization of sequential equilibrium outcomes with two or more suppliers. Although Proposition 4.1 shows that competition in the supply of public goods is consistent with a (second-best) welfare-maximizing outcome, we cannot really conclude that competition is efficient. According to Proposition 4.2, we cannot even say that competition in the supply of public goods is necesssarily more efficient than monopoly.

In our view the indeterminacy of sequential equilibria under competition cannot be removed by a further refinement of the equilibrium concept. To be sure, the inertia in voting that causes the indeterminacy may look like the inertia that supported the trivial Nash equilibria without trade in Section 2. However there is a major difference. In the case of the trivial no-trade equilibria the strategy of vetoing any nontrivial proposal was acceptable because each agent believed that his behaviour off the equilibrium path did not make a difference. In contrast, in the sequential equilibria of this section the voting strategies are chosen precisely because each agent acts as if his behaviour off the equilibrium path did make a difference.

To see this point, let $m=2$ and consider the voting stage when supplier 1 has proposed the monopoly mechanism μ^* and supplier 2 has proposed the second-best mechanism μ^S. Each consumer i must vote for one of the alternatives $V_i = 0,1,2$. If there are two consumers ($n=2$) and if we abstract from the problem of incomplete information, then the voting stage has the same structure as the noncooperative normal form game Γ in Table 1.[3)]

The game Γ has three equilibria in pure strategies: (0,0), (1,1), and (2,2). The constellation (0,0) is an equilibrium because each consumer believes that if the other consumer vetoes everything then his own vote does not matter. This is exactly the type of implausible consideration that supported the trivial no-trade equilibria in Section 2. If ever the consumer believed that there was the slightest chance that the other consumer might vote for supplier 2 or supplier 3, then he would strictly prefer to vote for supplier 2 or supplier 3 himself.

3) The analogy would actually be precise if consumers had to choose a supplier *before* they knew their valuations v_j. In the voting game that takes place *after* consumers know their valuations, the robustness considerations that we discuss in the text become much more complicated because for some values of the valuation v_j, e.g. for $v_j \in [0,1/3]$ in Figure 1, the consumer has nothing to gain from the profit-maximizing mechanism and will *always* vote for the second-best mechanism. It appears that for $c=0$ and $n=2$, this consideration is sufficient to eliminate the monopoly mechanism. However, for $n>2$, this effect can be outweighed by the argument that we give in the text.

Therefore the equilibrium (0,0) is not *perfect*, i.e. robust to some small perturbation of the game (see Selten (1975)). Similarly condition (2.15) in our definition of an equilibrium continuation rules out the possibility that consumers veto *both* the monopoly mechanism μ^* and the second-best mechanism μ^S merely because all other consumers also veto everything.

Table 1: The Game Γ

V_2 \ V_1	0	1	2
0	0,0	0,0	0,0
1	0,0	1,1	0,0
2	0,0	0,0	2,2

In contrast, *both* of the equilibria (1,1) and (2,2) in the game Γ are perfect. Indeed these equilibria are robust to *any* small perturbation of the game and hence stable in the sense of Kohlberg and Mertens (1986). For suppose that consumer 2 is expected to vote for supplier 1. Then consumer 1 will do likewise - not because he is indifferent, but because he has a *strict* preference for this alternative. If he has some small doubt about consumer 2's vote, this strict preference is not upset and he will still vote for supplier 1 rather than supplier 2. Given this remarkable robustness of the equilibrium (1,1), we do not see any refinement of the equilibrium concept that would eliminate this equilibrium. Similarly, we do not see any refinement that would eliminate the equilibrium continuations that support the profit-maximizing mechanism rather than the second-best welfare-maximizing mechanism in Proposition 4.2.

One might of course argue that the equilibrium (1,1) in the game Γ should be eliminated because it is strictly payoff-dominated by the equilibrium (2,2). However in the absence of cooperative pre-play communication, it is not clear that payoff-dominance can always be justified as an appropriate selection criterion. At this point we feel that the multiplicity of equilibrium continuations for a given offer constellation and hence the indeterminacy of sequential equilibrium outcomes under competition is in fact an important feature of our model.

However we must ask how robust this conclusion is to modifications of the model, in particular to modifications of the voting stage. Two aspects of the voting stage are important for our analysis: the *simultaneity* of voting and the *unanimity* requirement. We examine each of these in turn.

As an alternative to simultaneous voting, one might suppose that the potential users of the public good vote *sequentially*, first user 1, then user 2, etc. such that each voter knows the previous voters' decisions. To illustrate the impact of sequential voting, we reconsider the situation with two suppliers and two consumers in which supplier 1 has offered the profit-maximizing revelation mechanism μ^* and supplier 2 has offered the second-best revelation mechanism μ^S. With sequential voting the voting stage has the same structure as the extensive-form game Γ^* with perfect informationwhich is represented by the game tree in figure 2.

Figure 2: The Game Γ^*

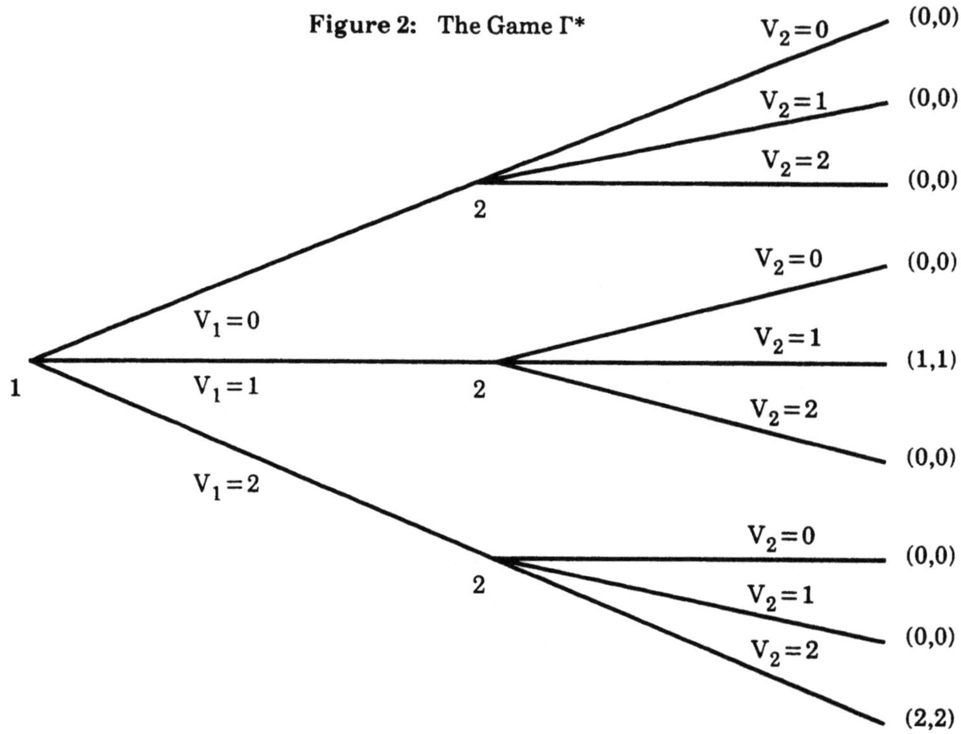

In the extensive-form game Γ^*, consumer 2 chooses not just a vote V_2, but a function $V_1 \rightarrow V_2(V_1)$ which indicates how his vote depends on the vote cast by consumer 1. Moreover, consumer 1 anticipates how his vote affects consumer 2's choice under the function $V_2(.)$.

One easily checks that the equilibrium (1,1) of the normal-form game Γ above is still an equilibrium outcome of the extensive-form game Γ^*. In this equilibrium, consumer 2 proposes to vote for supplier 1 regardless of consumer 1's vote, i.e. he chooses the constant function with $V_2(V_1) = 1$ for all V_1. Given this strategy, consumer 1 prefers to vote for supplier 1. Given that consumer 1 votes for supplier 1, consumer 2's strategy choice is justified because (i) for $V_1 = 1$ he strictly prefers the vote $V_2(V_1) = 1$, and (ii) for $V_1 = 0$ or $V_1 = 2$, he feels that the vote $V_2(V_1)$ does not matter because consumer 1 chooses $V_1 = 1$ anyway.

However, in the extensive-form game Γ^*, the equilibrium with outcome (1,1) is *not* perfect. If consumer 2 sees the slightest chance that consumer 1 might vote for supplier 2, then he would strictly prefer a strategy with $V_2(2) = 2$. But then consumer 1 would prefer the vote

$V_1=2$ with outcome (2,2) rather than $V_1=1$ with the outcome (1,1). Therefore the equilibrium with outcome (1,1) is not robust to small perturbations of the game Γ^*. The only equilibrium outcome which is robust to small perturbations of the game is the payoff-dominating outcome (2,2), which is supported by the strategies $V_1=2$, $V_2(2)=2$, $V_2(1)=1$, $V_2(0)$ arbitrary. Hence under sequential voting only the outcome (2,2) is perfect; all other outcomes of the game Γ^*can be eliminated by considerations of sequential rationality.

Similarly at the voting stage following the offer of μ^* by supplier 1 and μ^S (or something close to μ^S) by supplier 2, under sequential voting all outcomes other than a unanimous vote for supplier 2 can be eliminated by considerations of sequential rationality. In sharp contrast to Proposition 4.2, one can then show very easily that the profit-maximizing mechanism μ^* - or indeed any other mechanism that is dominated by μ^S - cannot be a sequential equilibrium outcome under competition when voting at stage 2 is sequential.

However with sequential voting, the second-best welfare-maximizing mechanism μ^S is not a sequential equilibrium outcome either. For consider a new revelation mechanism $\tilde{\mu}$ with the property that (i) consumer 1 prefers $\tilde{\mu}$ and the revelation continuation for $\tilde{\mu}$ to μ^S and (ii) $\tilde{\mu}$ and the revelation continuation for $\tilde{\mu}$ yield positive expected profits. Now consider the voting stage when firm 1 has offered $\tilde{\mu}$ and firm 2 has offered μ^S. With two consumers who vote sequentially, this voting stage has the same structure as the extensive-form game $\tilde{\Gamma}$ with perfect information which is represented by the game tree in Figure 3.

Figure 3: The Game Γ

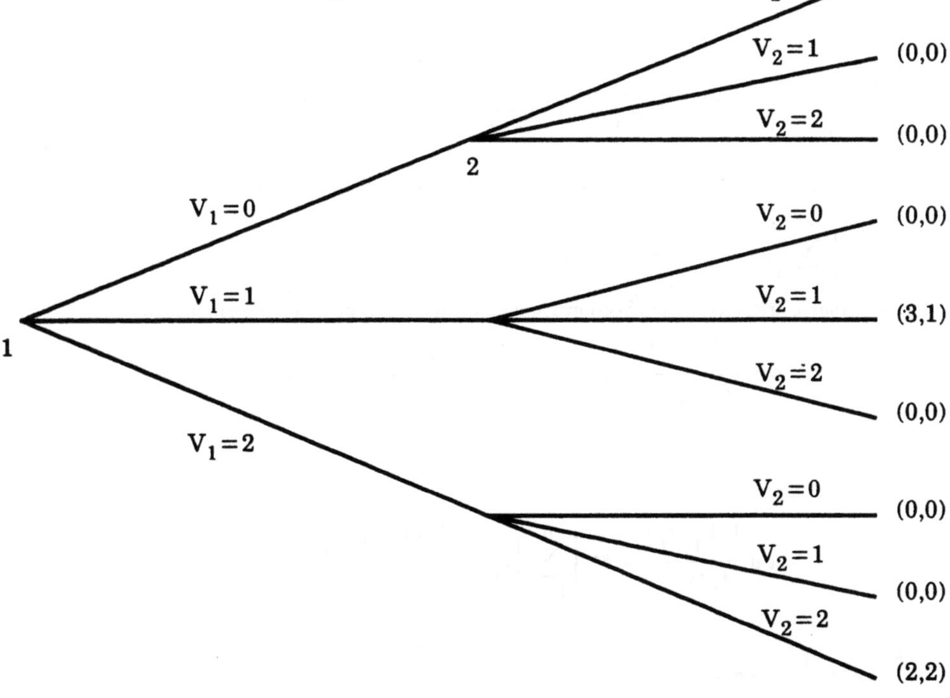

In the extensive-form game $\tilde{\Gamma}$, the condition of perfectness singles out the outcome (1,1) with payoff vector (3,1) rather than the outcome (2,2). The outcome (2,2) still corresponds to a Nash equilibrium. It is supported by the strategy constellation $V_1=2$, $V_2(V'_1)=2$ for $V'_1=0,1,2$. Given that consumer 2 votes for firm 2, consumer 1's best choice is to vote for firm 2 himself. Given that consumer 1 votes for firm 2, the votes $V_2(0)$ and $V_2(1)$ do not matter, and the vote $V_2(2)=2$ is strictly preferred to the alternatives $V_2(2)=0$ or $V_2(2)=1$. However a now familiar argument shows that the choice $V_2(1)=2$ cannot be maintained if consumer 2 sees the slightest possibility that consumer 1 might vote for firm 1 after all. In this case consumer 2 would prefer $V_2(1)=1$, which induces consumer 1 to choose $V_1=1$. Therefore the equilibrium outcome (2,2) is not robust to small perturbations of the game $\tilde{\Gamma}$. The only outcome which is robust is the outcome (1,1) which is supported by the strategies $V_1=1$, $V_2(2)=2$, $V_2(1)=1$, $V_2(0)$ arbitrary.

Similarly, at the voting stage following the offer of $\tilde{\mu}$ by suplier 1 and μ^S by supplier 2, under sequential voting all outcomes other than a unanimous vote for supplier 1 can be eliminated by considerations of sequential rationality. Hence *the second-best welfare maximizing mechanism μ^S cannot be a sequential equilibrium outcome under competition when voting at stage 2 is sequential.*

Indeed it is not difficult to show that under sequential voting *the only sequential equilibrium outcome is given by the revelation mechanism μ^*_1, which maximizes consumer 1's expected payoff subject to the condition that the supplier should not make a loss.*[4] The point is that

4) Formally, $\mu^*_1 = ([0,1]^n, q^*_1, p^*_1)$ is the solution to the Lagrangean problem

$$\max_{\substack{\underline{v}_1,\dots,\underline{v}_n \\ q(.)}} \int_Y q(v)\left[\frac{1-F_1(v_1)}{f_1(v_1)} + \delta\left\{\sum_{i=1}^{n}\left[v_i - \frac{1-F_i(v_i)}{f_i(v_i)}\right]-c\right\}\right] dF(v)$$

where $Y=[\underline{v}_1, 1] \times \ldots \times [\underline{v}_n, 1]$ and the Lagrange multiplier $\delta \geq 0$ must be such that at the optimal solution,

$$\int_Y q(v)\left\{\sum_{i=1}^{n}\left[v_i - \frac{1-F_i(v_i)}{f_i(v_i)}\right]-c\right\} dF(v) \geq 0.$$

Using the same arguments as in Section 3, one finds that μ^*_1 is given by the conditions

$$q_1^*(v) = \begin{cases} 0 \text{ if } \dfrac{1-F_1(v_1)}{f_1(v_1)} + \delta^*\left\{\displaystyle\sum_{i=1}^{n}\left[v_i - \frac{1-F_i(v_i)}{f_i(v_i)}\right]-c\right\} \leq 0, \\ 1 \text{ if } \dfrac{1-F_1(v_1)}{f_1(v_1)} + \delta^*\left\{\displaystyle\sum_{i=1}^{n}\left[v_i - \frac{1-F_i(v_i)}{f_i(v_i)}\right]-c\right\} > 0; \end{cases}$$

$$p_{1i}^*(v) = \int_0^{v_i} x \, dQ_{1i}^*(x),$$

(see next page)

under sequential voting the unanimity requirement gives consumer 1 a dictatorship position. Once consumer 1 has voted for a supplier, the other consumers can only agree with him or else vote for the non-supply of the public good. If the mechanism chosen by consumer 1 provides them with a positive payoff at all, then sequential rationality requires them to agree with consumer 1 rather than vote for the non-supply of the public good. Hence in any sequential equilibrium consumer 1 can expect that whatever he chooses will be accepted. Therefore he chooses what he likes best. Given this voting behaviour, competition forces the suppliers to offer the mechanism that is best for consumer 1.

The introduction of sequential rather than simultaneous voting has eliminated the indeterminacy of equilibrium outcomes only to yield a new type of monopoly solution. Competition with sequential voting replaces the supplier's monopoly by the dictatorship of the first, the pivotal voter.[5)] Like the monopolist's profit maximization, the dictatorship of the first voter leads to inefficient outcomes (compare the mechanism μ^*_1 in Fn. 4 to the second-best mechanism μ^S). There are two reasons for this. First, for some valuation vectors v, there may be an undersupply of the public good because the first voter wants the supplier to exploit his monopoly power over the other consumers in order to reduce the share of the supplier's cost that the first voter has to bear himself. Second for some valuation vectors v, there may be an oversupply of the public good because the first voter feels very strongly about it even though on aggregate the costs are not covered.

In summary, the replacement of simultaneous voting by sequential voting solves the problem of indeterminacy only to create another, more serious problem of inefficiency. Our pessimistic conclusion about the role of competition in the market for a public good is confirmed rather than reversed.

We therefore consider the effects of abandoning the requirement of unanimity. The most obvious alternative is a *majority rule*, possibly a qualified majority rule. To illustrate the impact of (simultaneous) majority voting, we again consider the situation with two suppliers

regardless of v_{-i} where

$$Q^*_{1i}(v_i) = \int q^*_1(v)\, dF_{-i}(v_{-i});$$

the Lagrange multiplier δ^* must be chosen so that

$$\int q^*_1(v)\left\{\sum_{i=1}^{n}\left[v_i - \frac{1-F_i(v_i)}{f_i(v_i)}\right]-c\right\} dF(v)=0,$$

5) To avoid this conclusion, one might consider randomizing the order in which consumers vote. But then firms might offer mechanisms that depend on the realizations of this randomization, such as a mechanism which is optimal for the first voter -whoever he may turn out to be. Even if such mechanisms are ruled out, say because firms cannot observe the actual order in which consumers vote, the second-best mechanism μ^S can still not be a sequential equilibrium outcome under sequential voting. If firm 2 offers μ^S, then firm 1 can still gain by offering the mechanism $\tilde{\mu}$ which is preferred by consumer 1 because if consumer 1 is the first to vote, then he will choose $\tilde{\mu}$ so that with positive probability $\tilde{\mu}$ must be chosen and earns a positive profit for firm 1.

when supplier 1 has offered the profit-maximizing mechanism μ^* and supplier 2 has offered the second-best mechanism μ^S. To distinguish majority voting from unanimity voting, we assume that there are three consumers. Then the voting stage has the same structure as the noncooperative normal-form game Γ' in which consumer i's payoffs for different strategy constellations (V_i, V_j, V_h) are given as:

Table 2: The Game Γ'

V_i / (V_j, V_h)	0	1	2
(0,0)	0	0	0
(1,0) , (0,1)	0	1	0
(1,1)	1	1	1
(0,2) , (2,0)	0	0	2
(1,2) , (2,1)	0	1	2
(2,2)	2	2	2

At first sight, we have the same embarassing multiplicity of Nash equilibria in Γ' as we had under unanimity voting in the normal-form game Γ. Specifically, the following strategy constellations (or permutations thereof) are Nash equilibria in Γ': (0,0,0), (1,1,1), (2,2,2), (2,2,1), (2,2,0), (1,1,0). To see that each of these strategy constellations is an equilibrium, it suffices to note that once two consumers vote for an alternative k, the third consumer can vote for anything that is no better than k without affecting the implementation of k or providing the others with an incentive not to vote for k.

However one can now use the same type of robustness consideration as before to eliminate all but the payoff-dominant equilibrium (2,2,2):

- The equilibrium (0,0,0) is not perfect because for any consumer i, the choice $V_i = 0$ is suboptimal whenever the consumer sees the slightest chance that one of the other consumers might vote for $k = 1$ or $k = 2$.

- The equilibrium (2,2,0) is not perfect because $V_3 = 0$ is suboptimal for consumer 3 if he sees the slightest chance that consumer 1 or consumer 2 might choose $k=0$ or $k=1$ rather than $k=2$; in this case, consumer 3 strictly prefers the vote $V_3=2$. By the same argument, the equilibria (2,2,1) and (1,1,0) are not perfect either.

- The equilibrium (1,1,1) is robust against some, but *not all* perturbations of the game Γ', i.e. it is perfect, but *not* strictly perfect (Okada (1981)); nor is {(1,1,1)} a stable set in the sense of Kohlberg and Mertens (1986). For suppose that consumer i has some doubts about the other consumers' votes. If he believes that there is a slight chance that consumer j or consumer h might deviate to $V_j=0$ or $V_h=0$, but not to $V_j=2$ or $V_h=2$, then he will still choose $V_i=1$ in order to raise the chances that the public good will be provided at all. However if he believes that consumer j or consumer h might deviate to $V_j=2$ or $V_h=2$, then he will prefer the vote $V_i=2$ to the vote $V_i=1$ because (i) in those cases where $V_j=V_h=1$, his vote does not make a difference, but in those -exceptional- cases where $V_j=2$ or $V_h=2$, the vote $V_i=2$ ensures a majority for the preferred alternative $k=2$. Therefore the equilibrium (1,1,1) is *not* robust against those perturbations of the game Γ' in which a deviation to a vote for $k=2$ is considered more likely than a deviation to a vote for $k=0$.

In contrast, one easily verifies that the payoff-dominant equilibrium (2,2,2) is robust against *all* perturbations of the game Γ'. This equilibrium is strictly perfect; indeed the singleton {(2,2,2)} is the only minimal stable set in the sense of Kohlberg and Mertens (1986)[6] Similarly, at the voting stage following the offer of the profit-maximizing mechanism μ^* by supplier 1 and the offer of the second-best mechanism μ^S (or something close to μ^S) by supplier 2, under simultaneous majority voting, all outcomes other than a unanimous vote for supplier 2 can be eliminated by robustness requirements. Again in contrast to Proposition 4.2, it follows that the profit-maximizing mechanism μ^* - or indeed any other mechanism that is payoff-dominated by μ^S - can be eliminated as an outcome of competition if voting follows the majority rule.

But once again, the same arguments that eliminate the monopoly solution will also eliminate the second-best solution. For consider a new revelation mechanism $\tilde{\mu}$ with the property that (i) consumers 1 and 2 prefer $\tilde{\mu}$ to the second-best mechanism μ^S and (ii) $\tilde{\mu}$ and the revelation continuation for $\tilde{\mu}$ yield positive expected profits. Consider the voting stage when firm 1 has offered $\tilde{\mu}$ and firm 2 has offered μ^S. With three consumers and simultaneous voting under the majority rule, this voting stage has the same structure as the normal-form game Γ'' in which consumer $i=1,2$ have the payoffs indicated in Table 3 and consumer 3 has the payoffs indicated in Table 4.

6) Alternatively, (2,2,2) is singled out as the only perfect equilibrium that remains perfect if the dominated strategies $V_i=0$, $i=1,2,3$ are deleted from the game Γ'. Indeed, (2,2,2) is the only strategy constellation that remains at all if one proceeds iteratively, eliminating first the strategies $V_i=0$, $i=1,2,3$, which are dominated in Γ' and then the strategies $V_i=1$, $i=1,2,3$, which in turn are dominated in the game that one obtains after elimination of the strategies $V_i=0$, $i=1,2,3$ from Γ'.

Table 3

(V_j, V_3) \ V_i	0	1	2
(0,0)	0	0	0
(1,0) , (0,1)	0	3	0
(1,1)	3	3	3
(0,2) , (2,0)	0	0	2
(1,2) , (2,1)	0	3	2
(2,2)	2	2	2

Table 4

(V_1, V_2) \ V_3	0	1	2
(0,0)	0	0	0
(1,0) , (0,1)	0	1	0
(1,1)	1	1	1
(0,2) , (2,0)	0	0	2
(1,2) , (2,1)	0	1	2
(2,2)	2	2	2

One easily verifies that in the game Γ" the following strategy constellations are Nash equilibria: (0,0,0), (1,1,1), (1,1,2), (2,2,2), (2,2,1), (2,2,0), (1,1,0). Moreover, the same robustness arguments as before show that the equilibria (0,0,0), (2,2,0), (1,1,0) are not perfect.

However, we now find that the equilibrium (2,2,2) is *not* strictly perfect, i.e. there exists some perturbation of the game Γ" under which the equilibrium (2,2,2) is not robust. To see this, suppose that consumer 1 sees a slight chance that consumer 2 might deviate from the strategy $V_2=2$ to the strategy $V_2=1$. Then he will choose $V_1=1$ rather than $V_1=2$: If consumers 2 and 3 stick to the choices $V_2=V_3=2$, then the deviation to $V_1=1$ does not make a difference. However in those instances where consumer 2 votes for firm 1 rather than firm 2, the vote $V_1=1$ contributes to a majority for firm 1, which consumer 1 strictly prefers to firm 2. Similarly, consumer 2 will prefer $V_2=1$ to $V_2=2$ if he sees a slight chance that consumer 1 might vote for firm 1 rather than firm 2. More generally, the equilibrium (2,2,2) is *not* robust against those perturbations of the game Γ" in which a deviation to a vote for $k=1$ is considered to be more likely than a deviation to a vote for $k=0$.

Unfortunately, the remaining equilibria, (1,1,2) and (1,1,1) are not strictly perfect either: Consumer 3 prefers $V_3=1$ or $V_3=2$ according to whether he considers consumers 1 and 2 more likely to deviate to the alternative $k=0$ or to the alternative $k=2$. In the first case, he prefers $V_3=1$ because he wants to make sure that the public good is provided at all. In the second case, he prefers $V_3=2$ because he wants to make use of the slight chance that he might contribute to a majority for firm 2. Therefore neither the equilibrium (1,1,1) nor the equilibrium (1,1,2) is robust under *all* perturbations of the game Γ".

However, the set of equilibria {(1,1,1), (1,1,2)} is stable in the sense of Kohlberg and Mertens (1986): Under *any* small perturbation of the game Γ", either (1,1,1) *or* (1,1,2) remains an equilibrium. Indeed, as a stable set, the set {(1,1,1) , (1,1,2)} is unique in the sense that any other stable set of equilibria must contain both (1,1,1) and (1,1,2).[7)]

In terms of what actually happens, the distinction between the equilibria (1,1,1) and (1,1,2) is irrelevant. In either equilibrium, the majority votes for the alternative $k=1$ with payoff 3 for consumers 1 and 2 and payoff 1 for consumer 3. Similarly, at the voting stage follwing the offer of the mechanisms $\tilde{\mu}$ and μ^S by suppliers 1 and 2, under simultaneous majority voting, the requirement of robustness against all perturbations - which we used before to eliminate the profit-maximizing mechanism μ^* - eliminates all outcomes other than a majority vote for firm 1 and the mechanism $\tilde{\mu}$. Hence *under the given robustness requirements, the second-best*

7) Alternatively, the equilibrium (1,1,2) may be singled out as the only perfect equilibrium that remains perfect after the dominated strategies $V_i=0$, $i=1,2,3$, are deleted from the game Γ". Again, (1,1,2) is the only strategy constellation that remains at all if the elimination of $V_i=0$, $i=1,2,3$ from Γ" is followed by the elimination of the new dominated strategies $V_i=2$, $i=1,2$ and $V_3=1$.

welfare-maximizing revelation mechanism μ^S cannot be the outcome of competition if voting at stage 2 is based on the majority rule.

More generally, we suspect that a pure-strategy equilibrium which satisfies the given robustness requirements at stage 2 may not exist at all. Given *any* offer constellation (μ^1, μ^2) of firms 1 and 2, the firm that does not get the franchise, say firm 1, should be able to find a mechanism $\tilde{\mu}$ that is preferred by a majority of consumers (the underdogs under the prevailing mechanism μ^2) and that makes positive profits. Given the new proposal $\tilde{\mu}$ by firm 1, the stable set of equilibria should involve a majority vote for firm 1 so that the deviation from μ^1 to $\tilde{\mu}$ is indeed profitable.

In summary, the introduction of majority rather than unanimity voting removes the indeterminacy of equilibrium outcomes only to introduce new problems, namely the displacement of the second-best solution and the possible nonexistence of equilibrium in pure strategies. Here too our pessimistic conclusion about the role of competition in the market for a public good is confirmed.

The different difficulties that arise under different specifications of the voting stage should be regarded as different manifestations of the same fundamental problem. The award of the franchise to supply a public good is a problem of social rather than individual choice. Therefore this decision is subject to all the well known difficulties that arise when the decision maker is a collective body rather than an individual. We cannot altogether rule out the existence of some voting scheme under which competition enforces the implementation of the second-best solution. However at this point we are quite skeptical about this possibility. Competition for the favours of a collective body simply seems to have much less force than competition for the favours of an individual.

References

(1) van Damme, E., (1985),
Fair Allocation of an Indivisible Commodity, mimeo, University of Technology, Delft.

(2) Dasgupta, P.S., P.J. Hammond, and E.S. Maskin (1979),
The Implementation of Social Choice Rules: Some General Results on Incentive Compatibility, Review of Economic Studies 46, 185-216.

(3) Demsetz, H., (1968),
Why Regulate Utilities, Journal of Law and Economics 11, 55-66.

(4) Goldberg, V., (1976),
Regulation and Administered Contracts, Bell Journal of Economics 7, 426-448.

(5) Güth W. and M. Hellwig (1986),
The Private Supply of a Public Good, Zeitschrift für Nationalökonomie, Supplementum 5, 121-159.

(6) Harsanyi, J.C., (1967-8),
Games with Incomplete Information Played by 'Bayesian' Players, Management Science 14, 159-189, 320-344, 486-504.

(7) Kohlberg, E. and J.F. Mertens, (1986),
On the Strategic Stability of Equilibria, Econometrica 54, 1003-1038.

(8) Kreps, D.M. and R. Wilson, (1982),
Sequential Equilibria, Econometrica 50, 863-894.

(9) Myerson, R.B., (1979),
Incentive Compatibility and the Bargaining Problem, Econometrica 47, 61-73.

(10) Okada, A., (1981),
On Stability of Perfect Equilibrium Points, International Journal of Game Theory 10, 67-73.

(11) Samuelson, P.A., (1954),
The Pure Theory of Public Expenditure, Review of Economics and Statistics 36, 387-389.

(12) Samuelson, P.A., (1955),
Diagrammatic Exposition of a Theory of Public Expenditure, Review of Economics and Statistics 37, 350-356.

(13) Selten, R., (1975),
Reexamination of the Perfectness Concept for Equilibrium Points in Extensive Games, International Journal of Game Theory 4, 25-55.

(14) von Weizsäcker, C.C., (1980),
Barriers to Entry, Lecture Notes in Economics and Mathematical Systems No. 185, Springer-Verlag, Berlin-Heidelberg-New York.

Comment on W. Güth und M. Hellwig: Competition versus Monopoly in the Supply of Public Goods

by

Eric van Damme

Güth and Hellwig consider the situation in which a group of producers (each one having access to the same technology) competes for the right to supply a public good. It is assumed that individual exclusion is impossible so one might prefer to speak of a collective good. The problem addressed is whether competition for the market will result in efficient supply. Efficiency is understood to be in the second best sense (maximize consumer surplus subject to a zero profit constraint) as it can be shown that in many cases any mechanism that maximizes consumer surplus imposes an expected loss on the supplier[1]. The authors show that competition might lead to efficiency, but that it need not. Specifically, the competition game played by the potential suppliers has multiple Nash equilibria, some of which are efficient and some of which are not. In particular, if there are at least 2 potential suppliers, then there exists an equilibrium resulting in the second best (Proposition 4.1), but independent of the number of potential suppliers, there also exists an equilibrium resulting in the same outcome as the (inefficient) one obtained in the monopoly case. (Proposition 4.2)[2].

To assess the importance of this result one has to ask how robust it is with respect to (i) the solution concept employed and (ii) the modelling of competition. The first point is relevant as it is well-known that in general not all Nash (or sequential) equilibria are viable. The second issue is important, since, whenever society persistently produces undesirable outcomes there will be an incentive to change the rules of the game so as to promote efficiency. Güth and Hellwig perform such a sensitivity analysis in section 4 and they conclude that, within their game, the inefficient outcomes cannot be removed by more refined equilibrium concepts. The authors also consider 2 variants of their basic competition game (replacing unanimity voting by, respectively, sequential voting and majority voting) and they find that both variants confirm their pessimistic conclusions about the forces of competition in markets for public

1) The first best mechanism μ^F imposes a loss on the seller whenever $n \geq 2$, $0 < c < n$ (Güth/Hellwig p. 198) *and* the distribution F_i of player i's value admits a strictly positive density f_i. The last condition is not satisfied in my incomplete information example and indeed in this example the first best can be implemented.

2) As the remarks below Proposition 4.2 and in Fn 3 in the Güth-Hellwig paper make clear, the latter result holds only if the monopoly mechanism yields almost all types of each player a positive payoff, a condition which is not satisfied in the example discussed in these comments. If the monopoly mechanism yields a non-null set of types zero profit one can perturb this mechanism by ε and obtain an equilibrium close to the monopoly mechanism.

goods. Of course, from 3 examples one cannot conclude a general theorem, but nevertheless the authors write that they are skeptical of finding a variant of the game forcing the second best.

The arguments Güth and Hellwig offer in Section 4 are to a large extent independent of the fact that there is asymmetric information (a consumer's willingness to pay is private knowledge) so that one might think that one should also be pessimistic in the complete information case. However, below I will argue that in this case, one should expect the first best to be reached. Secondly, I will consider an explicit example illustrating the paper's pessimistic conclusions in the incomplete information case. However, this example also shows that failure to reach the second best should not necessarily be viewed as market failure: The second best (or even the first best) welfare criterion may not be the appropriate one to use as consumers may have no interest in implementing a first best mechanism.

I. The Model

It will be convenient to slightly modify the basic model of Güth and Hellwig. There are m potential producers (P_1, ..., P_m) and n consumers (C_1, ... , C_n). Each producer has a cost c of supplying the public good, the willingness to pay of C_j is v_j. Cost are common knowledge, but v_j may be private information. The model I consider is the following 3 stage game:

(i) Each producer proposes a mechanism, i.e. a detailed description of the conditions under which he offers the public good and which (personal)prices he will charge/delet

(ii) Consumers vote for a producer (or veto supply).

(iii) If all consumers unanimously agree on a producer in a set I and if all producers in I propose the same mechanism, then a randomly selected producer from I supplies the public good according to the conditions he proposed; otherwise the public good is not provided.

The basic game of Güth/Hellwig differs from this one only to the extent that they restrict themselves to singleton sets I. The modification is proposed to exclude the situation in which 2 producers offer exactly the same favorable conditions but the public good is not provided since some consumers vote for the one, others for the other producer. Otherwise the change is inessential, however, and all arguments given by Güth and Hellwig also apply to my game.

II. The Complete Information Case

Assume that all v_j are common knowledge and that $c<\Sigma_j v_j$ so that provision is desirable. A mechanism of producer i in this case just corresponds to a vector of prices $p^i=(p_j^i)_j$ that i will charge in case he is awarded the right. Let $p = (p^1, \dots, p^m)$ be the mechanisms proposed in stage (i). We may assume $p^i_j < v_j$ for all i, j, since consumer j will never vote for i if $p^i_j \geq v_j$. Given p, the game faced by consumers in stage (ii) is an unanimity game G(p), on m+1 alternatives: the m proposed mechanisms and the alternative (say, o) of vetoing any proposal. Such a game has many equilibria, including many inefficient ones[3]. For example, for any $i = 1, \dots, m$, an equilibrium results when all consumers vote for producer i: If all other consumers vote for P_i, then C_j has a positive payoff $(v_j - p_j^i)$ when he also votes for P_i whereas unanimity will be lost if he deviates, in which case the public good is not provided and C_j's payoff is zero. Hence, any such equilibrium is strict, i.e. each player will loose by deviating. Consequently, existing purely noncooperative refinements (i.e. concepts that explicitly rule out communication) will not eliminate any of these equilibria[4]. Given that inefficient equilibria can result in G(p), there is indeed no reason why competition in the first stage should yield the second best and the negative Güth/Hellwig conclusion follows.

However, this negative conclusion crucially depends on the fact that communication between consumers has been ruled out. Furthermore, the argument ignores the fact that efficient equilibria might be focal points in the sense of Schelling (1960). In my view one cannot exclude communication, especially, when the number of consumers is small and I want to argue that in this case communication will result in an efficient equilibrium of G(p). For example, consider Table 1 in the Güth/Hellwig paper. Both consumers have an incentive to propose to vote P_2 and given such a proposal there is no reason not to follow it since there is no reason whatsoever to assume that the proposer himself will not vote for this producer. Unfortunately, one cannot turn to game theory for formal support of this argument as existing concepts fail to incorporate the meaning of ordinary language[5]. Of course, one could add efficiency as an axiom to the Nash postulate, but I agree with Güth/Hellwig that it is not clear that payoff dominance can always be justified as an appropriate selection criterion. Namely, consider the following variant of Table 1

0,0	0,x	0,0
x,0	1,1	x,0
0,0	0,x	2,2

$(1 < x < 2)$

3) An equilibrium is said to be inefficient if there exists another equilibrium that Pareto dominates it. Equilibria in mixed strategies are always inefficient as is the equilibrium in which all players veto any alternative. The latter is not perfect, but the former are, they are even stable.

4) Note that in the general case in which production cost differ there even exist strict equilibria in which all consumers vote for a producer having nonminimal cost.

5) All existing concepts treat the game including the message 'I will vote for P_2' as identical to the game without this message.

in which producer 1 offers a consumer a side payment of x in case this consumer is the only one who votes P_1. In this case, when C_1 proposes to vote P_2, C_2 has to decide whether C_1 really wants the more attractive producer to supply the public good or whether C_1 is a clever guy who has come to the conclusion that it is rational to vote P_1 but who, by manipulating C_2, tries to improve his payoff. If C_2 is not completely sure that C_1 is honest, he might prefer the 'safer vote' P_1, hence, it is not implausible that the final outcome will be (1,1). Note that, if $x=2$, then (1,1) is the unique perfect equilibrium).

The difficulty with the above game is that one cannot attach an unambiguous meaning to the phrase "I will vote P_2". In the games G(p) that Güth and Hellwig consider, all off-diagonal elements are zero, so that such a phrase always has unambiguous meaning. Consequently, I contend that payoff-dominance may be justified as a selection criterion in unanimity games[6] and that adding (nonbinding) communication to the game will eliminate all but the Pareto efficient equilibria in G(p) for any p. However, once this has been established, the standard Bertrand argument applied to stage (i) eliminates the positive profit equilibria from the 3-stage game. I conclude that communication forces a first best solution in the complete information case[7].

One might argue that, since a first best mechanism still leaves the distribution of the cost undetermined a conflict may result as a consequence of the fact that each consumer will vote for that mechanism in which he bears the smallest fraction of the cost. However, also this conflict will be resolved, as communication allows randomization. Realizing the danger of conflict, the consumers will amend the voting stage with a bargaining game, and they will finally come up with some correlated strategy over mechanisms. Equivalently, in this risk neutral case, consumers will agree to vote for the most preferred mechanism of some C_j in return for side payments from C_j to each of the other consumers. This bargaining problem has a well-defined conflict point as each player can veto supply of the public good. Hence, consumers have equal bargaining power and the final division of the cost will be such that, irrespective of which mechanisms the producers actually have proposed, each consumer has an equal utility gain. So, after side payments, the net price that j pays will be $p^N_j = v_j - (\Sigma_k v_k - c)/n$, the Nash bargaining solution (Nash (1950)). It should be stressed that to obtain this result, one need not assume any cooperative features of the bargaining game: All natural, noncooperative procedures will lead to the Nash outcome, (see Moulin (1982). (An especially simple procedure is random dictatorship: A randomly selected consumer proposes a producer and side payments, if consumers unanimously approve, the side payments are made and consumers vote for the proposed producer, otherwise conflict results). I conclude that with unrestricted bargaining, consumers will reach a specific first best mechanism, viz. the Nash mechanism $p^N = (p^N_1, \dots, p^N_n)$. Producers, realizing this, will presumably all propose this mechanism.

6) For this restricted class of games, efficiency may even be derived from more basic postulates, cf. Harsanyi and Selten (1987).

7) It should be remarked that *nonbinding* communication between firms does not alter this conclusion, but, of course, the solution might be completely different if firms can make *binding* agreements.

Of course, the above is nothing but an adaption of the Coase argument (Coase (1960)). However, now return to the case where communication is forbidden, so that consumers cannot coordinate their votes, let alone bargain on side payments. In this case, the Nash mechanism p^N provides the natural focal point whenever it is provided[8]. More generally, the Nash bargaining solution induces a 'Nash social welfare function' on mechanisms, a mechanism being socially preferred whenever it has a higher product of net utility gains. By the focal point argument, Bertrand competition will eliminate mechanisms yielding less social welfare, just as in the private goods case it eliminates mechanisms yielding less individual utility. I conclude that there are strong arguments to believe that in the complete information case, competition will force efficiency, specifically, that it leads to the same outcome as unrestricted bargaining among consumers[9].

III. The Incomplete Information Case

I will confine myself to illustrating several points of the Güth/Hellwig paper by means of a simple specific example[10], which is due to Myerson (1979, 1984).

The cost to provide the public good is 100. There are 2 consumers. Consumer 1 either has a willingness to pay of 30 (in which case I will refer to him as type 1L) or 90 (type IH). Consumer 2's willingness to pay is 90. Consumer 1 knows how high he values the public good, producers as well as consumer 2 assess 90 % probability that 1 is of type 1H. Note that, irrespective of 1's value, the sum of the values exceeds the sum of the costs, so that a first best mechanism always supplies the public good.

Suppose a monopolist considers offering a first best mechanism. The monopolist realizes that, if he charges 1L less than 1H, then consumer 1 will always claim that his value is 30. Hence, to guarantee incentive compatibility, both types of player 1 should pay the same price. This price cannot exceed 30 since in this case type 1L will veto the mechanism and this is suboptimal for a monopolist offering a first best mechanism. Consequently, the profit maximizing first best mechanism has consumer 1 pay 30 (irrespective of his type) while consumer 2 pays his reservation value of 90, with profit equal to 20. However, the monopolist can do better by not offering a first best mechanism. In the mechanism discussed above, the

8) An 'Independence of Irrelevant Alternatives' Argument establishes that p^N is the unique focal point, when provided. The feasible outcomes in the noncommunicating case are a subset of the outcomes obtainable by unrestricted bargaining. As long as the solution of the unconstrained problem is available, it should be the solution of the constrained one.

9) It should be pointed out that the solution theory of Harsanyi and Selten (1987) leads to the same conclusion (at least, for the model that I proposed). The arguments of Harsanyi and Selten are more formal and they differ from my focal point argument. Hence, the arguments are complementary and support each other.

10) This example (up to normalization) satisfies all the Güth/Hellwig conditions, except that uncertainty is a discrete random variable.

incentive compatibility constraint precludes that the monopolist extracts the entire surplus of type 1H. This surplus can be extracted in a mechanism in which the public good is not provided in case consumer 1 reports that his value is 30. Among all such mechanisms, the profit maximizing one is "Supply if 1 reports 1H and charge both consumers 90, do not supply if 1 reports 1L". This one results in an expected profit of 72 and it is not difficult to show that this is indeed the global optimum. Hence, we have verified that monopolistic provision may result in undersupply as compared to the first best.

Next, let us investigate which mechanisms will be offered under the sequential voting variant of Güth/Hellwig. To answer this question, we have to know which mechanism each consumer would want to implement if he were in a dictatorship position. Irrespective of his type, consumer 1 wants the public good to be provided and that consumer 2 pays his reservation value of 90 (hence, 1 only has to pay 10). So, consumer 1 would dictate a first best mechanism. If consumer 2 is the dictator, he is in more or less the same position as the monopolist discussed above. If he dictates a first best mechanism he can only extract 30 from consumer 1, so that it is better to demand that consumer 1 pays 90 with the consequence that the public good will not be supplied in the event that 1 has type 1L. Hence, 2 will dictate "Supply if 1 reports 1H and let me pay 10, do not supply if 1 reports 1L". In other words: 2 will insist on a mechanism that is not first best since in any incentive compatible first best mechanism he has to pay an unfair share of the cost. (Recall that is 90% likely that 1 has type 1H). This verifies the Güth/Hellwig claim that also sequential voting may lead to inefficient supply.

Finally, we come to the main question: Will competition lead to a second best solution, i.e. (in this case) a first best mechanism in which revenue equals cost. (Hence, the public good is always provided, consumer 1 (irrespective of his type) pays x, consumer 2 pays 100-x with $10 \leq x \leq 30$, so that no consumer pays more than his reservation value). First, however, we must consider whether a first best mechanism is desirable, i.e. whether free and unrestricted bargaining between the consumers will lead to a first best mechanism. Given that consumer 2 is very much opposed to such mechanisms (as they force him to pay an unfair share of the cost) the answer seems a clear no. Since both consumers have equal bargaining power, random dictatorship seems to be a reasonable compromise to resolve the conflict (as it was with complete information). Random dictatorship leads to the mechanism "if 1 reports 1L: supply with probability 1/2 and let 2 pay 90 if it is supplied, if 1 reports 1H: supply and let both pay 50). Although this mechanism is not first best, it is incentive efficient (i.e. it is not dominated by another incentive compatible mechanism), so that presumably consumers will agree on this mechanism as a fair compromise[11)]. The same arguments as in the complete information case, therefore, establish that competition will not lead to the second best: If competition works (and if it works in the complete information case, why would not it work here), it will produce this 'fair compromise' mechanism.

I conclude to there is no reason to expect that free bargaining between consumers will lead

11) Myerson's neutral bargaining solution indeed yields this mechanism, Myerson (1984).

to a second best mechanism, so that we should not be upset if it turned out that competition does not produce the second best: Of course, the challenging problem remains to formalize the focal point theory which guarantees that competition and bargaining lead to the same outcome, as well as to investigate the exact conditions under which this theory is valid.

References

(1) Coase, Ronald (1960),
The Problem of Social Cost, Journal of Law and Economics *3*, 1-44

(2) Harsanyi, John C. and Reinhard Selten (1987),
A general theory of equilibrium selection in games. MIT Press (forthcoming).

(3) Moulin, Hervé (1982),
Noncooperative implementation: A survey of recent results. Math Social Sciences *3*, 243-258.

(4) Myerson, Roger B. (1979),
Incentive compatibility and the bargaining problem. Econometrica *47*, 61-73.

(5) Myerson Roger B. (1984),
Two-person bargaining problems with incomplete information. Econometrica *52*, 461-487.

(6) Nash, John F. (1950),
The bargaining problem. Econometrica *18*, 155-162.

(7) Schelling, Thomas C. (1960),
The strategy of conflict. Harvard Univ. Press, Cambridge Mass.

MIX
Papier aus verantwortungsvollen Quellen
Paper from responsible sources
FSC® C105338

If you have any concerns about our products,
you can contact us on
ProductSafety@springernature.com

In case Publisher is established outside the EU,
the EU authorized representative is:
Springer Nature Customer Service Center GmbH
Europaplatz 3, 69115 Heidelberg, Germany

Printed by Libri Plureos GmbH
in Hamburg, Germany